# THE FIRST PRINCIPLE

*Talks on Zen*

# OSHO

## JAICO PUBLISHING HOUSE
Ahmedabad Bangalore Bhopal Bhubaneswar Chennai
Delhi Hyderabad Kolkata Lucknow Mumbai

Published by Jaico Publishing House
A-2 Jash Chambers, 7-A Sir Phirozshah Mehta Road
Fort, Mumbai - 400 001
jaicopub@jaicobooks.com
www.jaicobooks.com

Copyright © 1981, 2019 OSHO International Foundation.
All rights reserved

www.osho.com

THE FIRST PRINCIPLE: TALKS ON ZEN
ISBN 81-7992-128-X

First Jaico Impression: 2006
Tenth Jaico Impression: 2019

All rights reserved.
No part of this book may be reproduced or transmitted
in any form or by any means, electronic or mechanical,
including photocopying, recording, or by any information
storage and retrieval system, without prior written
permission from OSHO International Foundation.

The material in this book is a transcript of a series of original
OSHO Talks on Zen, given to a live audience.
All of Osho's talks have been published in full as books, and are
also available as original audio recordings. Audio recordings and the
complete text archive can be found via the online OSHO Library at
www.osho.com/library

Photos: Copyright © OSHO International Foundation

OSHO is a registered trademark of OSHO International
Foundation, used under license. www.osho.com/trademarks

Page design and layout: Yogesh Typesetting, Pune

Printed by
Repro India Limited
Plot No. 50/2, T.T.C. MIDC Industrial Area
Mahape, Navi Mumbai - 400 710

# Contents

| | | |
|---|---|---|
| Chapter 1 | Catching the First Principle | 1 |
| Chapter 2 | Greed Behind Greed Behind Greed | 25 |
| Chapter 3 | The Only One Who Has Not Talked | 52 |
| Chapter 4 | Go With The River | 78 |
| Chapter 5 | Beyond The Prism of the Mind | 107 |
| Chapter 6 | The Irrational Rationalist | 137 |
| Chapter 7 | The Song of Sound and Silence | 164 |
| Chapter 8 | The Profound and the Trivial | 189 |
| Chapter 9 | You: The Greatest Lie There Is | 218 |
| Chapter 10 | All Going Is Going Astray | 245 |

## Chapter 1
# Catching the First Principle

*Once a tyro asked a Zen master, "Master, what is the first principle?" Without hesitation the master replied, "If I were to tell you, it would become the second principle."*

Yes. The *first principle* cannot be said. The most important thing cannot be said, and that which can be said will not be the first principle. The moment truth is uttered it becomes a lie; the very utterance is a falsification. So the Vedas, the Bible, and the Koran, they contain the second principle, not the first principle. They contain lies, not the truth, because the truth cannot be contained by any word whatsoever. The truth can only be experienced – the truth can be lived – but there is no way to say it.

The word is a far, faraway echo of the real experience; and it is so far away from the real that it is even worse than the unreal because it can give you a false confidence. It can give you a false promise. You can believe it, and that is the problem. If you start believing in some dogma, you will go on missing the truth. Truth has to be known by experience. No belief can help you on the way; all beliefs are barriers. All religions are against religion – it has to be so by the very nature of things. All churches are against God. Churches exist because they fulfill a certain need. The need is: man does not want to make any efforts; he wants easy shortcuts. Belief is an easy shortcut.

The way to truth is hard; it is an uphill task. One has to go through total death – one has to destroy oneself utterly, only then is the new born. The resurrection is only after the crucifixion.

To avoid the crucifixion we have created beliefs. Beliefs are very cheap. You can believe and you remain the same. You can go on believing, and it doesn't require any basic change in your life pattern. It does not require any change in your consciousness, and unless your consciousness changes, the belief is just a toy. You can play with it, you can deceive yourself with it, but it is not going to nourish you.

Visualize that a child is playing in the garden of his house, playing with imaginary lions, and then suddenly he has to face a real lion who has escaped from the zoo. Now he does not know what to do. He is simply scared out of his wits. He is paralyzed; he cannot even run. He was perfectly at ease with the imaginary, but with the real he does not know what to do.

That is the situation of all those people who go on playing with beliefs, concepts, philosophies, theologies. They ask questions just to ask questions. The answer is the last thing they are interested in. They don't want the answer. They go on playing with questions, and each answer helps them to create more questions. Each answer is nothing but a jumping board for more questions.

The truth is not a question. It is a quest! It is not intellectual; it is existential. The inquiry is a gamble, a gamble with your life. It needs tremendous courage. Belief needs no courage. Belief is the way of the coward. If you are a Christian or a Hindu or a Mohammedan you are a coward. You are avoiding the real lion, you are escaping from the real lion. If you want to face the real, then there is no need to go to any church, there is no need to go to any priest, because the real surrounds you within and without. You can face it – it is already there.

I have heard:

A Zen master, Shou-shan, was asked by a disciple, "According to the scriptures, all beings possess the buddha-nature; why is it that they do not know it?"

Shou-shan replied, "They know!"

This is a rare answer, very rare, a great answer. Shou-shan said, "They know! But they are avoiding it." It is not a question of how to know the truth. The truth is here, you are part of it. The truth is now, there is no need to go anywhere. And it has been there since the beginning, if there was any beginning, and it will be there until the end, if there is going to be any end.

And you have been avoiding it. You find ways to avoid it. When somebody asks, "What is the way to truth?" in fact he is asking, "What is the way to avoid the truth?" He is asking, "How can I escape?"

You may not have heard:

Says that old rascal Bodhidharma: "All know the way, few walk it, and the ones who don't walk cry regularly, 'Show me the way! Where is the way? Give me a map! Which way is it?'"

Those who don't walk, they go on regularly crying and shouting, "Where is the way?" And all know the way because life is the way, experience is the way. To be alive is the way, to be conscious is the way. You are alive, you are conscious. This is the first principle.

But it cannot be said, and I am not saying it!

And you are not hearing it.

The truth, by its very nature, is a dumb experience. All experiences are dumb because they happen only in deep silence. If you love a woman the love happens in deep silence. If you create poetry it descends in you in deep silence. If you paint a picture you disappear. The painter is *not*, when the painting is born, there is not even a witness to it. It happens in utter silence and utter aloneness. If you are there then the painting cannot be of any value. If the poet is there then the poetry will be nothing but a technical thing. It will have all the rules fulfilled, it will follow the grammar, the rules of melody, but there will be no poetry. It will be a dead corpse. It will not be a real woman; it will be a nun.

I have heard:

At an isolated part of the beach of Cannes a beautiful French girl threw herself into the sea. A young man off at a distance noticed it and dashed into the water to save her, but it was too late. He dragged the seminude body ashore and left it on the sand while he went in search of some official. When he returned he was horrified to see a man making love to the corpse.

"Monsieur!" he exclaimed, "that woman is dead!"

"Sacré bleu!" muttered the man, jumping up. "I thought she was a nun."

To be a monk or to be a nun is to be dead. And there are millions of ways of how to die and not live.

Truth surrounds you. It is in the air, it is in the fragrance of the flowers, it is in the flow of the river, it is in the green leaves, it is in the stars, it is in the dust, it is in you. Only truth is! But you go on avoiding it and you go on asking questions – How to attain to truth? Where is the map? Which way is it? And even if the map is given to you, the map does not help you in any way. In the first place the map cannot be given, because the truth goes on changing. It is not a stagnant phenomenon; it is continuously changing. It is alive, it is breathing. It is never the same; it is never the same for two consecutive moments.

Says old Heraclitus, "You cannot step in the same river twice." In fact, you cannot even step once; the river is flowing, the river is flowing so fast. And not only is the river flowing, you are flowing. You cannot step in the same river twice: the river changes. You cannot step in the same river twice: because *you* change.

Truth is dynamic. Truth is not something dead. That's why it cannot be contained in words. The moment you utter it, it has passed, it has gone beyond, it is no more the same. The moment you say it is so, it is no more so. Words lag behind.

To be with truth there is only one possibility: drop words. Language lags behind. Language is lame. Only silence can go with truth, hand in hand. Only silence can move with truth. Only silence can be so fast, because silence has no weight to carry. Words are loaded; they carry weight. So when you are carrying words, great theologies in your head, great abstractions, then you cannot walk with truth. To walk with truth one has to be weightless. Silence is weightless; it has nothing to carry. Silence has wings. So only in silence is the truth known, and only in silence is the truth transferred, transmitted.

The tyro asked the master:

*"Master, what is the first principle?"*

He must have been a tyro, a beginner; otherwise the question is foolish, the question is stupid. Either a stupid person can ask it or a philosopher. The question is meaningless because "first" means the most fundamental. The mind cannot contain it, because it contains the mind! The "first" means the basic; it was before the mind, so how can the mind comprehend it? Mind came out of it, mind is a by-product of it. The child cannot know the father; the father can know the child. The reality can know you, but you cannot know the reality. The part cannot know the whole; the whole can know the part. And the part cannot contain the whole. Now the mind is a very tiny part. It cannot contain the vastness of reality. Yes, the person who asked must have been a beginner.

*"What is the first principle, master?"*

And the master said:

*"If I were to tell you, it would become the second principle."*

Then it will be an echo, it will be a reflection, it will be a mirror image.

Do you know who you are? You don't know, but you know a mirror image. You know your name, you know your address, you know the name of your family, the country, the religion, the political party you belong to. You know your face reflected in the mirror. You don't know your real face. You have not encountered your original face yet. The Zen masters continuously persist, they go on hammering on the heads of their disciples, "Look into your original face – the face that you had before even your father was born, the face that you will have when you are dead, the face that is yours, originally yours." All that we know about our face is not really about our face. It is the mask of the body, the mask of the mind. We don't know who lives in the body. We know truth as secondhand, borrowed.

Whenever something is borrowed it becomes ugly. Only the firsthand experience is beautiful, because it liberates. The secondhand thing is ugly because it becomes a bondage. If you become religious you will be liberated. If you become a Christian or a Hindu or a Mohammedan you will be in a bondage. Mohammed was liberated because for him Islam was a firsthand experience. So was Jesus liberated because for him his experience was *his* experience – authentically his. Buddha was liberated; he came upon the experience. It was not handed to him by somebody else – it was not borrowed, it was not thought out, it was not a logical syllogism, it was not an inference. It was an experience!

Beware of inference. You have been taught inference to avoid experience. There are people who say, "God exists because if God is not there, who will create the world? God must exist because the world exists."

Just the other day I was reading a story about a rabbi. Must have been utterly unenlightened. Rabbis are like that – priests. A man came to the rabbi. The man was an atheist, and he said, "I don't believe in God, and you talk about God. What is the proof?" And the rabbi said, "You come after seven days, and come wearing a new suit." The man said, "But what does that have to do with my question?" The rabbi said, "It has something to do with it. You just go to the tailor, prepare a new suit, and come after seven days."

The man came, reluctantly, because he could not see any relationship between his question and the answer that had been given. But he still came; he was wearing a new suit. The rabbi said, "Who has made this suit?" And the man said, "Have you gone mad? What type of a question are you asking? Of course the tailor." The rabbi said, "The suit is here; it proves that the tailor exists. Without the tailor the suit would not be here. And so is the case with the world. The world is here: there must be a tailor to it, a creator."

This is inference.

Change the scene. In a small Indian village a mystic is sitting with his disciples. Silently they are sitting; there is tremendous silence. It is a *satsang* – the disciples are drinking the presence of the master. And there comes an atheist, a scholar, a well-known logician, and he says, "I have come to ask one question. What is the proof of God?" The mystic opens his eyes, and he says, "If you want the proof of

God, look into the eyes of the devotees. There is no other proof."

God exists in the eyes of the devotees. God exists in the vision of the lovers. It is an experience of the deepest core of your being, the heart. There is no other proof. God is not a concept. God is a reality, an experience, a deep subjective experience, the deepest there is. All else is peripheral. God is the experience of your innermost center. When you are centered you know.

But you have been taught to believe in the God of the philosophers. That is a way to avoid the real God! The real God is very wild! The real God is very crazy! The real God is very unknown and unknowable. And the real God cannot be controlled. The real God can possess you; you cannot possess the real. That is the fear: the mind is always afraid of anything that can possess it. The mind goes on playing games with words, ideas, philosophies. It can remain the master there. With the false, the mind is the master; with the real, the mind becomes a slave, and the mind does not want to become a slave. So the mind is completely contented with the secondhand.

Your God is secondhand. Your love too is secondhand. Your poetry is secondhand. Your dance is secondhand. Your singing is secondhand. And of course all these secondhand things make *you* secondhand; then you lose all originality.

Religion has nothing to do with logic. Religion has something to do with the first principle. Logic deals with the secondhand. Logic deals with the junkyard, the used – used by many people. Logic deals with inference. And remember, it is good as far as the human world of intellectual garbage is concerned; the moment you go beyond that boundary logic fails utterly, it falls flat on the ground.

I have heard a very beautiful anecdote:

The safari had struck camp in dangerous territory and to protect themselves from wild animals they built a high fence around the camp. To be really sure, they dug a deep ditch around the fence. One evening a member of the group, who was a professor of philosophy and a world-known logician, carelessly went out for an evening stroll without his gun and got attacked by a lion. He ran back to the camp with the lion after him and fell down into the ditch. His friends inside heard a terrible yelling and screaming from outside, and when they ran out to look they saw the poor man – the poor philosopher – running round and round in the ditch closely followed by the lion. "Watch out, he is right behind you," they yelled down to him.

"That's all right," the philosopher yelled back. "I am one round ahead of him."

Logic is meaningless as far as life is concerned. Life is not logical at all; life is illogical. Logic is man-made, manufactured by the human mind. Life is absurd.

So if you go through inference you will reach the secondhand. If you go through experience you will reach the firsthand.

And religion is radical. Churches are not radical. The word "radical" means "belonging to the roots". Religious is radical, religion is rebellion. And churches are not rebellious; they are orthodox. Hence, I will repeat again, all churches are against religion. All so-called religious people are against religion. They deal in a false entity; they deal in pseudo coins, counterfeit coins. That's why so many people look religious and there is not even a trace of religion on the earth. So many people talk about God, but it remains an empty talk.

Have you ever felt God? You have heard the word again and again and again. You are bored with the word. It has almost become a dirty word. From the very childhood people have been conditioning you for the word. Have you ever had any glimpse of God?

This is something very strange. How can we miss him? If he is the totality, if he is all over the place, how can we miss him? How did it ever become possible for us to miss him? We must have been doing great work to miss him. We must be doing much work to miss him. We must be really avoiding him. We must be creating many barriers and hindrances and obstacles so that he cannot reach us.

And then these empty words: God, love, peace, prayer. All beautiful words have become empty. All ugly things are very real. War is very real; love is very unreal. Madness is very real; meditation is very unreal. Beauty is not there at all; ugliness, everywhere. You can come across the ugly any moment. And God is beauty, God is truth, God is love.

So what has happened? We have been trained for empty words, and we have become contented with these empty words.

Drop this contentment! If you really want to know what is, become discontented with all that you have been taught, become discontented with all that you have been educated for! Become discontented with your education, with your society, with the power structures around you, the churches, the priests. Become discontented! Become discontented with your own mind. Only in that discontent comes a moment when you become capable of dropping all this mind and all this nonsense with it... and suddenly God is there, the first principle is there.

A naive young man who had lived a sheltered life finally decided he could not take any more. He arranged an appointment with his doctor and poured out the whole story.

"It is this girl I have been going with," he said. "I suspected she was fast, but I never dreamed she was a sex maniac. Every night now for weeks and weeks on end, I keep trying to break off the romance, but I haven't got the will power. What can I do? My health just can't stand the pace."

"I see," said the doctor grimly. "Tell me just what happens; you can trust me."

"Well, every night I take her driving in my car. We park in some secluded street. Then she asks me to put my arms around her. And then, every night, she reaches over and holds my hand."

"And then?"

"What do you mean 'and then'?" gasped the youth. "Is there more?"

That's what has happened to religion. The moment the word "religion" is uttered you remember the serious long faces in the churches, the very sad-looking priests, the very serious theologians, trying to split hairs, chopping abstract words, nobody knows why, for what. Religion is broke. The religion of the philosophers is bankrupt. The religion of the intellectuals is relevant no more; it has lost all relevance.

The old religion is dead! And it is good that it is dead. The old God is dead! And it is good that it is dead because now the door opens and we can search for a new God, a God more real, not conceptual, more existential, not philosophical, a God who can be seen, loved, lived, a God who can transform your life, a God who is really life and nothing else.

A totally different kind of religion is needed in the world, a gut-level religion, a religion which has blood, life, a religion whose heart still beats. The old religion is simply dead, and people are worshipping the corpse. And people carrying the corpse, by and by, become just like the corpse they are carrying.

The first principle means a gut-level religion, a religion that you can experience in your innermost core, in the interiority of your being. You are the shrine for the first principle. No Bible, no Koran, no Veda. You are the shrine for the first principle. So the only way to reach to the real is to go within, is to go in. Turn in.

That's what meditation is all about. That's why Zen is not interested in any dogmas. It is interested in helping you to contract your own being.

*When the fifth patriarch of Zen, Hung-jen, was asked why he had chosen Hui-neng as his successor out of the five hundred monks in his monastery, he replied: "Four hundred and ninety-nine of my disciples understood Buddhism very well, and only Hui-neng had no understanding of it whatsoever. He is not a man to be measured by any ordinary standard. Hence, the robe of authentic transmission was given to him."*

Because he has "no understanding of it whatsoever". An intellectual understanding is not an understanding. It is a deception, it is an illusion, it is a dream, it is a substitute.

Because you are missing the real and because you are not courageous enough to accept the fact that you are missing the real, you substitute it. It is a plastic flower. You substitute it with a false thing and then you feel very good. You start thinking that you have it. And you don't have it! Your hands are empty.

Those four hundred ninety-nine disciples of Hung-jen were all scholars. For years they had studied, they had studied all the scriptures. They had all the scriptures on their tongue. And he had chosen a man who has no understanding whatsoever. The man he had chosen, Hui-neng, was not known at all in the monastery. Nobody even was aware that he existed there.

When Hui-neng had come to the master, the master had asked him one thing: "Do you really want to know? Do you? Do you want to know about truth, or do you want to know truth itself?" And Hui-neng said, "What will I do by knowing *about* the truth? Give me the real thing." And the master said, "Then go to the kitchen and clean the rice for the mess – and never come again to me. Whenever the right moment has come I will call you."

Twelve years passed, and Hui-neng was simply working in the kitchen, at the back. People did not even know about him. Nobody knew his name. Who bothers to think about a man who simply goes on working in the kitchen from the morning till late in the night? The monastery was not aware. There were great scholars, famous people; all over China their names were known – there were celebrities in the ashram. Who bothered about Hui-neng?

Twelve years passed, and then one day the master declared, "My time has come and I will be leaving this world, so I have to choose a disciple as my successor. Anybody who thinks himself ready, capable of becoming my successor, should write four lines in front of my door to show his understanding. The greatest scholar went there in the night and wrote four lines, beautiful lines, really beautiful the very essence of the *second* principle. You cannot reach higher through the mind than that. He wrote: "The mind is like a mirror. Dust gathers on it. Clean the dust, and you know what is." Perfectly true, absolutely okay. What more can there be?

The whole monastery was agog. People were discussing, debating whether the master would choose this man as the successor or not. And everybody was trying to improve upon it, but nobody could find anything wrong in it. There was nothing wrong....

That is one of the most difficult things about the intellect. What is wrong in a plastic flower? Nothing is wrong. In a way – in many ways – it may be better than a real flower. A real flower is born in the morning and by the evening it is gone. A plastic flower is more stable, more permanent – gives the idea of the eternal! The real flower is momentary. The real flower is born and dies, and the plastic flower knows no death. It is the closest that you come to the eternal. And what is wrong in it? It can have as much color as the real – can have more color because it is in your hands to make it so. And you can make it perfumed too; there is no problem about it. But something basic is missing; it is dead.

Nobody could find anything wrong. And people were trying to improve it, but they were all intellectuals. You cannot improve more than that; this is the last point the mind can reach. And it seems logical: "The mind is like a mirror. Dust gathers on the mirror, and then it cannot reflect" – that's what has happened to the mind.

Then two, four monks were discussing it, and they passed Hui-neng, who was doing his work in the kitchen. He heard it – they were talking about these beautiful lines, the essential of all the scriptures – and he laughed. For twelve years nobody had even seen him laughing. He laughed. Those monks looked at him, and they said, "What? Why are you laughing?" And he said, "It is all nonsense. It is not true." They could not believe their ears. This man, the rice cleaner, for twelve years just cleaning rice.... Nobody had ever seen him even meditating.

How can you see Deeksha meditating? Impossible.

And one never knows.... This man, has he become enlightened or something? But they could not believe it. And they were scholars, so they laughed at the absurdity of it, and they said, "All the great scholars are there, and you, a rice cleaner, for twelve years nobody has seen you reading scripture, studying – nobody has ever seen you sitting by the side of the master, inquiring about anything – can you improve upon it?" He said, "I can, but there is one problem. I cannot write. I knew twelve years ago, I used to write a little bit, but I have forgotten."

This happens, this unlearning happens. Unlearning is the process of becoming enlightened. Because you have learned wrong ways, and those wrong ways are the barriers, they have to be unlearned. You are born enlightened, and then you are forced into unenlightenment. Then you are conditioned for an insane society. Then you are forced to adjust to an insane society. If you remain miserable there is no wonder in it. You will remain miserable because this is not your real nature. This is not the flowering of your being.

So he said, "I cannot write. I have completely forgotten. If you can write, I can say something; you go and write it." And he didn't go there; he simply said, "The mind is not a mirror at all. Where can the dust gather? One who knows it knows it."

The mind is not a mirror. Where can the dust gather? One who comes to know this has known, has become enlightened, has looked into the deepest core of his being.

And when these words were written on the door of the master, the master became very angry. Listen carefully. The master became very angry. He said, "Bring this Hui-neng immediately, and I am going to beat him." And the scholars were very happy; they said, "That's how it should be. Bring that fellow."

The guy was brought, and the master took him inside and told him, "So you have got it! Now you escape from this monastery. This is my robe, you are my successor. But if I tell it to people, they will kill you. It will be too much against their egos to accept a rice cleaner as the head of the monastery. You simply escape. That's why I was angry, excuse me. I had to be. You simply escape from this monastery as far away as possible. You are my successor, but these people will kill you."

Scholars are very, very ambitious and political. You can go to any university and you can see. You can go to any academy and you can see. You will never see men anywhere else backbiting so much as in a university. Each professor against all, and each trying to pull everybody else down, and each thinks he is the only one capable of being the vice-chancellor or the chancellor. And all are fools.

This Hui-neng escaped. Within two, three days people got the idea that something has happened. Hui-neng is missing, and the master's robe is missing. They started searching for him. The greatest scholar, who had written the first lines, went in search. Hui-neng was caught in a forest, and Hui-neng when caught said, "You can take this robe. I am not interested in this robe at all; this is absolutely unnecessary. I was happy cleaning rice. Now I am trying to escape and hide for no reason. You take this robe."

He dropped the robe on the ground, and the scholar tried to pick it up, but it was too heavy. He could not pick it up. He fell on the ground perspiring, and he said to Hui-neng, "Excuse me. I had come for the robe, but even the robe is not ready to go with me. I am incapable. And I know it that I am incapable because all that I know are words and words and words. Excuse me...and teach me something."

And Hui-neng said, "Teaching is your problem; you have taught yourself too much. Now unteach, unlearn. Now drop all that you know. Knowledge is your barrier in knowing."

That's why the master says "...and only Hui-neng had no understanding of it whatsoever." When you don't have any intellectual understanding there arises a great understanding which is not of the mind, which is of your total being. That understanding gives you the first principle, the first taste of Tao.

I have heard:

A wealthy horse-owner died and left a large fortune to a university. A provision in the will, however, was that the school must confer a degree of Doctor of Divinity upon his favorite horse. Since the university was anxious to receive the money – it was a really big sum – the Dean set a date for the animal to receive a degree of DD.

This unusual occasion was attended by the press, and one of the reporters asked the Dean, "What is your reaction to this strange arrangement?"

"Well," replied the Dean, "in my experience I have awarded

many degrees. However, I must admit that this is the first time I have awarded a degree to a *whole* horse."

All others were donkeys, not whole horses.

The mind cannot have any contact with reality. To live in the mind is to live like an idiot. To live with the mind, in the mind, as the mind, is to live a stupid life. The moment you become a little loosened from the mind: celebration. The moment you become a little loosened from the mind: joy. A little you become loosened from the mind: and God. And suddenly the doors are open. They have never been closed; only your mind was blocking the way.

The mind can give you the second principle. The first principle is possible only through no-mind. Meditation means a state of no-mind. Meditation does not mean "to think about". Meditation means not to think at all. It does not mean, of course, to fall asleep. It means to fall *awake*. It means thoughts should disappear and only pure consciousness should be there, a presence, a luminous presence: you see; there is clarity, transparency.

Thoughts don't allow you to see. Or, even if they allow, they distort. Or they interpret. They never allow the reality to come to you raw. They decorate it, they change it, they color it. They make it digestible to you. They make it according to you. And you are false, you are a mask, so when reality is cut according to you it becomes unreal.

That's why the Master said, "If I tell you the first Principle it will become the second principle. You are asking the question from the head." The disciple was asking the question from the head. It was an intellectual question: "What is the first principle? "If the master answers it, the head will take the answer – and the head will spin philosophy around it and it will become the second principle.

The real, the true cannot be conveyed through words. It can be conveyed – yes, it can be conveyed – but the way to convey it is totally different. It is like measles: you catch them. Nobody can give them to you, but you can catch them. Truth cannot be taught but can be caught.

Look at me. I have the measles. Now, if you don't resist,

you will catch it, so lower your resistance. If you resist, you may not catch it. If you are really stubborn and hard and you close your being utterly, totally, if you are not vulnerable at all, you will not catch it. But I cannot give it to you. You can catch it, or you can not catch it, but I cannot give it to you.

It cannot be given, but it can be taken, and that is the whole art of being with a master: to learn how to take. Because he will not give. He cannot give. He makes it available. A master is a catalytic agent, he is a presence. Something is possible around him. You have to be vulnerable, you have to be in an attitude of surrender, you have to be in an attitude of receptivity: you have to be feminine.

*Hui-k'o, another Zen master, made his way northward to H'sin-yeh, where he began teaching, and among those who came to hear him was Tao-ho, a noted teacher, a very well-known author, a famous scholar on Buddhist philosophy.*

*But Hui-k'o's teaching was not like that of any other Buddhist school's, and Tao-ho was very much disturbed....*

The teaching was absurd, almost sacrilegious, because Huik'o used to say, "Kill your parents." A beautiful saying – but don't take it literally. The parents are within you. You can ask the T.A. people – Transactional Analysis people. The parents are within you. The mother, the father – their conditioning is within you. They go on controlling you from within you. So when Hui-k'o said, "Kill your parents; only then come to me," he was uttering a great insight.

That's what Jesus says. Christians have not yet been able to explain it. He says, "Unless you hate your mother, unless you hate your father, you cannot come to me." Hate? And the utterance is coming from the man who says, "God is love"?

And Hui-k'o used to say, "If you meet the buddha on the way, kill him immediately!" Because when you start meditating you will meet your parents, you will meet all the people who have been related to you. You will have to kill them, you will have to disassociate yourself from them; you will have to learn aloneness. And finally you will meet the buddha, your master, and you have to kill the master too.

But these are dangerous things to say. And the way he used to say them. This scholar Tao-ho became very angry. He said, "This man will destroy all religion." That's what people say about me.

...He determined to destroy this unholy doctrine and to that end dispatched several of his best students to dispute with Hui-k'o....

Hui-k'o is the successor of Bodhidharma, and of course he was a worthy successor, of a great master. He was a great disciple. Hui-k'o was attacked by this man Tao-ho in many ways, and he used to send his disciples to dispute with and to defeat this man.

...Tao-ho awaited their return with high expectations of hearing that they had won a notable victory over the hated interloper, but they did not come back....

Not a single person ever came back. Whosoever went to Hui-k'o simply disappeared. These people are dangerous people. One should avoid them if one really wants to avoid them. Sometimes you may go as an antagonist, and you may fall in love with them. And these people are like dragons; once you are close to them they will suck you in.

...He sent out other emissaries, and still others, but none came back to report the expected victory. It was only after some time had passed that he met some of his messengers and said to them: "I had opened your eyes to the Tao; why were you such faithless emissaries?"

One of them spoke up for the rest: "The original eye is perfect in itself, but your teaching has rendered us half blind."

"The original eye is perfect in itself." Each child is born with that original eye – it is perfect – that innocent eye. It is perfect! It needs no improvement! And the whole effort of all the masters down through the ages has been one;

whatsoever the society has done, they have to undo. Whatsoever the society has put into your mind, they have to take it away. They have to dehypnotize you, they have to uncondition you. They have to make your childhood again available to you.

But remember, religion is not a teaching, is not a learning. You can catch it. Yes, it is like measles. And you have to be in a mood to catch it. That mood is what is meant by being a disciple. A disciple simply shows a gesture, a great gesture, a *mahamudra*, that "I am ready, master," that "I am open," that "I will not resist. If you are going to kill me, I am ready. Whatsoever you are going to do to me, I am available – my availability is total." That's all a disciple has to do. And the Master has to do nothing; he has just to be there.

The Master there – the one who has become enlightened, the one who has come to know his real nature – his presence, and the availability of the disciple, and something catches fire, something simply happens. And that is the first principle. It cannot be asked, it cannot be answered. That which can be asked and that which can be answered will be the second principle; it will be a carbon copy, an echo.

Of course, the priests won't like such a rebellious meaning to be given to religion. They will not like people to become awake. Neither will the politicians like it. The politician and the priest is the very, very ancient conspiracy against the innocence of man. They corrupt. Their whole business depends on this: that man remains unconscious, that man does not become aware. Because the moment a man is aware, he is freedom – freedom from all politics and freedom from all religions. He is religious, but free from all religions. You cannot say that he is a Mohammedan, you cannot say that he is a Hindu.

To call Zen people Buddhist is wrong. It is as wrong as to call Sufis Mohammedans. It is as wrong as to call Hassidim Jews. The real people are simply real people. Zen, Sufi, or Hassid, there is neither Buddhist nor Mohammedan nor Jew.

But the priest will not like it. It will be destroying his whole business. It will be dismantling his whole shop, his whole market.

Two waiters were standing at a table over which a loaded customer had fallen asleep. Said one, "I have already awakened him twice. Now I am going to awaken him for the third time."

"Why don't you chuck him out?" asked the other waiter.

"The devil I will," said the first waiter. "I got a good thing going for me. Every time I wake him up he pays his bill."

If humanity remains asleep, if humanity remains unconscious and hypnotized, then the politician can remain in power and the priest can go on exploiting you. If humanity becomes awake, then there will be no need for these priests and politicians. There will not be any need for any country, state, and there will not be any need for any church, any Vatican, any pope. The need will disappear. There will be a totally different quality to human consciousness.

That quality needs to be born. We have come to that point in the evolution of human consciousness where this new consciousness is tremendously needed, desperately needed – this new consciousness which makes man free from politics and free from religion.

And let me remind you again and again, that will be the only religious world: free from religions, but not free from religion; free from churches, dogmas, but not free from the first principle; free from all the second principles.

A girl told her friend she had just become engaged to a traveling salesman.

"Is he good looking?" asked the friend.

"Look, he would never stand out in a crowd."

"Does he have money?" continued the friend.

"If he does, he won't spend it."

"What about his bad habits. Does he have any?"

"Well, he drinks an awful lot," said the future bride.

"I don't understand you," said the friend. "If you can't say anything nice about him, then why are you marrying him?"

"He is on the road all the time," she replied, "and I will never see him."

That's the only good thing about it – and that is the good

thing about the god of the priests: you will never see him. That's why you go on following the priest. To avoid God you follow the priest. To avoid God you read the Bible. To avoid God you chant Vedas. To avoid God you become scholars, thinkers. To avoid God you are doing everything that is possible

But why do you want to avoid God? Why in the first place do you want to avoid God? There are reasons. The very idea of God creates tremendous fear because God will mean death to your ego. You will not exist if God is there.

The great Indian mystic Kabir has said, "Look at the irony of it. When I was, God was not; now God is, I am not. Anyway the meeting has not happened." Because for the meeting, two are needed. "When I was, God was not; now God is, I am not."

The fear is that you will have to lose yourself. You are afraid of death; that's why you are afraid of God. And that's why you are afraid of love, and that's why you are afraid of all that is great.

You are too attached to this false ego – which never gives anything but misery, but pain, but at least gives you a feeling that you are. Just watch. Meditate over it.

If you want to be, then you will always fall into the trap of the priest. In fact you are not. The whole idea is a false notion. How can you be? The waves exist, but not separate from the ocean. So exist we: not separate from the ocean of consciousness. That's what God is. The leaves exist, but not separate from the tree. Everything exists, but nothing exists separately. No man is an island, and no part can exist independently. We exist in deep interdependence. We are members of one another, of each other. We penetrate each other. This whole existence is a great penetration. Trees penetrate you; you penetrate the trees. Stars penetrate you; you penetrate the stars. You penetrate the earth; the earth penetrates you. Everything is penetrated.

God is this totality. You cannot exist separately. If you want to exist separately, then you are a politician. All politics is nothing but the shadow of the ego. Then you will live in misery and in madness.

But if you look, if you watch deeply, you will be surprised.

You are not! Not that you have to dissolve! Simply you are not. It is just a false notion that you have been carrying, the notion that you are. Any moment of silence and you will suddenly see there is emptiness within you, nothingness within you. Buddha has called this nothingness *anatta*, nonbeing, *shunya*, nothingness. If you look within, you will not find yourself. That's why people don't look within; they are afraid.

Once it happened I was traveling with Mulla Nasruddin in a train. Came the ticket collector and Nasruddin became very hectic. He looked in his suitcase, he turned over all the things, he looked in the bed, turned over everything, he looked in his many pockets, and he started perspiring and he could not find the ticket. I saw that he had not looked in one pocket, so I told him, "Nasruddin, you have not looked in that pocket." He said, "Don't mention that." I said, "But why? The ticket may be there." He said, "Don't mention it at all. If I look in it and the ticket is not found, I will fall dead. I will drop dead! I cannot look in that! If the ticket is not there, then finished. There is a hope that it may be there."

That's why people don't look inside: a hope one may be there. The day you look in, you are not. The day you look in, suddenly there is vast emptiness...and it is tremendously blissful, beautiful, peaceful. You are not there; then there is no noise.

That's what Hui-neng means when he says, "There is no mirror of the mind. Where can the dust gather? To know this is to know all."

Look within. People think "We are bad" but you are not, so how can badness gather? People think "We are good," but how is it possible? You are not there; how can you be good? People think "We are moral and immoral and this and that," but everything hangs on the idea of "I". To be good the "I" is needed first, to be virtuous the "I" is needed first. To be a sinner or to be a saint the "I" is needed first. Without the "I" you will not have anything to hang anything upon. Where will you hang your goodness, your sin or your saintliness?

That's why Zen goes on insisting there is nobody who is a sinner and there is nobody who is a saint, nothing is good and nothing is bad. All distinctions are ego created. Distinctions are created so that the ego can exist through the distinctions. When you look within there is neither saint nor sinner, neither good nor bad – neither life nor death. All distinctions disappear.

In that nothingness one becomes one with God. One is one with God – one has been from the very beginning.

So the fear is that if you want to know God you will have to disappear; so you don't look into your own being. The fear is that if you look within yourself you may become happy...

People go on saying that they want to become happy, but I rarely come across a person who really wants to be happy. People cling to their misery. Again the same game. With the misery you have something to do. With the misery, some occupation. With the misery you can avoid yourself, you are engaged. With joy there is nothing with which to be engaged, there is nowhere to go. In joy you again disperse and disappear. In misery you are there – you are very much there. Misery gives you a very solid experience that you are. When you are happy, you start disappearing. When you are really happy, you are not, again you are not. In a state of bliss, again you disappear.

You talk about heaven, but you go on creating hell because only in hell can you exist. You cannot exist in heaven. George Bernard Shaw is reported to have said, "If I am not going to be the first in heaven, then I would not like to go to heaven. I would like to be in hell, but I would like to be first; I don't want to be second." Hell is okay, but the ego says, "Be first, be a leader." Hell is okay if the ego remains; heaven is not okay if the ego has to be dropped.

You would like to be in heaven with your ego. You are asking the impossible. That cannot happen.

The religion that exists on the earth is false, it is a make-believe, it is just for the name's sake, but it fulfills your demand. It fulfills a certain demand, that you want to pretend that you are religious. You don't want to become religious but you want to pretend. And you want to pretend in such a way that not even you yourself can catch yourself pretending. You want to pretend in such a way that you don't ever come across your pretensions, so a great structure is created. And that great structure is the church. Avoid that structure if you really want to become religious. And unless you are religious you are not!

Now let me tell you this paradox; You are only when you are not, because you are only when the ego has disappeared and you are God. That is the first principle. I am not telling it to you, and you are not hearing it from me.

It happened:

The car suddenly broke down in the middle of nowhere. He crawled underneath to see what the trouble was. She crawled underneath to hold the torch for him. It was quite cozy under there and, after a while, they forgot about car repairs. Suddenly a voice said, "And just what do you two think you are doing?"

Looking up they saw the local village constable.

"Why we are – er – repairing the back axle," the young man stammered.

"Well, while you are down there, you had better look at the brakes as well," replied the law. "Your car has been at the bottom of the hill for the past half hour."

That's what has happened to churches. Jesus is not there, the Buddha is not there. People are doing something else in the name of Jesus, in the name of Buddha, and they are thinking Buddha is there. Church is the last place where you can meet Jesus, and the temple, the Buddhist temple, is the last place where you can meet a Buddha. But you go to the church, you go to the temple...and you think you are going to Buddha and to Jesus.

You are great pretenders. You want to pretend. You want to be respectable. You want to show to everybody that "We are religious people." So we have created a Sunday religion; every Sunday you go. Six days for the world; one day – not the whole day – one or two hours – for God. Just in case something goes wrong or maybe really God is or maybe one survives death. These are all perhapses. And a perhaps never changes anybody's life; only a certainty changes somebody's life.

Hence my insistence, if you cannot find an alive master, go on searching and searching. There are always alive masters somewhere or other; the earth is never empty of them. But never go to the places where conventionally you expect them. There they are not. Jesus was not in the synagogue. Buddha was not in any Hindu temple; he was born a Hindu, but he was not in any Hindu temple. Jesus was a Jew, but he was not in the synagogue. And so has been the case always. Don't go on worshipping ideas. Find a living reality.

And the moment you find a living reality, become vulnerable, become open. And you will have the first principle, which cannot be said, but you can get it.

Chapter 2

# Greed Behind Greed Behind Greed

*Is God really dead?*

If not dead, then seriously ill, on his deathbed. Which is far worse.

I have heard:

There was a small synagogue somewhere in some obscure village in central Poland. One night when making his rounds, the rabbi entered and saw God sitting in a dark corner. He fell upon his face and cried out, "Lord God, what art thou doing here?"

God answered him with a small voice, "I am tired, Rabbi. I am tired to death."

God is tired of man's inhumanity to man. God is tired of man's immense stupidity. God is tired of man's unawareness. Only man seems somehow to be a misfit. The whole existence goes on harmoniously; the whole existence is a dance. Man is out of step. And the reason is that only man is free to be out of step. The glory of man is that he is free, totally free. Nobody else has that freedom. Because of the freedom, man can choose. He can choose either to be with God or he can choose to be against – and man has chosen to be against. There is a reason for it.

Each child has to choose to be against his parents. That is the only way for the child to attain his ego. If the child goes on saying yes to the father, yes to the mother, and says always yes and never says no, then the child will not have any backbone. Then the child will not have any soul. Then the child will be just an extension of the parent. That hurts, that humiliates. And it is not just accidental that we have called God the father. It is the same drama played on a more cosmic scale.

Man is still childish. To be, he still needs to say no. A man is mature when he can be and can say yes too. Try to understand it. A child has to say no to the parents, a thousand and one times he has to say no, because that is the only way he can feel "I am." Sometimes he has to say no against his own welfare; sometimes he has to say no in spite of himself. Sometimes he wants to say yes, but he cannot say it, because to say yes means not to be. And each moment the struggle: to be or not to be. The moment he says yes, he is not; parents are. The moment he says no, he is. So the child has to say no. He has to rebel, he has to go against, he has to go astray to be.

But one need not be a child forever. Adam was a child; Jesus was a mature man: Adam went out of paradise. In fact, he was not expelled, he expelled himself. That was the only way to have individuality. That is the childish way to have individuality. Now, Jesus was so certain about his integrity he could say yes and yet remain himself.

Do you follow it? When you can say yes and yet remain individual, you are mature. Then there is no necessity of saying no, because if you say no and then you become individual, your individuality has a negative taste to it. It is not real individuality; it is not yet positive. It is just a no deep down, a wound, a hole. And through the no you can become an individual, but your individuality will never be satisfying. There will be no contentment in it, there will be no bliss, because bliss flows only out of yes. When you can say yes to existence, you start flowing blissfully. No cripples, paralyzes. No makes you an enemy of the existence; no gives resistance. Yes makes you nonresistant; yes makes you vulnerable.

God is dead or dying because man has not yet grown. There have been millions of Adams and Eves, and only very rarely Christs – a Buddha here, a Christ there, a Lao Tzu – only few and far between. The people who have really said yes, they give life to God. By saying no, you give life to yourself. By saying yes, you give life to the total, to the whole; you pour your life into the whole. So if you really want God to be alive, you have to say yes.

Man has killed God – almost killed him – by saying no, continuously saying no.

I love this story. The rabbi asked, "Lord God, what art thou doing here?" God answered him with a small voice, "I am tired, Rabbi. I am tired to death." Yes. God is tired. In fact, God cannot die. God can die in *your* life. There are millions of people in whose lives God is dead, in whose lives God has disappeared. That is the meaning when I say God is dead. Look into people's eyes and you will not find God alive there. And where else can God be alive? Millions and millions of hearts are completely empty of God. That's what I mean when I say God is dead.

God lives in a Jesus, in a Buddha, in a Krishna. Is God living in you? The question is not basically about God, whether God is dead or alive. The question is whether God is alive in *you*! If he is not alive in you, then what difference does it make if he is alive somewhere in heaven? It does not make any difference. For you it is practically the same: God is dead.

Nietzsche is right about modern humanity when he says God is dead. Not that God is dead! How can God be dead? God means the eternal element, the first principle. God cannot be dead. But you can be so against God, you can be so empty of God, that for you he is dead.

You have to pour your life into him, you have to make God alive in you, so he can beat through your heart, he can pulsate in you, he can love through you, he can *be* through you. That's what sannyas is all about: an effort to allow God to live in you, an effort to become a shrine of the divine.

Look into your own being and search there. You will be fortunate if you can find in a dark corner of your being somewhere God sitting, tired – tired to death. You will have to revive him. You will have to breathe for him, live for him. You will have to surrender your life for the whole. A religious person is one in whom God has come alive again.

*How can I be nothing and unique?*

You can be unique only when you are nothing. If you are something, you are comparable. If you are somebody you can be compared with others, and that which can be compared cannot be unique. Unique means incomparable. Unique means you are alone, there is nobody like you. So if you are somebody.... If you are a man there are millions of men; you are comparable. If you are rich, then there are millions of rich people; you are comparable. If you are good you are comparable. If you are bad you are comparable. If you are a painter you are comparable. If you are a singer you are comparable. If you are somebody you are comparable, and by being comparable you cease to be unique.

The moment you attain to a nothingness, when the "I" disappears.... The "I" is comparable; the "no-I" is incomparable. That's why I say if you become nothing you become unique. If you become nothing you become incorruptible; the nothing cannot be corrupted.

You have heard Lord Acton's saying, "Power corrupts; and absolute power corrupts absolutely." Why does power corrupt? Because power makes you somebody. It gives you a definition. It says who you are – you are a prime minister of a country or a president of a country. Power gives you a definition; it demarks who you are. If you have money, it demarks you. If you don't have money, it demarks you. If you are a musician or a poet or a singer, it shows who you are. The moment you know who you are, you are limited, you are finite – and you are comparable.

But if you are nobody – just a pure nothingness, pure sky with not even a particle of dust – then how can you be compared.?

God is unique because God is nothing. You cannot find God anywhere. Either you can find him everywhere or nowhere, but you cannot find him somewhere. Either he is the whole or he is nothing.

When you are nothing you also become the whole. When you are nothing you also become divine. By being somebody you remain human. By being nobody you attain to divinity, you become divine. Hence I have said that the moment nothingness arises in you, you have become unique.

Buddha is unique not because he is the great saint, because there are millions of saints. Jesus is unique not because he is the most virtuous man. That's all nonsense. He is unique because he is nothing. He is unique because he is ready to crucify his ego. And the moment his ego is crucified, he resurrects – he resurrects as the whole. He dies as the part and resurrects as the whole. He dies in time and is resurrected in eternity.

*I belong to the intelligentsia; I believe in intellect and reason. Is there a way out for me?*

It is going to be difficult. The intellect has no way out; the intellect is a cul-de-sac. The intellect moves in a vicious circle. It creates its own world of concepts, words, theories, and lives there. There is no way out from the head. The way out is from the heart, because the heart opens – so the way out is possible. Intellect lives in a closed way. Intellect has no doors to go out from; it is a closed existence, encapsulated.

It is very difficult to communicate with an intellectual, almost impossible. You say something; he hears something else. You show something; he sees something else. His intellect is a constant interference. It is very difficult to communicate; there is no bridge. Communication is possible only between two hearts, not between two heads. Two heads simply collide with each other, conflict – confusion, but no meeting, no communion. Only hearts meet.

But the intellect has been praised down the centuries because intellect is very useful. The intellect is capable of exploitation. The intellect is capable of domination. The intellect is capable of cheating nature, of oppression. The intellect is very, very useful as far as the world of things is concerned. So man has cultivated his intellect and has denied his heart, because the heart is dangerous. You cannot exploit if you are a heart man. You cannot use somebody's life as a means if you are heart-oriented. The other becomes an end unto himself. You cannot become a politician and you cannot become a scientist. The politician exploits other human beings, and the scientist exploits nature. Both are destructive. The politician has destroyed humanity, and the scientist has destroyed nature.

Now the whole of existence on this earth is collapsing – because of the politician and the scientist. And they both are together. The atom bomb became possible because Albert Einstein and Roosevelt joined together. It would not have been possible if Roosevelt had wanted it alone. It would not have been possible if Albert Einstein had wanted it alone. It becomes possible only when politics and science meet. Then there is a Hiroshima and a Nagasaki, and then there is destruction. And the politician and the scientist have been in cooperation down the ages. They have been helping each other.

The heart-oriented man can become a poet, but of what use is a poet? Of what use is poetry? A heart-oriented man can become a musician, but of what use is music? A heart-oriented person can become a lover, but the world does not need lovers. It needs soldiers; it needs people to kill and to be killed. It needs butchers. It needs mad people. It does not need sane people, who love, who live – who live peacefully and who help others to live peacefully. The world does not believe in rose flowers. It believes in swords, in rifles in atom bombs.

Intellect has been very destructive. I am not saying that intellect has to be dropped completely. That will be foolish. Intellect has to be used – but not as a master, rather as a slave. The mind is very beautiful as a slave, but it is a very lousy master. Never make the intellect your master. Use it. It is a beautiful instrument, a biocomputer. No computer yet made by man is so delicate, so evolved as the human mind. The human mind is such a beautiful, delicate mechanism. It can be of much use, but it should be in the service of love.

The head should be in the service of the heart; then you are really intelligent. Remember the difference. I don't call an intellectual an intelligent person. An intelligent person is one whose intellect is in the service of the heart, whose logic is in the service of love, whose reason is in the service of life, which is more than reason. Otherwise your so-called intellectuals are just stupid people.

One story:

Five men are on a military plane crossing the North

Atlantic – President Jimmy Carter, former President Ford, Kissinger, a Catholic priest, and a hippie....

Maybe the hippie was my sannyasin.

...The plane is suddenly buffeted by a thunderstorm and the pilot rushes into the passenger section. "We have just been hit by a lightning bolt. The co-pilot is dead. Our power is gone. Here are four parachutes. Decide among yourselves who will use them."...

There are five persons and four parachutes.

...With that, the pilot bails out.

President Carter speaks first: "I have the burden of the whole free world on my shoulder. I am sure you will agree I must carry on." He dons a parachute and bails out.

Ford speaks up: "I have never done any harm to anyone. Besides, I have a golf date." And he bails out.

Henry Kissinger declares: "I am sure you will agree that I am the smartest man in the world. Obviously I must be spared." And he jumps.

The priest turns to the hippie, "I have led a full life. I am not afraid to meet my maker. Go ahead, my son, and take the last parachute."

"But Father," says the hippie, "there are two parachutes left. The 'smartest man in the world' just bailed out wearing my knapsack."

Please don't be the smartest man in the world. Intellectuals are not very intelligent people.

*What is the reason that I find it difficult to enforce rules? Part of me gets angry and insists that sannyasins follow simple rules like no smoking or eating in the gardens. Teertha has called me "the commandant of the garden," but deep down I hate the whole authority trip; it is the only part of my work that is not enjoyable. How can one be a nobody when put in a position of having to enforce rules?*

*Could Chuang Tzu lay down his fishing pole and come to Pune to play Laxmi's role?*

The question is asked by Nirgun.
Who do you think is playing Laxmi's role? It is Chuang Tzu.
A few things to be understood about the question. It's certainly difficult to play an authoritative role, but the difficulty arises not because of the role but because of the unconscious desire to dominate. You can repress the desire, you can avoid any authoritative role; the desire will remain there. Whenever the authoritative role is given to you, the desire hidden in the unconscious, the repressed desire, becomes alive, jumps on the role.

It is beautiful to watch it and get rid of it; rather than getting rid of the role, rather than trying to avoid the role itself, it is better to get rid of the desire to be authoritative. So Nirgun, it is good that you are placed in a role where again and again you will have to say to people, "Don't do this."

But this can be said in a very nonauthoritative way. There is no need to be authoritative about it. Don't make it a trip. And then the situation will be a great opportunity to grow. I have put many people in authoritative roles. That is the only way to get rid of any repressed desire. When the situation is there and the opportunity is there, the desire comes up, surfaces.

And Nirgun has that desire deep down; hence the fear. She would like to escape from the situation. She would like some work where there is no need to say to anybody, "Don't do this." But how will you get rid of the desire? It is easy to avoid children, but it is very difficult to get rid of the parent role. It is very easy never to be in a position where you have to say to people, "Do this. Don't do this." Very easy. But how will you get rid of the subtle aggressive energy in you?

I would like you to use these situations. And this ashram has to be a constantly ongoing group. Every situation has to be used in such a way that it helps your spiritual growth.

She refers to Chuang Tzu, the famous story that Chuang Tzu was asked by the emperor to come to the palace and to become his prime minister. I have commented on the story. I love Chuang Tzu.

Two messengers came from the emperor. Chuang Tzu was fishing, and they came and they said, "The emperor wants you to become the prime minister of the country." Chuang Tzu said, "Do you see that turtle there, wagging its tail in the mud?" They said, "Yes, we see." "And do you see how happy he is?" They said, "Certainly. He looks tremendously happy."

And then Chuang Tzu said, "I have heard that in the king's palace there is a turtle, three thousand years old, dead, encaged in gold, decorated with diamonds, and he is worshipped. If you ask this turtle who is wagging his tail in the mud to change his role, to become that turtle in the palace – dead, but encaged in gold, decorated with diamonds, and worshipped by the emperor himself – will this turtle be ready to accept that?"

The messengers said, "Certainly not. This turtle will not be ready."

So Chuang Tzu said, "Why should I be ready? Then be gone! I am happy in my mud, wagging my tail, and I don't want to come to the emperor's palace."

Now, this is a beautiful story, but if I meet Chuang Tzu I will say that he is still afraid, he still has a certain fear. If I had been in Chuang Tzu's place, I would have gone to the palace. You can wag your tail in the palace too, and it will be fun. But Chuang Tzu must have been a little afraid, a little fear that maybe he will become imprisoned there, maybe he will have to lose his freedom, life, aliveness, maybe he will start going on a power trip, ego trip. But that fear simply shows that something in the unconscious is still lingering on.

A man should be so free that if the situation demands him to be in a power role, he can be in a power role – without being powerful. If the situation demands it of him, he can easily accommodate himself to the new situation without any trouble. A man should not have a fixed role in life. He should be fluid. And the question is not of roles; the question is of consciousness.

So Nirgun, be more conscious, be more loving. Don't allow that urge to dominate to become an unconscious trip, that's all. Become conscious of it. Through consciousness, it will be dropped.

Because of this fear, millions of people down the ages

became monks and nuns. What was their fear? Why were they afraid of the world? They were afraid not of the world, they were afraid of their unconscious desires. They knew well that if opportunity is given to them they will fall from their pedestals. But what type of awareness is this? If you can be happy only in the forest and cannot be happy in the marketplace, your happiness is not worth much. If you can be celibate only when there is no woman available, your celibacy is not of any worth, not worth much. If you can be nonpossessive when there is nothing to possess, then what is the point of your being nonpossessive? When you have the whole world to possess and you remain non-possessive, this is attainment, this I call *siddha*, this I call real achievement.

So my sannyasins are not to become escapists. They have to live in the world, and they have to live above the world – in the world and yet above it, in and yet not in it. My sannyasin has to face more than Mahavira's sannyasin or Buddha's sannyasin. My sannyasin has to remain liquid, flowing – and yet uncontaminated.

*I am no politician, no diplomat, and I feel like a clown. I want to dance on the desk and sing on the phone "Hello-lujah" rather than "Hello". May I sign up for the ashram fool?*

It is too early. To be really a fool one needs to be very wise. To be a fool one needs to be *truly* wise. That's why all wise people have something of foolishness in them. Jesus was known as a fool, so was Buddha, so was Francis of Assisi. They were known as fools.

There is a certain quality of foolishness in a real wise man. Why? Because a real wise man contains the opposite. He is both together. He is more comprehensive. A wise man who has no foolishness in him will be dry, dead. His juice will not be flowing. He will not be green. He will not be able to laugh; he will be serious; he will be a long face. A wise man who is just wise and in whose being the fool has not been integrated will be very heavy. It will be difficult to live with such a wise man. He will be very boring. He will be boring to you and he will be boring to himself. He will not have any fun; his life will not know any joy. He will be completely unacquainted with laughter. And when laughter is missed, much is missed.

And one can never know God without laughter. One can never know God without joy. One can never know reality just by being wise.

The fool has something to contribute too – the laughter, the joy, the nonseriousness, the quality of fun, delight. The fool can dance, and the fool can dance for any reason whatsoever – any excuse will do. The fool can laugh. And the fool can laugh not only at others, he can laugh at himself.

When the wise man and the fool meet together in a consciousness, then something of tremendous value happens. There are foolish people and there are wise people. The fool is shallow; the wise man is serious. The fool does not know what truth is, and the wise man does not know what joy is. And a truth without joy is worse than a lie. And a joy without truth is not reliable. A joy without truth is momentary, cannot be of the eternal.

My approach is that of great balance. You have to be very, very balanced. Delicate is the balance, difficult to achieve, but once achieved you will know that there is a quality of consciousness which can absorb wisdom and foolishness together, and there is no contradiction. They both become two aspects of your energy.

Then you are sincere, but not serious. Then you are truthful, but not joyless. Then you have joy, but the joy is not of the momentary, it is of the eternal. It is not within time; it is beyond time.

So it is too early. To really become the ashram fool, you will have to become almost enlightened. Don't think that it is easy to become a fool.

I am not talking about the common variety of fools. Gurdjieff used to talk about eighteen varieties of idiots; they come in all sizes and all shapes. But I am talking about the ultimate. Gurdjieff used to say God is the ultimate idiot. Looks very profane. The ultimate idiot, God? And Gurdjieff used to say if he was not an idiot, why should he have created you all? Some idiocy, some trait of foolishness must exist in him; otherwise why man? And not only you. Men like Adolf Hitler, Genghis Khan, Nadir Shah; men like Joseph Stalin, Mao Zedong. Why in the first place? God must have some trait of foolishness. He must be fooling around; he must be trying trial and error. Yes, sometimes he turns up with a Buddha too, that's okay – but rarely, very rarely.

God must be a fool. Otherwise there cannot be so much joy in existence. Just think: a mahatma ruling the world. All joy will be simply prohibited. Can you laugh in a Christian heaven? Have you asked this question to your ministers, priests? Can you have a belly laugh, standing in front of God? No, that doesn't seem proper.

But I tell you, you can have. And if you don't have, God will have, looking at your seriousness.

Look at trees, the birds, the animals, the stars. There seems to be tremendous joy. Life is not serious. Life is very, very playful.

So when I say become a fool and wise together, I mean don't think of life as a duty, but as a play. Always remember, if your prayer is without laughter, you are missing something. If your laughter is without prayer, you are again missing something. A prayer without laughter is dead, and a laughter without prayer has no depth. Can you pray and laugh together? Can you be prayerful and dance too? Can you meditate and love together?

That is the synthesis I am trying. That is the highest possibility a man can arrive at, the greatest symphony, when you can love and meditate together. There have been meditators, but they were against love, and there have been lovers who were against meditation. There have been people who say eat, drink, be merry, but they are against God. The Charvakas, the Epicureans – they say eat, drink, be merry, there is no God. They help you to be joyful, but that joy cannot be very deep. Without God your joy cannot go very deep.

Your joy – on your own – cannot be real joy. It will be very shallow and superficial. It will not have the quality of the ultimate in it. It will not throb with eternity. And you will get fed up with it sooner or later.

That's what is happening in the West. The West has

followed the Epicurean tradition – eat, drink, be merry. Now people are fed up, really fed up; nothing seems to satisfy. The superficial cannot satisfy long. One day or other it is exposed; you come to know that it is not much and it is a repetition. The West is fed up with the Epicurean ideology, the ideology that says, "Just enjoy. There is no need to seek and search."

And the East is fed up with the opposite ideology, the other polarity that says, "Don't enjoy," that says, "'Eat, drink, be merry' is the ideology of the sinners. Wear long faces, be ascetics, mahatmas. Do yoga. Fast. Destroy the body and the senses. And be seriously after God: the only thing that is worth achieving is God-realization; everything else has to be sacrificed."

The East is fed up, tired. The West is fed up and tired. It is natural because both have chosen one aspect. God is all the aspects together. God means totality.

My approach towards God is Epicurus plus Buddha. Be as Epicurean as possible, and be a meditator, a seeker, as authentic as possible. And I don't see that there is any conflict. There is no conflict in meditation and love. In fact, the more you meditate, the more you become capable of love; the more you love, the more you become capable of meditation.

And there is no conflict between being a fool and being wise. If you can have both, that is the best. And don't settle for one; otherwise one day you will repent. The missing one will take its revenge, and with vengeance.

But to Vani I would like to say it is too early. Get a little ready.

I have heard:

Once there was a fellow who was too forward. He would meet a girl and within two seconds say, "Honey, let us make love." His buddy took him aside and explained that he should act suave and carry on a friendly conversation for a while before he suggested such things. On his next date he remembered the words of wisdom. He started the conversation by saying, "Honey, have you ever been to Africa?" just to create a conversation.

She said, "No." So he said, "Well, let us make love."

Vani, it is too early. Wait a little more. The hello has to become hello-lujah, but wait a little more.

*One beautiful day when love was humming in the air, even Winnie the Pooh forgot his constant fruitless search for a pot of honey and just sat down. When his eyes opened he was bowled over to see all around him huge pots overflowing with more honey than he could ever eat.*
*When he rolled into Eeyore's later that night, all sticky and content and full of his discovery, Eeyore looked wise and said, "Honey is always there – but you can only find it when you are not looking."*
*Pooh Bear thought he understood, but for days after when he made sudden surreptitious glances out of the corner of his eye – no honey! He even tried sitting down again and saying very loudly, 'I am not looking for honey!" but when he opened his eyes, the honey still was not there.*
*Dear Eeyore, how can I drop my greed and my expectations, and just be?*

Yes, it is one of the most fundamental questions. When you are not looking, the honey is everywhere. When you start looking for it, suddenly it disappears. This is a great truth. The moment you start looking for it, you become tense. The moment you start looking for it, you become very, very concentrated, you become closed and narrow. And the honey is possible only when you are open, not closed, not narrow. The honey overflows all around you when you are also overflowing, in every direction.

To look means to be directed in one direction. Not to look, not to seek, then you are available to all directions – you are available to every direction possible, you are available to the whole existence.

But the difficulty is that if I tell you not to look you say, "Okay, we will not try," but an unconscious effort goes on. You even try not to look, but that too becomes just an effort to look.

The question is very fundamental. Buddha says, "If you are desireless, all desires will be fulfilled." Now, one monk asked one day, "Since you have said that all desires will be fulfilled if you become desireless, I have got only one desire: to be desireless. Now what to do about it?" But the desire to be desireless is still a desire; it is on the same plane. Whether you desire money or you desire power, prestige, or you desire desirelessness, it makes no difference at all: only the object of desire changes; the desire remains the same. And the desire is the problem, not the object.

If you desire money, people will call you very worldly, materialistic. If you desire God, people will call you spiritual, other worldly, religious. But those who know, for them, there is no difference at all: you are still worldly. It is not that a few desires are worldly and a few desires are otherworldly! Desire, as such, is worldly. There can be no otherworldly desire.

So God cannot be desired. If you desire, you miss. If you seek, you will not find. The more you seek, the more miserable you will become. Don't seek, and find. Just be – in an attitude of non-seeking. Not that deep down you still go on thinking "Now he must be coming because I am not seeking"; then you are in the same trap again.

The question is what should be done: "How can I drop my greed...?" But why do you want to drop your greed? Why in the first place do you want to drop your greed? There must be some greed behind it – to attain to God, to nirvana, to enlightenment, to this and that, all sorts of rubbish things, all nonsense.

Enlightenment *happens*. You cannot desire it. When one day suddenly you find all desires have disappeared, enlightenment is there. It has always been there; just because of desires you could not see it. The desire becomes a curtain on your eyes. You lose clarity, you cannot see what is. How can you see what is when you want something to be there? When you expect something, the expectation does not allow you to see that which is. With the expectation you have already moved into the future.

You want a beautiful woman, and you have a fantasy. Because of that fantasy, you will miss your woman, who is just in front of you, but because of the fantasy you cannot see her. The fantasy goes on driving you away.

You ask, "How can I drop my greed?" I would like to ask why in the first place you want to drop greed. And suddenly you will find some greed hidden behind. Greed behind greed behind greed. This is not going to help.

So I will not tell you how to drop it. I will tell you how to understand it. In understanding, it drops on its own accord. Not that you drop it. You cannot. You are greed; how can you drop greed? You are desire; how can you drop desire? You are the search; how can you drop seeking and searching? This *you* is the center of all your madnesses. You ask how to drop greed. Who is asking? The "I". Now the "I" wants even God to be possessed. The "I" wants enlightenment to be possessed. The "I" does not only want the world, it wants the other world too. The "I" is getting more insane.

Just understand. There is no need to drop anything. Man cannot drop anything. Just try to understand. Try to understand the ways of greed. Try to understand how greed functions. Try to understand how greed brings more and more misery, more and more frustration, how greed goes on creating new hells for you, ahead of you, goes on creating new hells so when you are there, they are ready. Just look into the very phenomenon of greed – with no idea of dropping it, because if you want to drop it, a part of greed will remain unobserved. The part that wants to drop greed will remain unobserved, will remain in the dark.

There is no need to think in these terms. Simply try to understand. That is what Socrates means when he says, "Know thyself." It does not mean that you sit silently and repeat "I am soul", "I am God"; it doesn't mean that. "Know thyself" means whatsoever is the case, go into it deeply, layer by layer. Expose it to your understanding. Go to the very bottom of it, to the very root of it. Look through and through.

And the day you have looked through all the layers.... The layers are just like an onion. You go on peeling an onion. So peel your being like an onion, go on peeling. Fresher layers you will find; go on peeling, go on peeling.... One day suddenly you have peeled through and through and nothing but emptiness is left in your hand. In that emptiness greed has disappeared, and in that emptiness enlightenment has happened. In that emptiness God is. That emptiness is God.

So rather than asking how to drop greed, ask how to understand greed. The whole thing hangs on one thing: understanding. When the understanding of anything is perfect, it liberates. That's what Jesus means when he says, "Truth liberates." When you know the truth of greed you are liberated. When you know the truth of sexuality you are liberated. When you know the truth of anything whatsoever you are liberated from it. To know is to be free; not to know is to be in bondage.

So don't ask how to drop. There is no hurry. In fact, go deep into it, watch it deeply before it drops; otherwise you will always miss that understanding. If it drops before understanding, something will remain missing. That's why it never drops, it clings to you. It clings up to the last moment, when you understand it, when you have looked into it so deeply that nothing is unrevealed, you have seen the ways of greed, the subtle ways of greed.

Now, this question is a subtle way of greed: how to drop it? That was the problem of Pooh; he thought he understood: "...but for days after when he made sudden surreptitious glances out of the corner of his eye – no honey!" You will also make surreptitious glances from the corner – unless you understand greed totally.

"He even tried sitting down again and saying very loudly, 'I am not looking for honey!' " And you will say the same too. You have said it already many times, that "I am not looking for God and I am not looking for enlightenment. Osho says nirvana is the last nightmare. I am not looking for it" – and then surreptitiously, from the corner of the eye, you are looking for it. You are waiting and you say, "What is the matter? And Osho has said, 'When you drop all desire it happens,' and it has not happened yet." You have not dropped the desire yet.

But you *cannot* drop the desire! I insist on it! My emphasis is absolute on it. There have been other teachers who say, "Drop it!" I don't say drop it, because I know you cannot drop it. Nobody has ever dropped it. Not even a Buddha was able to drop it. It dropped on its own accord one day – when Buddha understood it.

If you drop something, the ego now feels very enhanced. "I have dropped it" – and the ego is the root cause. It will create a new greed; it will find new ways. It is very inventive.

Because of this inventive ego, you cannot discover that which is. Because of too much inventiveness, the reality is being missed. It will find some other way; from the back door it will come back. So don't ask how to drop it. I am not here to help you to drop it. I am here to help you to understand it. If it is still there, it simply shows one thing: that you have not understood it. You have not done your homework yet. Do the homework. Don't be in a hurry to drop it. Just look, watch.

Watch in small things of life. You are walking on the road; a car passes by. Just look into yourself: some greed has arisen. The moment you say the car is beautiful, a subtle greed has arisen to possess it. A beautiful woman passes by, or a man, and suddenly a desire to possess.

I have heard:

A woman sat in her doctor's waiting room alongside of a mother and her child of five. The child sat very quietly while the woman and his mother exchanged pleasantries. The woman was very much impressed by the child's good behavior....

He was really graceful, sitting silently like a small Buddha.

..."I wish," she said, "I had a little boy like you."

"Well," countered the child – the little Buddha, "why don't you get pregnant?"

The moment you see something – a beautiful child – and a deep desire arises: you should have a child like this. And the child is saying, "Why don't you get pregnant?" And he is right. In fact, if you look deeply in your desire, you will find that the desire to become pregnant has arisen in you. On the deepest layer it is there. On the surface you simply say, "How beautiful a child. I wish I had a little boy like this." On the surface it is very simple, as if you have simply complimented the child, but deep down many things have happened.

In small things of life.... You are eating, you know your appetite is gone, and you continue to eat. Watch. Greed is there. Now you are not eating out of hunger; you are eating out of greed. One day in meditation something beautiful happens –

a breeze comes into your being, suddenly there is light, suddenly there is fragrance, and you sway with that fragrance – and then it is gone. Now you want every day in every meditation that that has to happen now. Now you are frustrated; and the more you are frustrated, the less is the possibility. Now that window will never open again. And when it doesn't open, you hanker for it too much; then you become very miserable – "Why is it not happening?"

I have been observing so many meditators, thousands. When for the first time meditation really goes deep, immediately, for months, that glimpse disappears. And then they come to me, saying, "What is happening? I had seen something, and it was tremendously beautiful. Why has it disappeared? What wrong have I done?" You have not done anything wrong: you became greedy. When it happened for the first time, you were not greedy, because you had not ever known it. How could you have been greedy about it? It was unknown; it came from out of the blue. It simply came; you were caught unaware. Now watch. It came when you were not asking for it – you had not known it, so you could not have asked for it. It came on its own. Now you are asking for it. Now you are asking for something which had come without your asking. You are creating the whole trouble – the greed has entered.

Sometimes it has happened that a man has come very close to satori, very close, and then he went astray because of the greed.

So watch. Eating, watch. In the morning, you know that the sleep is over, but you still want to turn over and have a little nap. Now it is greed. If your body is fresh and you are feeling good and the tiredness is gone, then watch. It is everywhere. Eating, sleeping, meditating – it is everywhere.

One day you make love to your woman or to your man, and it is ecstatic. Now you hanker, now you start repeating, but that ecstasy never happens again. You are miserable. You don't know what has happened, what has gone wrong? Why am I not attaining that peak.?" You will never attain it again, because you are looking for it. The first time it happened, you were not looking for it.

This is a fundamental law. Things happen and they happen on their own accord; you cannot manage them to happen. Great things cannot be managed by you; they are beyond you. You can, at the most, allow them to happen. At the most, you can keep your doors open so that they can happen, but you cannot force them to happen.

If you force, then nothing happens. Then you can go on making love to the woman and nothing will happen; in fact, you will start feeling nauseous about the whole thing. You will start hating the woman, you will start hating the man; you will think that the other is cheating you. And you will start looking for another woman, for another man, somewhere else to go – "It is not happening here anymore." And you will become suspicious as to whether it had ever happened or you had imagined. How can it happen with this woman? It is not happening now. So you will become doubtful even about the experience that had happened.

People come to me and they say, "Now for months nothing is happening in the meditation," and they say they have become doubtful. Had they imagined the first time? They had not imagined; it had happened. Now they want it to happen and they are imagining and they are creating an idea around themselves.

So what is to be done? You have to watch all the ways of the mind. Greed, desire, ambition, jealousy, possessiveness, domination – you have to watch everything. And they are all interconnected, remember. If greed disappears, then anger will disappear. If anger disappears, jealousy will disappear. If jealousy disappears, violence will disappear. If violence disappears, possessiveness will disappear. They are all intertwined. In fact, they are spokes of the same wheel, and the hub that supports them all is the ego. So watch the ways of the ego.

Watching, watching, watching...one day suddenly it is not there. Only the watcher is left. That moment of pure watching is the moment of transformation.

*My parents deceived me with Father Christmas. Are you real, or will I be disillusioned again?*

The question is from Anand Nitya. Why she has asked has to be understood.

Since she has been here in this ashram, she has not been able to become part of the family. She has been resisting in many ways. I tolerate these things for a time, but I cannot tolerate them forever; otherwise I will not be able to help you at all. A day is bound to come when I will start hammering. The day I start hammering, you start feeling negative, you start feeling against me. If I go according to you, then everything is beautiful, then Osho is beautiful. The moment I start going in some other direction when it is not easy for you to go with me, then negativity arises.

And I have to go against all of you! Because I love you. I have to go against all of you; otherwise I will not be of any help to you. If I simply go on consoling you and simply go on patting your heads and simply go on saying, "You are good, everything is good"....

I say that for a time. In the beginning I say that. If you are not yet a sannyasin, I will continue saying, "Very good!" The moment you are a sannyasin things change. Then I have to be more truthful to you, even if it hurts. It hurts, truth hurts, because you have become so untrue.

So the day I started hammering on Nitya, she must have started thinking, "Where have I come to? Is this man really a Osho or not?"

Hence the question: "My parents deceived me with Father Christmas. Are you real, or will I be disillusioned again?"

First thing: Father Christmas is far more real than I. I am absolutely unreal, because I don't exist as an ego. I am not solid at all. If you go through me, you can pass through me without coming across anybody. I am empty.

The second thing: Because of this emptiness, I can function as a screen for any sort of projection. You can project anything on me. There are people who think I am a saint, and there are people who think I am a rascal. There are people who think I am the greatest sinner there is, and there are people who think I am the greatest master there is. And both are right and both are wrong, because I am neither. You project. There are some people who come and they say, "Osho, you have such beautiful eyes." And just the other day I was reading an article by Rahul Singh in *The Illustrated Weekly Of India*, and he says, "This man has hypnotic and sinister eyes." Good!

It is difficult for you not to project, that I know. But I have to help to destroy all your projections. Once your projections are destroyed, you will be freed.

Father Christmas is far more real. If you look into him, you will find a real person there. If you look into me, there is no person. In the East we call God the imperson. There is no personality. I am just a window; you can look through me. There is not even a glass; there is nothing. But you can project. So it is very easy for you to project because, whatsoever you project, there is nobody to deny it. There is nobody to say, "No, your projection is wrong." You are playing the game alone.

You will know my reality only when you have stopped all projections, when you have become empty, when you have attained to meditative energy. The meditative energy is a non-projective energy. It does not project anything; it simply looks at things as they are.

If a meditator comes across a flower, he will not even say it is a rose flower, because the word "rose" becomes a projection. With the word "rose" all the roses that you have known before come between you and this rose. With the word "rose" all that you have heard about roses, all the poetry that you have read about roses – all that arises between you and the reality. A real meditator will simply look at the rose without even saying the word "rose" inside his being; there will be no language. There will be no idea what it is. He will simply see that which is, the nameless. And that is the only way to see the real rose.

If you want to see me, my reality – I am not a person, but if you want to see my nothingness – you will have to come to me without any ideas. And that's how, if you come closer and closer, more and more projections will fall.

"Are you real, or will I be disillusioned again?" You will be disillusioned, and this time disillusioned forever. That's my hope. If you cooperate with me, you will be disillusioned forever. Then you will never project again. And that's all a master can do: to help you not to project again.

## Greed behind greed behind greed

I have heard:

Two Martians were walking along Piccadilly. One of them nudged the other and pointing to a traffic light said, "How would you like her for a girlfriend?"...

A traffic light! But you can think about Martians – they can project.... "Wow!" said his friend. "What a beauty! I think I will go over and chat her up."

After about ten minutes he rejoined his companion, who asked, "Well, how did you get on?"

"Not bad," replied the second Martian. "She did not actually say anything, but she keeps winking at me."

A traffic light, but you can project.

All your projections are yours, Nitya, and they have to disappear. You have to be disillusioned. Only in that moment of disillusionment does reality explode.

*The Zen masters say, "Kill your parents," and even, "If you meet the Buddha on the way, kill him immediately." Is it not shocking? Is it not irreverent?*

It is shocking, but precisely, that is the purpose. A master has to shock you to awake you. A master is not a lullaby. A master is not a tranquilizer. A master has to be like a sharp knife in your heart. To be with a master is painful. And the master has to destroy all possibilities of projections.

First the child learns to project on the mother and the father. Then for the whole life one goes on projecting. Have you watched it in your own being? Whenever you are attracted by a woman, you may be again looking for your mother. Whenever you are attracted by a man, just watch. Are you again looking for your father? Because the first man the child has known was the father and the first woman was the mother. The child is imprinted with the first form of the woman and the first form of the man. That imprint is very deep.

You all know that suddenly one day you see a woman and something clicks. What clicks? The mother in you. When you see a woman and something reminds you deeply of your mother.... It may not be conscious, you may not be aware of it, you may not be able to figure out what it is, you may not be able to put your finger on it, but if you go deep into your unconscious you will find that the way the woman walks, the long nose of the woman, or the black eyes of the woman or the style of her hair, or her voice, or something, suddenly has clicked your unconscious and the unconscious knows, "This is the woman." People fall in love so suddenly, without knowing the woman, who she is – love at first sight. How is it possible? What psychological mechanism is functioning there? Your mother. And so it is true about the father.

When Zen masters say, "Kill your parents," they are saying, "Destroy the imprint of your mother and father from your unconscious." Once that imprint is destroyed you will be free.

Christianity, Islam, or Judaism or Hinduism are not as perfect religions as Zen, because they still talk of the Father God or the Mother Goddess. The imprint continues. Not only in this world, it goes on being projected in the sky too – God the Father or Kali the Mother. You are still looking for your parents. Now, even in the ultimate reality you are looking for your parents. When will you become adult? When will you become mature? Zen is a process of maturity: so kill the parents.

There is a saying among Zen people that a man becomes really mature when his father and mother are dead. Have you not watched? If your father and mother have died, you are shocked. You have never thought that they would ever die. Although many times you have wished that they should die – an unconscious wish – because they are heavy on you, because their very presence is a restriction.

Have you watched, whenever you go to talk to your father you start stuttering, perspiring, you become nervous? Because he reminds you again that you are helpless, a small child, and he is a powerful man. Have you watched, when you go to your mother it is so difficult to communicate? It is so difficult to say anything. It becomes so difficult to talk to a mother, to sit and chitchat is almost impossible. What to say? She is puzzled and you are also puzzled. Both are embarrassed.

So deep down sometimes you have thought, "They should

die, so I should be free of them." And when the father and mother die, suddenly you feel you are a child no more.

But when Zen people say it, they mean something else. They are not talking about the father and mother on the outside. They are talking about the inside. When the father and mother in the inside die, you become mature, you become free.

And remember, if you are free from your father and mother in the unconscious, you will be capable of communing with your father and mother for the first time, because then there will be no barrier. In fact, you will be able to love them for the first time. You will be able to forgive them for the first time. You will be able to feel compassion for them, how much they have done for you. When you are mature, when you are free of them, when their presence is no more a heavy weight on your heart, you can feel them for the first time. You can be with them in a loving space.

So it is shocking, but it is not irreverent, one thing.

The second thing: they say, "If you meet the Buddha on the way, kill him immediately." And these people who have said these things, they were worshipping Buddha every day in the temple. They may have said it sitting at the feet of the statue of Buddha.

The man who said this was a priest in a temple. He lived in the temple, worshipped in the morning, evening, would bring flowers and incense, and he said one day to his disciples, "If you meet the Buddha on the way, kill him immediately!" One disciple asked, naturally, "What do you mean? And you have been worshipping Buddha." And the man said, "Yes, I have been worshipping him because he has helped me. Even to kill him he has been helpful! It is he who has helped me to kill him. It is he who has helped me to be free of him." The ultimate work of the master is to make you free of himself.

Zarathustra is leaving his disciples and they ask him, "What is your last message?" And he says, "Beware of Zarathustra." Without any comment he escaped into the forest. "Beware of Zarathustra" – the last message. Beautiful. Tremendously Zen. "Beware of me; otherwise you may become a slave to me" – that's what he means.

The same I say to you. Forget about Buddha. because you can kill Buddha very easily. Kill me. That will be far more difficult. With Buddha you have no relationship at all, so you can take it, "Okay, if he comes on the way, we can kill him." But I say to you, kill me when I come on your way. And I will come.

At the last moment, when everything has been cut off, the master remains, because that is the deepest relationship. You can cut your relationship even with your mother because that is only biological, physical. You can cut your relationship even with your beloved because that is psychological. But to cut your relationship with the master is the most difficult thing. You will need a really sharp sword, a really, really sharp sword, and you will need great courage, because the disciple-and-master relationship is a spiritual relationship. It goes deepest in your being. You will start trembling.

When I will stand on your way.... And that is going to be the last barrier: the master is the passage to God and the last barrier too. You will have to leave the master also. And these things are of the inward journey, remember again and again. At the last moment when you are disappearing into emptiness, the last hand that you will have to leave will be the master's hand.

So it is not irreverent. It is with great respect that it has been said.

One thing more. The Zen people are totally different from Christians. You cannot think of a Christian saying to another Christian, "Kill Jesus when he comes on your way. Kill him immediately!" That will look very sacrilegious because Christians have not yet been able to be nonserious about their religion. Their religion is very serious. Hence it misses much. Zen has the quality of laughter, it can laugh. And Zen has the quality of rebelliousness, nonauthoritativeness. And Zen goes on keeping a balance: surrender to the master, and yet remain independent. Very difficult, almost impossible. But when you do the impossible, only then does the ultimate happen to you. Surrender to the master, and yet remain independent. Be sincere in your search, but don't lose your laughter. Become wise, but let foolishness also flower. And Zen people are very,

very absurd in that way. They can say things which will shock you.

A Zen master is weighing flax, and a man comes, a seeker, and he asks, "What is Buddha? What is buddhahood? What is buddha-nature?" The master is weighing the flax, and he says, "Three pounds of flax. That is what Buddha is."

Three pounds of flax! – and he is talking about Buddha? Looks very sacrilegious.

A Zen master, on a cold night, burned a Buddha statue, a wooden statue, because he was feeling cold. No Christian can do that. No Hindu can do that. No Mohammedan can do that. Hence they lag behind. In the night he burned the Buddha statue because it was too cold, and in the morning he was worshipping again.

This playfulness, this nonseriousness, is of tremendous value. With me also, remember that: you have to surrender and yet you have to remain independent. In fact, your surrender is needed so that I can make you independent. Paradoxical of course, but this is how one grows.

I have heard one beautiful story – very shocking, but tremendously beautiful. The story is from Sheldon Kopp:

One Sunday afternoon after church, God and St. Peter went to play golf. God teed up on the first hole, swung his driver mightily, and sliced the ball off into the rough beside the fairway. Just as the ball hit the ground, a rabbit came running out from beneath a bush, picked up God's golf ball in his mouth, and ran with it out onto the fairway. Down from the sky swooped a hawk and pounced on the rabbit. The hawk picked up the rabbit in its claws and flew with it over the green. A hunter spotted the hawk, took aim with his rifle, and shot the bird in mid-flight. The hawk dropped the rabbit onto the green. The golf ball fell from the rabbit's mouth and rolled into the cup for a hole in one.

St. Peter turned to God with exasperation, saying, "Come on now! Do you want to play golf, or do you want to fuck around?"

This is perfect Zen.

Chapter 3

# The Only One Who Has Not Talked

*The pupils of the Tendai school used to study meditation before Zen entered Japan. Four of them, who were intimate friends, promised one another to observe seven days of silence.*
*On the first day all were silent, but when the night came and the oil lamps were growing dim, one of the pupils could not help exclaiming to a servant: "Fix those lamps."*
*The second pupil was surprised to hear the first one talk. "We are not supposed to say a word," he remarked.*
*"You two are stupid. Why did you talk?" asked the third.*
*"I am the only one who has not talked – thank God!" concluded the fourth.*

In the search for the first principle silence is the door – the only door. And except it there is no way to approach the first principle. The first principle can be known only when you move to the primordial state of your being. Thinking is secondary. Existence precedes thinking, existence comes first. First you are, and then you start thinking. Thinking is secondary. Thinking is a shadow activity; it follows you. It cannot exist without you, but you can exist without it. Through thinking you can know secondary things, not the primary things. The most fundamental is not available to thinking; the most fundamental is available to silence.

Silence means a state of consciousness where no thought interferes.

The first principle is not far away, it is not distant. Never think for a single moment that you are missing it because it is very far away. No, not at all. It is the closest thing to you. It is the obvious thing. It surrounds you. It surrounds you just like the ocean surrounds a fish. You are in it. You are born in it and born out of it. You live in it, you breathe in it, and one day you disappear in it. It is not far away, not that you have to travel to it. It is there. It is already there around you, within and without. It is your very existence, that first principle.

Zen people call it the first principle; other religions call it God. There is no difference. The Zen approach is far better because with the word "God," trouble starts. The first principle becomes personified; then you can create an image. You cannot make an image of the first principle, but that's what all the religions do. They say, "God is the first cause, the uncaused cause, the most fundamental, the substantial, the substratum." Zen people call it the first principle. It is beautiful to call it the first principle because nothing preceded it. Everything has followed it.

So if you want to have a communion with the first principle, you will have to seek and search for a reality within yourself which is original, which has not been preceded by anything else.

Silence is primordial. Sound exists in silence. Sound comes and goes, silence remains. Sound is like light, and silence is like darkness. Darkness remains; light comes and goes. Light needs some cause to be. Darkness needs no cause. No fuel is needed for darkness; it simply exists without any fuel. It exists as primordial existence. Darkness is eternal; light is momentary. In the morning the sun rises and there is light. By the evening the sun is gone, the light is gone. Don't think that the darkness comes. Darkness never comes; it is always there. Light comes and goes. You burn a lamp and there is light. You blow out the lamp and light is gone. Not that darkness comes; darkness is there. Light is accidental; darkness is existential.

Silence is there. You can create sound; you cannot create silence. The moment sound is no more created there is silence. Thinking is sound; meditation is silence. So all the religions of the world have been searching for and seeking in one way or another that silence which has not been preceded by anything else, which is the first.

Now a few things before we analyze this state of silence.

First thing. Man is missing this first principle not because he is not a skilled thinker but because he is, not because he is not a trained logician but because he is. Thinking creates a screen around you, a screen of smoke, and because of that smoke the obvious is lost. To see the obvious, you need clarity, not thinking, not logic. You simply need clarity, you need transparency. Your eyes should be completely empty, naked – naked of all clothes, naked of all concepts, empty, empty of all thoughts. When the eyes are just empty, you can see the first principle, and not only can you see it as an object outside you, you see it as your own interiority, as your own subjectivity.

In fact, it is thinking that creates the distinction between the subject and the object. It is thinking that creates division. It is thinking that creates a split. It is thinking that makes things separate. Once thinking is dropped, existence is one, it is one unity, it is one orgasmic experience where duality is totally lost. All boundaries lose themselves into each other, merge into each other. Everything is joined to everything else. The smallest leaf of grass is joined to the greatest star. And then there is nothing high, nothing low, nothing good, nothing bad, because all is joined together. The greatest saint is joined to the greatest sinner; they are not separate.

Nothing is separate. With the disappearance of thinking, schizophrenia disappears, this existential schizophrenia of dividing everything: this is man, this is woman, this is good, this is bad, this is beautiful, this is ugly, this is mine, this is thine. All distinctions create neuroses. Man is mad because he thinks too much, and he goes on missing the obvious.

God is very obvious.

I have heard about a great philosopher:

He married a beautiful girl many years his junior. After a while he began to be torn by doubts as to her faithfulness...

Natural for a philosopher to be torn by doubts. A philosopher lives in doubts; doubt is his trade. He doubts, and he goes on doubting. Through doubt he creates questions and then answers, and through doubt he makes more questions out of the answers. His whole life is a procession of doubts. Naturally, "he began to be torn by doubts as to her faithfulness."

...so he hired a private detective to watch her while he left on a trip. On his return he called the detective.

"Out with it, out with it!" shouted the philosopher. "I can take it. It is the element of doubt that is driving me crazy."

"It looks bad," said the detective. "As soon as you left the house a handsome fellow called for your wife. I followed them to a night club. They had four or five drinks and then danced – and very close. Then they went back to their table and held hands. Finally they took a cab back to your house. The lights were on, and I saw them walk into the bedroom and embrace. Then the light went out and I could not see any more."

"What did I tell you?" shouted the philosopher. "That damned element of doubt!"

Now, even the obvious – "That damned element of doubt!" Even the obvious is not obvious to a philosopher. The greater the philosopher, the more doubts he has. He has doubts about everything. He doubts even his own existence – which in fact cannot be doubted. How can you doubt your own existence? Even to doubt, you are needed to be there. The doubt cannot exist in the air. The doubt cannot exist without you. The doubt can exist only if *you* are there, but philosophers have been doubting even their own existence: Who knows whether we are or we are not?

Doubt is the only outcome of thinking. Nonthinking gives you trust, nonthinking gives you faith, nonthinking brings you closer to reality, face to face with reality. So the first thing to be understood: thinking is not a way to the first principle. Not through philosophizing will you arrive at the first principle, because philosophy is secondary. You can know secondary things through the secondary. To know the primary, you will have to achieve the primary within yourself. You can know only that which you are.

If you live in thinking, you will be able to know only secondary things. You will be able to know the shadow world, what Hindus call the world of maya. Through the mind you can know only the world of maya, the shadow world, the world of illusions. You will be surprised. In Sanskrit we have two terms. One is *vidya*; Vidya means "knowledge". Another is *avidya*;

*Avidya* means "non-knowledge". And you will be surprised, in Sanskrit "science" is called *avidya* – "non-knowledge". Science is called *avidya*. Why? Science knows more than anything else, but in Sanskrit they call science *avidya*. Why? Because science knows only the shadow world – knows the secondary, the nonessential; knows the object, misses the subject; knows the body, misses the soul; knows the world, misses God; knows the secondary.

To know the primary, you will have to become primary. You will have to fall into that wavelength where the primary pulsates, that silence. That is the state of no-mind. No-mind preceded your mind.

A child is born. He comes without any mind whatsoever; he simply exists. His existence is pure, unhampered by any thought, unhindered by any cloud. Look into the eyes of a child. They are so innocent, they are so transparent, so crystal clear. From where comes this clarity? This clarity comes from no-thought. The child still has not learned how to think, how to accumulate thoughts. He looks, but he cannot classify. If he looks at the trees he cannot say they are trees, he cannot say they are green, he cannot say they are beautiful. He sees the trees, but no classification, no category. He has no language yet to be clouded with. He simply sees. Color is there, but he cannot say it is color; green is there, but he cannot say it is green. Everything is purely clear, but he cannot label it. Hence the innocence of the eyes.

A man of understanding again attains the same eyes. He again becomes a child, as far as the clarity is concerned. Jesus is right when he says, "Become like small children; only then will you be able to enter into my kingdom of God." He is not saying become foolish like children; he is not saying become childish; he is not saying learn tantrum again; he is not saying that a child is the last stage. No, he is saying simply one thing. He is not saying become a child; he is saying become like a child. How can you become a child again? But you can become like a child. If you can drop thinking, if this cloak of thinking is dropped and you become nude, again you will have the same clarity.

It happens sometimes through drugs. Not a very good way to

attain it – very dangerous, very costly, and illusory – but it happens. Hence the appeal of the drugs down the ages. Drugs are not new in the world; even in the Vedas they talk about *soma*. Soma seems to be one of the most powerful drugs ever discovered by man. It must be something like LSD. Aldous Huxley has said that in the future, when the ultimate drug will be known, we will call it soma. From the Vedas, the ancientmost book in the world, to Timothy Leary, man has always been attracted by drugs – alcohol, marijuana, opium. Why this attraction? And all the moralists have been against it, and all the puritans have been against it, and all the governments have tried to curb and control, but it seems beyond any government to control it. What has been the cause of it? It gives something...it gives a glimpse into the innocent mind of the child again.

Through chemical impact, the mind becomes loosened for a few moments or a few hours. Under the impact of the drug your thinking slips. You start looking into reality without thinking; again the world is colorful, as it is for the child; again in a small pebble you can see the greatest diamond; ordinary grass looks so extraordinary; an ordinary flower looks so tremendously beautiful; an ordinary human face looks so divine. Not that anything has changed. The whole world is the same. Something has changed in you – and that too only temporarily. Through the forceful drug your mind has slipped down. You don't have the mask; you can see into things with clarity. That is the appeal of the drugs down the ages.

And unless meditation becomes available to millions of people, drugs cannot be prevented.

Drugs are dangerous because they can destroy your body's equilibrium, they can destroy your nature, they can destroy your inner chemistry. You have a very delicate chemistry. Those strong drugs can destroy your rhythm. And more and more drugs will be needed and you will become addicted – and less and less will be the experience. By and by, the mind will learn how to cope with the drugs, and then, even under the drug, you will not attain to the state of innocence. Then you will need even stronger drugs.

So this is not a way.

The mind can be put aside very easily. There is no need to depend on anything chemical, on anything artificial. There is a natural possibility to get out of the mind, because we were born without minds. Deep down we are still no-minds. The mind is only on the periphery. That's why I say it is just a cloak, a dress that you are wearing. You can slip out of it.

And one moment of slipping out of it will reveal to you a totally different world: the world of the first principle.

So the real fight in the future is going to be between meditation and drugs. In fact, that has always been the case: the real fight is between drugs and meditation, either drugs or meditation.

So it is not coincidental that when you start meditating by and by the pull of the drug becomes less and less. If it is not becoming less and less, then know well you are not meditating yet, because when you know the higher, the lower is dropped automatically.

But one thing has to be understood. Drugs do something; they *undo* something in you. They help you to get out of the mind. They give you courage to look into reality without thinking. For a moment the curtain slips, and suddenly you are aware that the world has a splendor. It had never had it before. You had passed through the same street and you had looked through the same trees and at the same stars and the same people, and today now everything suddenly is so luminous and everybody is so beautiful and everybody is afire with life, with love. A saint – one who has attained – lives in that state continuously, without any effort.

You were born as a no-mind. Let this sink into your heart as deeply as possible because through that a door opens. If you were born as a no-mind, then the mind is just a social product. It is nothing natural; it is cultivated. It has been put together on top of you. Deep down you are still free; you can get out of it. One can never get out of nature, but one can get out of the artificial any moment one decides to.

Existence precedes thinking. So existence is not a state of mind; it is a state beyond. To be is the way to know the fundamental, not to think. Science means thinking, philosophy means thinking, theology means thinking. Religion does not mean thinking. The religious approach is a nonthinking approach. It is more intimate, it brings you closer to reality. It drops all that hinders, it unblocks you; you start flowing into life. You don't think that you are separate, looking. You don't think that you are a watcher, aloof, distant. You meet, mingle, and merge into reality.

And there is a different kind of knowing. It cannot be called "knowledge". It is more like love, less like knowledge. It is so intimate that the word "knowledge" is not sufficient to express it. The word "love" is more adequate, more expressive.

In the history of human consciousness, the first thing that evolved was magic. Magic was a combination of science and religion. Magic had something of the mind and something of the no-mind. Then out of magic grew philosophy. Then out of philosophy grew science. Magic was both no-mind and mind; philosophy was only mind; and then mind plus experimentation became science. Religion is a state of no-mind.

Religion and science are the two approaches to reality. Science approaches through the secondary; religion goes direct. Science is an indirect approach; religion is an immediate approach. Science goes round and round; religion simply penetrates to the heart of reality.

A few more things. Thinking can only think about the known – it can chew the already chewed. Thinking can never be original. How can you think about the unknown? Whatsoever you *can* manage to think will belong to the known. You can think only because you know. At the most, thinking can create new combinations. You can think about a horse who flies in the sky, who is made of gold; but nothing is new. You know birds who fly in the sky, you know gold, you know horses; you combine the three together. At the most, thinking can imagine new things, but it cannot know the unknown. The unknown remains beyond it. So thinking goes in a circle, goes on knowing the known again and again and again. It goes on chewing the chewed one. Thinking is never original.

And the first principle means to come upon reality originally, radically, to come upon reality without any mediator, to come upon reality as if you are the first person to exist and you come upon reality. That is liberating. That very newness of it liberates.

And when you come to know reality directly, it is never reduced to the known; the mystery remains. In fact, it becomes a deeper mystery than ever. The more you know, the more you feel that you don't know. The more you know, the less you feel you know. The more you know, the more vast is the mystery of it. Religion is mysticism, religion is magic, because religion is a no-mind approach.

Thinking can think only about the known; it is repetitive. Philosophy is repetitive. You can go into the books of philosophy, into the history of philosophy, and you will see the same thing being repeated again and again – new phraseology, new words; new terms, new definitions, but nothing fundamentally different. From Thales to Bertrand Russell you can go on, but you will find the same thing being repeated again and again. The wheel moving: the same spokes come to the top again and again.

Science can experiment only with the objective; experimentation is possible only with the objective. You cannot experiment with the experimenter himself; there is no way. The subjective reality remains outside science. Einstein may know much about matter, but he does not know anything about himself. Newton may know much about gravitation, but he does not know who he is. One goes on accumulating knowledge about the objective world, and one remains in deep darkness within one's own self. One's own light is not yet there, and one goes on groping, experimenting.

Science can experiment only with the objective, philosophy can think only about the known, and the reality is beyond both. The reality is unknown – not only unknown, but unknowable – and the reality contains the subjective element. So the very methodology of philosophy and science prohibits coming to the fundamental, to the first principle. To come to the fundamental, you will have to find another door, a door other than science and philosophy. That door is religion.

And religion can be reduced to one word, and that word is "meditation," or call it silence – to be in such a silence that you are almost not, there is no noise within you, the stillness is absolute. Only in that stillness something stirs, only in that stillness do you start hearing the still, small voice of the first principle – call it God or call it soul. Only then life calls forth life. Only then the source calls forth the source. Only then are you close to reality, hand in hand with the fundamental. And that is the search, that is what we are seeking; and without knowing it, without realizing it, there is going to be no fulfillment.

The last thing; then we enter into this small parable. When thinking disappears you are left with the first principle. It has always been there; you were not there just because of your thinking. Now you are also there: two presences meet. Ordinarily you are absent, you are somewhere else. In your thoughts you are lost. When there is no thought you are herenow; then there is no way to go from herenow. Thought functions as a bridge to go away from yourself. The moment a thought has come in, you are already far away from yourself. When there is no thought, where can you go, how can you go? When there is no thought you have to be in the present. Thought can take you to the past, thought can take you to the future; no-thought brings you to the present. And only the present is. This moment is all there is.

When you are herenow, absolutely herenow, how can you miss the real, how can you miss God? When thinking disappears you are left with the first principle.

But when I say "when thinking disappears," I am not saying "when you fall asleep," because in deep sleep thinking does disappear. In the East we have divided human consciousness into four phases. The first phase we call "waking," *jagrat*. Waking means "consciousness plus thinking"; you are conscious, but your mind is crowded with thoughts. The second state we have called "dreaming," *swapna*. The second state means "unconsciousness plus thinking"; you fall asleep, but the thinking continues so there is dreaming. Dreaming is a way of thinking in sleep, and thinking is a way of dreaming while awake. Thinking and dreaming are not two separate things. Dreaming is only thinking in a very primitive language – the language of images. Then the third state we call *sushupti*: sleep, deep sleep, dreamless deep sleep. The third state is "unconsciousness minus thinking"; you are unconscious – you don't know where you are, who you are, all consciousness has disappeared, you are at rest – and with the consciousness has disappeared thinking too, dreaming too.

These three are ordinary states: waking, dreaming, sleeping. We all know these three. The fourth is the state of meditation. The fourth is called *samadhi*, *turiya*. It means "consciousness minus thinking".

So four stages: consciousness plus thinking is waking, consciousness minus thinking is samadhi, unconsciousness plus thinking is dreaming, unconsciousness minus thinking is sleep.

So samadhi has something similar to waking and something similar to sleep; hence Patanjali has defined samadhi as "waking sleep" – sleep and yet not sleep. Sleep in the sense that there are no thoughts now, no dreams. And not sleep in the sense that you are perfectly aware, that the light of your awareness is there, that you are conscious, that you know that there is no knowledge now, that you are aware that all thinking has disappeared, that you are aware that now there is no dream lurking in your field of consciousness, that you are absolutely zero, *shunya*.

This is the state that the East has been trying to achieve. The West has been too involved with science; hence it has missed religion. The East's involvement is with samadhi: hence it has missed science.

These four states can be thought of in some other ways also. Consciousness plus thinking means waking. Science is a waking activity, so is philosophy, so is theology. Second, dreaming: unconsciousness plus thinking. That is what art is, poetry, painting, music. It is a dream activity, so it is not just accidental that we call the poets dreamers, that we call the artists dreamers, that we don't trust them much – they are not reliable, they cannot be the guides to reality. We enjoy them, it is fun, but we cannot accept them as guides to reality – they are not. They live in fantasy. They dream while awake. Their eyes are full of dreams. So waking is science, philosophy, theology, logic; and art, all kinds of art, is dream activity.

Unconsciousness minus thinking means sleep. Of course all

activity ceases in sleep, so nothing is born out of sleep – no science, no art.

Consciousness minus thinking is *samadhi*. *Samadhi* gives birth to religion. When Jesus attained to *samadhi* Christianity was born. When Nanak attained to *samadhi* Sikhism was born. When Buddha attained to *samadhi* Buddhism was born. Religion is born out of samadhi, the fourth state. What is *samadhi*? If you can stop your thinking and yet remain alert and don't fall asleep. Difficult, arduous, one of the most difficult things, almost impossible. It is easy to be awake and thinking, it is easy not to think and fall asleep, but to remain awake and not think is the most difficult thing, because it is not part of evolution. It is a revolution. It is not given by nature automatically. You have to attain it.

That is the task man has to solve. That is the challenge given to man, and very few have accepted that challenge. And those who have accepted it, only they are man; others are man only for the name's sake. We exist as potential man, not as actual man. It is our potentiality. We can become a Buddha or a Christ, but it has not happened yet. We are just seeds. That's our misery because a seed can never be satisfied unless it becomes a tree and blooms. A seed will remain miserable because there is a feeling deep down that "I am not yet that which I am meant to be; my destiny is not fulfilled."

Have you not observed this in you? If you had not observed it, you would not be here. You are here only because you feel something is missing. You are here only because you continuously feel that something has to happen and it is not happening, that something is just there by the corner and yet you cannot grasp it, seems to be not very far away, yet seems to be beyond reach. The tree is not very far away from the seed. If the seed finds the right soil, falls into the soil, relaxes, surrenders to the soil, dissolves into the soil, dies into the soil, then the tree is not very far away. In the right season the seed will sprout, a tender plant will be born, and the seed will be able to see the light.

Only when the seed has become a plant will it be able to feel the wind and the ecstasy that the wind is and be able to feel the sunrays and the ecstasy that the sun brings and be able to live and be able to accept the challenges and start growing. Come storm, come wind, come rains, and the small, tender plant will become stronger and stronger. Every challenge will give it strength and integration; and one day there will be a great tree whispering to the skies, it will bloom, and the fragrance will be released to the winds in all directions. Then there will be jubilation.

When Jesus says again and again to his children, to his disciples, "Rejoice!" what he is saying is true because he has become a tree and he has bloomed. But his disciples must have looked here and there, they must have thought, "What does he mean? Why does he go on saying again and again, 'Rejoice'?" They are seeds; how can they rejoice?

When I say to you, "Celebrate!" you start thinking, "For what? Why? What have we got to celebrate?" You cannot celebrate because celebration is possible only when you bloom. I know it! But I go on saying, "Celebrate!" And Jesus knows it and he goes on saying, "Rejoice!" In fact, he wants to create such a thirst in you to know what this rejoicing is that out of that thirst you start seeking and searching for the right soil.

To find a right master is to find a right soil because only through the master will you be able to dissolve, only through the master will you be able to surrender. A seed needs to surrender. A seed has to die; only then is there a new life born out of it. Death makes it possible. Death is tremendously beautiful: it makes it possible that a man can be new, a man can be reborn.

*Samadhi* is celebration, *samadhi* is rejoicing. *Samadhi* is your gratitude towards God, your thanksgiving.

How can you thank God right now? You have nothing to thank him for. You can complain, you cannot thank him; so your prayers are more of complaints, less of thanks. You cannot say, "Thank you." How can you? For what? In fact, you are very angry with God. Why has he given birth to you? Why has he created so much misery? Why has he put you in such anguish and turmoil? Why in the first place? What wrong have you done? If suddenly you come across God you will jump upon him. That's why he goes on hiding. You will kill him. You will say, "What have you been doing? For what are we suffering?

What wrong have we done? Why did you make us in the first place? Not to be would have been better — no anxiety, no anguish. Not to be would have been more peaceful. Why did you create us?"

The whole existence seems to be mischievous. It seems as if somebody, a sadistic God, is sitting there, torturing people, creating a thousand and one ways to torture them.

Right now you cannot thank him because right now you are not. When you are, you will be able to thank him. And the way to be goes through death, through surrender. And the way goes through silence. But it is not easy to be silent; it is the most arduous thing to be silent.

Now this small story:

> The pupils of the Tendai school used to study meditation before Zen entered Japan. Four of them, who were intimate friends, promised one another to observe seven days of silence.
> On the first day all were silent, but when the night came and the oil lamps were growing dim, one of the pupils could not help exclaiming to a servant: "Fix those lamps."
> The second pupil was surprised to hear the first one talk. "We are not supposed to say a word," he remarked.
> "You two are stupid. Why did you talk?" asked the third.
> "I am the only one who has not talked — thank God!" concluded the fourth.

What happened? The Tendai school is a school of meditation. Before Zen entered Japan, Tendai was very much prevalent. But that too was a school of meditation. In fact, because of Tendai and its roots in Japan, Zen could enter Japan. These things don't happen suddenly; you need a climate. A country does not become suddenly interested in meditation. It needs a climate. The climate is born out of long tradition.

In the Tendai school a seven-day silence was ordinarily prescribed to every disciple. Why a seven-day silence? It is very symbolic; the number is symbolic. Man has seven centers, and each center has to attain silence. You may not have looked at it in that way. When the sex center becomes silent it is *brahmacharya*, it is celibacy. When the heart center becomes silent it is compassion. If the heart center is in turmoil there is anger. If the sex center is in turmoil, shouting, there is sexuality. All the seven centers of man have to become silent. When all of them are chained in silence, then this whole being of man falls silent. In that silence one knows the first principle – one *is* the first principle.

So these disciples must have been told by some master to be silent for seven days. But man functions in a mechanical way. If you sit silently that doesn't mean you will Become silent. In fact, just the reverse will happen: if you sit silently you will find a rush of thoughts coming to you. You will be more crowded by thoughts than ever. All sorts of thoughts – relevant, irrelevant, meaningful, meaningless – they all will jumble together. It will be rush-hour traffic. And they will all claim your attention. Your attention will become fragmentary; you will almost feel like going mad. You will be torn apart. You will feel you are being pulled and pushed in so many directions...you will start feeling crazy.

Just to sit does not help. One has to be very aware. These four disciples were not aware at all, so when the one said, "Fix those lamps" to a servant who was passing by, he must have done it in a very unconscious way; otherwise he was to keep silent. It was none of his business whether the lamps were getting dim or not. He had to remember that he was in silence, but he forgot.

The story is not humorous; it is tragic. That's how things are with you, with everybody.

It happened after twenty-four hours. Try it. Just take your wristwatch today and sit silently, put your wristwatch in front of you, look at the second hand. The second hand moves one complete circle in one minute. Just watch the second hand and remember that "I am to remember the second hand moving; I am not to forget it." And it will be difficult for you even to remember for fifteen seconds; you will forget. After two, three seconds you will start thinking something else; then again you will remember; then again you will forget. In one minute you will forget at least four, five times. You will not be able to remember for one continuous minute that you are to remember the second hand moving, that you are not to go anywhere else.

So please don't laugh at this story. The first reaction is laughter, but it is very tragic. It is how we are.

For twenty-four hours they are sitting silently; then suddenly one servant is passing and one of the pupils says, "Fix those lamps." Not that he is interested in the lamps. Anything would have provoked him; anything would have become the excuse. He wanted to say something! He must have been getting crazy. That's why the second cannot tolerate it; he says, "What? We are not supposed to say a word!" And the third says, "You two are stupid! Why did you talk?" And the fourth says, "I am the only one, thank God, who has not talked yet." They all wanted to say something, to release, to get a little relief. It must have been getting too heavy on them.

So one thing, when you sit silently, all doors for your thoughts to be released through are closed, so they hammer within you, they start gathering within you. They become a mob. Their presence becomes heavy; then you will find any excuse and you will say something.

In many traditions a mantra is given, chanting is given. The master gives you a mantra. That is just to help you so you don't go mad, nothing else. It is just a help for the beginners. A mantra is given – go on repeating, "Ram, Ram, Ram...." That will help; this will remain a release. Other thoughts will not bother you too much; at least one passage is open so something can flow. You can go on repeating, "Ram, Ram, Ram..." and this will help you in the beginning, but this is not real meditation. It is just a preparation for meditation. What Maharishi Mahesh Yogi calls "transcendental meditation" is neither meditation nor transcendental. It is just a cleaning; a beginner prepares himself for meditation.

Meditation starts with silence, not with a mantra; but a mantra can be helpful if you are very alert. Otherwise even the mantra can become dangerous; you may get too addicted to it. Then you remain outside the temple. The mantra is a help if you know that it is just to make you ready by and by to become silent.

Many thoughts are there; then one thought is allowed to you – "Ram, Ram, Ram...." Ninety-nine thoughts are not allowed, one is allowed. If you can attain this, then one day that one has to be dropped too. But if this one becomes very strong – and there is every possibility it will become strong because your whole attachment that was divided in a hundred thoughts will now fall on one thought – it will become a very deep attachment. It will become your very soul. If somebody will say, "Drop it," you will be angry. "This is my mantra," you will say. "How can I drop it?" Even a man like Ramakrishna found it very difficult to drop his Mother Kali, at the last moment.

Difficult. You have cultivated it so much; you have put so much into it. All your desires, all your projections, all your thoughts, you have poured into it. It becomes one of the strongest thoughts in your being. It will be very difficult. So unless you are alert from the very beginning, a mantra can poison you rather than help you.

In the Tendai school there is no mantra, so these four disciples must have been getting very volcanic. They must have been sitting on a volcano; they must have been ready to explode. The passing of the servant and the oil lamps growing dim was just an excuse.

The mind is so habituated to thinking, so habituated to expressing itself that it is almost impossible to get out of it – unless you put your total energy in getting out of it, unless you make it a life-and-death problem. If you are just trying so-so, it will not help. If you are just making a lukewarm effort, it will not help. Unless it really becomes a life-and-death problem it is not going to help.

A man came to Sheik Farid and said, "I would like to know God. Can you give me some method?" Farid said, "I am going to the river to take my bath; you come with me. And if I get a chance I will give you the method." They went to the river. The man was very curious as to what he was going to give him at the river. At the river Farid said, "Now you also unrobe and get down into the river with me. Let us first take a bath." So the man got down into the river, and when he came close to Farid, Farid jumped on top of him, pushed him down into the river. Farid was a very strong man. The seeker could not understand what was happening. He had come to ask how to attain God, and this man was trying to kill him!

But when it is a question of life and death, even the seeker, who was not a very strong man, also tried hard. He threw Farid away, and when he came out of the water he said, "What nonsense! I had always thought that you are a pious man. You have fame as a mystic, and what were you doing? Are you a murderer? And I have not done anything to you; I have just asked a question, how to attain to God." And Farid said, "That's what I was doing – giving you a method. Just now tell me one thing first, in case you forget. What happened when I was pushing you down into the river? How many thoughts were there in your mind?"

He said, "Thoughts? There was only one thought – how to get rid of you. And by the end even that disappeared. Then there was only an effort, not a thought – no thought. My whole life was at stake. It was just an effort to get out of the river somehow. And I had put all my energies – known, unknown, conscious, unconscious, whatsoever – because this seemed to be the last moment."

Farid said, "That is the method. When God become a life-and-death problem – not a question, not a curiosity, but a life-and-death problem – when your life and death hang on the very question, on the very quest, only then will you be able to know."

Now these four seekers are sitting there. Lukewarm they must be. They don't know what they are doing. Somebody has told them to sit silently; they are sitting. Mind functions mechanically. To get out of it you will have to use all your energy. The possibility is there; you can get out of it.

Gurdjieff used to say that man is a machine. Then somebody asked, "Then what is the difference between a real machine and man?" And Gurdjieff said, "The difference is if man wants, he can go beyond the machine too. The machine cannot." Otherwise there is no difference. As man exists he is a machine. The only difference is in the future, in the possibility, potentiality. If man wants to get out of the mechanical world he can, but great effort will be needed.

A city fellow bought a place in the country recently and was going to raise livestock, but when he arrived at his farm, all he found was a large, ancient sow. "Hell of a note," he muttered and stamped off to the general store. The storekeeper was sympathetic and volunteered that he should breed his sow with Farmer Jones' boar, and soon he would be in the livestock business. "Great idea," said the slicker.

So he loaded his sow in a wheelbarrow and took her to Farmer Jones'. The next morning he rushed out of bed and looked into the pigpen, but no piglets. Disgusted, he went back to the store, and the storekeeper tolerantly recommended Farmer Smith's boar now.

Once again the sow was loaded in the wheelbarrow and taken down the road, and once again the next morning the slicker found no piglets. This routine went on for a week, and finally on the eighth day, the slicker refused to get out of his warm bed in the early morning. Rolling over to his wife, he said, "Look out the window and see if there are any piglets in the pen."

His wife looked. "There aren't any piglets in the pen," she said, "but the sow is back in the wheelbarrow."

That's how the mind functions – mechanically. It goes on doing things which it has been doing. It goes on repeating.

If you really want to become a man, get out of your repetitions. There are no bad habits and no good habits. because all habits are bad. To live through habits is to live a mechanical life. Get beyond, become aware.

Now, all these four men just said things out of habit, not knowing what they were saying.

And it is very easy for you to see others committing mistakes, errors, because you can look at others objectively. It is very difficult to look at yourself. The moment you start looking at yourself, you are becoming nonmechanical. To become aware of your habits is the beginning of a nonmechanical life, is the beginning of life itself. To exist as a machine is not to exist at all.

Three small stories of how man is. Because of mechanical habits he lives unconsciously. You do a thousand and one things, but you simply go on doing them because you have been doing them.

First scene:

One of the two drunks standing beside a lamp post asked his companion, "Say, you gotta match?"

"I think so," said his companion. "Let me see." He reached in his pocket, withdrew a stick match and rubbed the unsulphured end on the lamp post several times. "No good," he said finally, and threw it away. He pulled out another and tried again to strike the unsulphured end. "No good," he said again, and threw it away. He reached into his pocket, found another match, and fortunately tried to light the proper end. It blazed up, but immediately he blew it out and thrust it into his pocket. "Ah," he beamed. "That's a good one. Gotta save it."

The second scene:

A cop approached three drunks on a park bench. The one in the middle was snoring peacefully, apparently passed out, but the two on either side were going through the motions of fishing, casting out their lines, jerking them, and reeling them in swiftly. The cop watched for a while and then shook the middle man awake.

"Are these nuts friends of yours, buddy?"

The drunk nodded.

"Well, get them out of here and make it snappy."

The drunk agreed, saluted, and began rowing vigorously.

The third scene:

Mort and Leo wandered into one of those newfangled bars and sat down in a booth. The sign on the wall of their booth said, "Push button to call the waiter." Mort pushed the button, and sure enough the waiter appeared. "Two beers," ordered Mort and the waiter brought them their beers.

This kept up for a good four hours, and it was hard to say which pleased them more, drinking beer or pushing the button for the waiter. Finally, full of fun and good cheer the two parted and went home. The next morning Leo's wife had him on the carpet. "What the hell did you think you were doing last night?"

she demanded. Leo was puzzled. "I don't know. What was I supposed to have done?"

"All night long," remonstrated his wife, "you kept poking your finger into my navel and calling for two beers."

A mechanical mind is an unconscious mind. You go on doing things, but not knowing what you are doing and why you are doing them. And while doing them there is no awareness. Walking, you walk, but there is no awareness. Eating, you eat, but there is no awareness. Talking, you talk, but there is no awareness.

The story is significant. It says the first did it unconsciously – and the second could see the error – but the second did something unconsciously himself. The third could see the error of them both, but himself committed the same error! And the fourth could see the error of all three and thanked God that "I am the only one who has not yet broken silence." It is very easy to see the error of somebody else because that is not *your* mechanical thing. You can be aware of it. When it comes to your own mechanical things you become completely unaware.

Can't you see? Somebody is eating too much and you can say very easily, "Don't eat too much." Somebody is angry and you can say, "What are you doing? Going mad?" Somebody is in love and doing foolish things and you can say, "Are you going mad? What are you doing?" But the question is, "Can the man who has fallen in love see it?"

Just the other night, one beautiful sannyasin told me that she has fallen in love with a man and things are going really fantastically; the relationship is beautiful. I told her, "Every beginning of a relationship is beautiful. That is not something to brag about. The question is, 'Can the beautiful relationship remain beautiful?' All relationships start in beauty, in sweetness, in harmony. All relationships start as they should be, but sooner or later things start falling. Sooner or later the negative asserts, sooner or later the ugly comes up – then is the question." But the woman said, "It will not come." All that she said, summarized, will mean that she is an exception; it is not going to happen. And that is the foolishness of all lovers.

That's how all lovers think, that it is not going to happen to them.

And when it has happened, then it is too late. Then you cannot put things right again. When things start going wrong, there is no way to put them right again. Even if you put them right, they will never be the same. It is as if a cup has broken. You can put it right; you can glue it together. But it will never be the same again. It is better to handle it carefully from the beginning. And the first thing to know is that every relationship starts good and every relationship ends bad. Yours included, mind you! It is very easy to see that others are just unaware. "But we two who have fallen in love, we are different," – that is the idea of everybody.

Now, the woman was very confident – and in that very confidence is the problem. In that very confidence she will miss because when you are so confident you don't take any precautions. When you are so confident you don't try to be aware of what is happening. Then you move unaware, and all that is in you, by and by, will come up – is bound to come up.

In the beginning when two lovers meet, they show their beautiful faces. Their gracefulness is infinite. Their care about each other is absolute. It has to be so because both are showing their beautiful parts. But when they will be together for twenty-four hours, then it will be impossible. It will be too heavy to keep the ugly parts always hidden; by and by the ugly parts will take revenge. They will start coming up.

When you fall in love, why do we call it "fall"? It is called "fall" because it helps you to be unconscious. It is a fall. You become unconscious. We say somebody has "fallen" asleep, somebody has "fallen" in love. "Fall" means now you are no more conscious; you are behaving very mechanically. Love in itself is mechanical. Then, when the hate starts coming, you will be a victim of that too.

If you really want to change your life, start immediately. If you have fallen in love, make it an awareness. Do things with full awareness. See that you are showing the positive aspects of you and you are hiding the negative. See well that this cannot last long, so something has to be done. If the relationship has to become really intimate, if it is to go long, then something has to be done. And that something has to be done in you, not in the other! Otherwise the woman thinks the husband has betrayed, the husband thinks the woman has betrayed. That's what these four people thought: the other is doing the wrong.

Whenever you throw the responsibility on the other, you are avoiding awareness. Let this be a very fundamental law. Whenever you throw responsibility on the other, you are saying, "I am doing perfectly well; the other is doing wrong." A man who is trying to be aware will always see that "I am responsible; I am doing something wrong." It is not a question of whether the other is doing wrong or not. That is *his* problem. That is not your problem. Your problem is whether you are doing something unconsciously. If you are doing something unconsciously, then things cannot go on being beautiful forever. Then all that is there is going to be temporary; it cannot have the quality of the eternal; it cannot have the timeless beauty and divinity in it.

So always remember, when you see somebody doing something wrong, somebody committing an error, rather than jumping on him, look into yourself – what you are doing. If you can watch everybody's error and everybody's error becomes a remembrance of your own errors, your life will be transformed. Then everybody will become a teacher to you. Then the whole of life becomes your master. Everywhere you will find arrows pointing to you. The whole of life will be arrowed towards you, saying, "This is unconscious...this is irresponsible."

We have found a very easy trick: we turn the arrows towards others. Others go on throwing the arrows towards us; we go on throwing the arrows towards others. In this game, life is lost. Don't continue playing this game.

Your world is created by your consciousness or your unconsciousness. It has nothing to do with your wife, your husband, your children, your friends, your society. Your world is *you*. Bring light to your world. Bring more awareness to your world. And start existing less like a machine, more like a man. Otherwise one has been going from one life to another, repeating the same.

You have repeated enough! Are you not yet bored? Are you not yet fed up with it? Start changing a few fundamental things.

One, stop looking at others' errors, and each time you see somebody else committing an error, a mistake, start finding out immediately somewhere some mistake in yourself. In fact, to look at the mistake of the other is a way of avoiding your own mistake. One feels very good: "Somebody else is committing the mistake and I am perfectly okay." Start analyzing, observing. Become more critical about your habits, about your ways, about your style of life.

I have heard about one man who married eight times. Each time he thought, "I have found the wrong woman." And he was not wrong. After each marriage there was misery. He divorced the first woman, tried to find another, and again after a few months the same misery. And he was surprised at how he managed to find the same type of woman again and again! Eight times he married, and all the times he married the same type of woman. And each time he was trying to be more alert not to fall in the trap again, but he fell – because when you choose a woman the chooser is the same. How can you change the woman!

If the chooser is the same, the choice is going to be the same. Again the same thing will appeal to you. Maybe the face is a little different, the hairstyle is a little different, the color of the hair is a little different – that is not the point. These are irrelevant things. A marriage does not depend on the color of the hair, a marriage does not depend on the color of the eyes, and a marriage does not depend on the length of the nose. These are superficial things. After two days, who looks at the size of the nose? Or who bothers about the color of the hair? In fact, if your wife suddenly goes and changes the color of her hair, the husband will be the last one to note it. Who bothers?

But more essential is why you choose a certain woman, why you choose a certain man. Why? What fits with your mind? Again you will choose the same type of woman – for the same reasons. Those reasons are unconscious. So you can go on changing women and you will not find the woman you are searching for. You can go on changing your job and you will not find the job you are searching for. And you can go on searching among the masters – from one to another you can go on moving – and you will not find the master you are searching for, unless you become more alert about your mechanical habits.

Once you become aware of your mechanical habits things start changing. Then the first ray of light has entered. Then you will choose a different kind of woman, because you have become different. Then you will choose a different kind of master, because you have become different. Then you will choose *everything* in a different way, because you are different. And if a person chooses out of awareness, he chooses rightly.

People come to me and they ask, "What is right and what is wrong?" I say, "Awareness is right; unawareness is wrong." I don't label actions as wrong and right. I don't say violence is wrong. Sometimes violence can be right. I don't say love is right. Sometimes love can be wrong. Love can be for a wrong person, love can be for a wrong purpose. Somebody loves his country. Now, this is wrong because nationalism is a curse. Somebody loves his religion. He can kill, he can murder, he can burn others' temples. Neither is love always right nor is anger always wrong.

Then what is right and what is wrong? To me, awareness is right. If you are angry with full awareness, even anger is right. And if you are loving with unawareness, even love is not right.

So let the quality of awareness be there in every act that you do, in every thought that you think, in every dream that you dream. Let the quality of awareness enter into your being more and more. Become suffused with the quality of awareness. Then whatsoever you do is virtue. Then whatsoever you do is good. Then whatsoever you do is a blessing to you and to the world in which you live.

Ponder over this small story. It is a story of four unconscious people who are trying to be silent. But they have not understood the laws of thought, they have not understood the law of being unconscious. They don't know that man is a machine. They don't know that to look at the other is a way of avoiding oneself. They are not yet conscious of what they are doing. Even though they are sitting in meditation and trying to be silent, they are not aware of the science of silence, of the yoga of meditation. Hence this foolish anecdote became possible.

You will be repeating the same thing. All, the whole of humanity, are repeating. Don't think that you are an exception! Don't think that if you were one of these four people you would not have committed this. Know well you would have committed it! This story is about you. It has nothing to do with the Tendai school. These four can be Rajneesh sannyasins.

Watch each step that you take – in action or in thought. The only goal is awareness...and then your whole life is transformed. Then your whole life attains to a new quality, to a new dimension. And that dimension leads to the first principle.

*You* are the first principle!

## Chapter 4
# Go with the River

*It seems to me that I don't understand anything.*

That's far out. If it is really true, then it is great. If you don't understand anything, then the door is open, then there is nothing to hinder your way, to hinder your vision. It is knowledge that is obstructing. Ignorance is an opening. Ignorance is very blissful. It is knowledge that creates noise. It is knowledge that does not allow you to see. If your eyes are completely rid of knowledge, then what is there to hinder you from seeing the truth? The truth is obvious. You just need a clarity to see it. Ignorance gives that clarity.

To be consciously ignorant is to be in satori. A child is ignorant, but not conscious of his ignorance. A saint is ignorant, but is conscious of his ignorance. He knows that he knows not. That's the only difference. The child also knows not, but he does not know it. The saint knows that he knows not. His whole knowledge consists of one single thing: that there is nothing to be known and there is no possibility to know, that the whole effort towards knowledge is futile, that existence is such a mystery that it can never be reduced to knowledge.

All that we know is superficial, arbitrary. All that we know has nothing to do with reality. The reality remains untouched by our knowledge. The reality remains mysterious.

If it is really true that you have become aware of your ignorance, then there is nothing else to be sought, nothing else to attain. Relax in this ignorance. Accept this ignorance. And feel blissful.

But it may not be true. That's why I say *if* it is true. It may again be just a hankering to know. Then you have not understood, then you are not at ease with your non-knowing.

The question seems to be because you are worried; otherwise why a question? You are worried. Something is gnawing at your heart. You are worried that "I don't understand anything, and I have to understand." In fact, when Vidya had come, she must have thought that she knows. Now by and by I have been hammering on her, and her knowledge has disappeared. Now she is worried.

When you come to me you come full of knowledge. You come with much luggage, and that luggage has to be destroyed, burned utterly, so that you cannot find it again. When you lose your luggage you start feeling as if you are missing something. Naturally so. You have been carrying the load so long; now suddenly it is gone; you feel you are missing something. The question has arisen because of your feeling that something is being missed: "I don't know anything?" The knowledge has disappeared and ignorance has not yet been accepted.

If you don't accept ignorance, sooner or later you will attain to knowledge again, you will start gathering and hoarding. And this time you will hoard in a more subtle way so that it cannot be easily taken away from you.

Beware. These are the moments when you need a master to say to you, "Accept and relax into this ignorance." I am not here to impart knowledge to you. I am here to take it away from you.

In one of the most ancient books in India, *Shivasutra*, there is a tremendously significant sutra: *Gyanam bandham* "Knowledge is bondage." When there is no knowledge, a man is free. It is such a radical statement: all knowledge is bondage. The moment you know that you don't know, the bondage falls, but if you have lived in the bondage for long, you start accepting it as part of you.

If a man has lived in prison for many years with chains on his hands and on his feet and then you suddenly take away the chains – he will not even be able to sleep in the night. He has become accustomed to them; he needs that weight, that noise. When he used to turn in the night, those chains used to make noise; now suddenly the noise will not be there. He will become awake again and again in the night: something is missing. Walking, he will feel as if he is naked: something is missing. He has become accustomed to that weight, and that's how everybody has become accustomed to the weight of knowledge. Knowledge is a bondage.

The question arises only because the acceptance has not arisen yet. You can miss this great opportunity of being ignorant.

Relax, love it, embrace it, feel one with it, and there will arise a new sort of innocence. You were innocent when you were a child. This will be a new birth and a new sort of innocence. Again you will become a child, and yet your childlike quality will not be childish; it will have a maturity in it.

Sometimes reading, sometimes listening, and particularly listening to Zen, you may start feeling, "I don't know anything." Because the Zen people are very much against knowledge, you may start clinging to the idea of not knowing. But that idea is not going to help. That idea is again part of knowledge. Listening to the Zen masters, you may start getting attached to the very idea of not knowing. Then this idea of not knowing becomes your knowledge.

To be really in deep ignorance means you don't even have the idea of non-knowledge. You are simply innocent. The knowledge has disappeared, and nothing has appeared in its place.

Let me tell you this famous anecdote:

Traditionally Zen monasteries will only admit wandering Zen monks if they can show proof of having solved a koan.

And you can solve a koan only when you have fallen into deep ignorance, not before it, because a koan is not a puzzle. Or if it is a puzzle, then it is not an ordinary puzzle. An ordinary puzzle can be solved by the mind; if you put your mind to it you can find a way to solve it; it has a solution. A koan is such a puzzle that it has no mind solution possible; you cannot solve it. It is not a question of what you do, it is insoluble. Mind cannot give any answer to it.

For example, Zen masters say, "Listen to the sound of one hand clapping." Now, one hand cannot clap, and unless it claps there will not be any sound, so to what are you going to listen? The mind will work out many solutions, and all will be meaningless, and the master will send you back again and again. Again listen. Meditate. The solution will happen one day when the mind disappears. When you work hard with the mind and the mind finds no way to reach any solution, out of sheer tiredness the mind falls flat on the ground. Suddenly you are in a state of no-mind, and you hear the sound of one hand clapping.

The mind hears only the sound of two hands clapping because the mind lives in duality. The mind can hear only a created sound. When the mind disappears, you hear the soundless sound, what the Hindus call *anahat nad*. The word *anahat* means exactly the same as what Zen people call the sound of one hand clapping. If you clash two things there is a sound that is called *ahat nad*, a sound that comes out of conflict. And there is a sound permeating existence itself – which is not created, uncreated. When you become so silent that the mind has disappeared, disappeared with all its noise, suddenly that soundless sound is heard, that *aumkar*, that anahat nad is heard. But that happens only when the mind has gone.

Traditionally Zen monasteries will only admit wandering Zen monks if they can show proof of having solved a koan.

It seems that a monk once knocked on a monastery gate. The monk who opened the gate did not say "Hello" or "Good morning" but "Show me your original face, the face you had before your father and mother were born."...

This is a koan. And the host is asking the guest to show some sign that he can solve a koan; otherwise he is not worthy of being allowed to stay in the monastery; then he will have to go away.

...The monk who wanted a room for the night smiled, pulled a sandal off his foot and hit his questioner in the face with it. The other monk stepped back, bowed respectfully, and bade the visitor welcome. After dinner, host and guest started a conversation, and the host complimented his guest on his splendid answer.

"Do you yourself know the answer to the koan you gave me?" the guest asked.

"No," answered the host, "but I knew that your answer was right. You did not hesitate for a moment. It came out quite spontaneously. It agreed exactly with everything I have heard or read about Zen."

The guest did not say anything, and sipped his tea. Suddenly the host became suspicious. There was something in the face of his guest which he did not like.

"You *do* know the answer, don't you?" he asked.

The guest began to laugh and finally rolled over the mat with mirth.

"No, reverend brother," he said, "but I too have read a lot and heard a lot about Zen."

Hearing me, there are many things you will start imagining, many things you will start believing. Beware, because those things won't help. Hearing Zen, reading Zen is not going to give you Zen. Zen is a quality that you have to attain to. It is a new vision of life and reality. It is a new penetration into the mystery of existence. It is not intellectual; it is existential. You have to throb with it, your heart has to beat with it, you have to breathe it in and out. It is not going to be just an intellectual understanding.

Listening to me, the understanding will come to you intellectually very easily because whatsoever I am saying is simple. There is nothing difficult about it. It is not very complex. I am not spinning any philosophical theories here. I am simply stating simple facts.

Now, this fact is simple that a child has an innocent clarity. And one day if you also attain consciously to that childhood – what Jesus calls, "When you are reborn," that is rebirth – then you will be able to see what is. But listening to me, you may start thinking, "Yes, that's right. I also don't know anything." But is it your understanding, or just a reflection of my understanding? Is it your experience, or just an imitation?

It happens – in the presence of every master it happens – because man is naturally imitative. Darwin is right. Man comes from the monkeys, and is very imitative. He can imitate anything.

I have heard there was a great master:

The master would sit for hours alone in his cave meditating, his only companion being a favorite cat which he tied to a post in his cave during his periods of meditation. As years went by his fame spread and he soon had a number of pupils who came to learn from him and who made him their guru or their master. He instructed his pupils to meditate as he did. Soon each pupil could be observed meditating with a cat tied to a post by his side.

The master died, so what did the pupils do? They had known always of one cat being tied to a post by the side of the master. Naturally they thought the cat must have something to do with meditation. And cats are very esoteric people. The cat must have something to do with meditative energy. Somehow the cat must have been a help; otherwise why? The master used to do it continuously. For years they had seen it. Whenever he was meditating, the cat was there tied to the post.

He had to tie the cat; otherwise the cat would disturb his meditation! The cat may jump into his lap, might like to play with him. Cats don't bother whether you are meditating or not, so the cat has to be tied to the post. But what about the disciples? They watched. And you can see only the outward; the inner remains invisible. Naturally they also tried to imitate it.

It happens. Beware of that too. Don't be imitative. Just because I am saying something, you need not repeat it. If you repeat it, it will not be helpful for your own growing understanding. Don't repeat it. Let it sink into your being. Experience it.

If I say something, there is no need to believe in it. There is no need to disbelieve either. Remain open. If I say something, then try it. Then look at the trees without any ideas whatever. Look at the birds and the sky with no knowledge. Drop language and see whether what I am saying gives you clarity.

If you can drop the word "rose" and then see the rose flower, what happens? You will immediately feel a new kind of relationship arising between you and the flower. Don't even call it a flower; there is no need. Your language is not needed to support it; it exists without language. Why bring language in? Put language aside. Put aside your continuous gibberish that goes on inside the mind. Just look.

In the beginning it is difficult – the language will come up again and again, just out of old habit – but sooner or later it comes easily: you can remain at least for a few moments without language. Listening to the song of the birds or the murmur of the wind passing through the trees, or the river, you can remain without language for a few seconds. And in those seconds will be the proof of what I have been saying to you. Suddenly you will see as if a great darkness has disappeared and everywhere is light. You can see as if the doors of perception have been cleansed.

Ordinarily we are looking through dark curtains. The glass we are looking through is too dusty. Only fragments of reality appear, not the totality.

Experience what I am saying, don't imitate, and then this is going to happen to you: one day you will suddenly see you don't know anything. But this will be a vision, a realization. Then it is great. If it is truly happening, it is great.

*Meher Baba has talked about God descending in man (Avatar, Rasool, Christ) and man rising to be God (the perfect master, satguru, qutub, tirthankara). Would you please talk to us about the same?*

God is. He neither ascends nor descends. Where can he ascend to and where can he descend to? God is all. There is nothing into which God can ascend or descend. There is nobody else other than God. All that is is divine. So the first thing: there is no ascendance, no descendance.

But when Meher Baba says it, there must be some meaning in it. The meaning is something quite different. Let me explain it to you.

God is, remember. God is a pure isness, pure existence, and

there is nowhere for God to go or come. The whole is full of him. He fills his existence, one thing. Second thing: but Meher Baba must be true. Then there must be some other meaning to it – not God descending and ascending. What can be the meaning? The meaning is there are two ways of man approaching God.

What do I mean by "man" when God is the only reality? Man is the God who has forgotten that he is God; man is a God who has forgotten himself.

Man can remember his godliness in two ways. One way is that of surrender, devotion, love, prayer; another way is that of will, effort, meditation, yoga. If a man tries to work his way through will, then he will feel he is ascending towards God or he is reaching towards God through his will. Hence Jainas call the man who attains to godliness a *tirthankara*. *Tirthankara* means consciousness has reached the peak; man has arrived by ascending, as if there has been a ladder, the ladder of the will, the ladder of effort and yoga. So is the concept of the buddhas; that too is the path of will. Avatar means God descending; that is another approach, when a man surrenders. He cannot ascend. He simply opens his heart and waits, prays and waits, and suddenly he starts feeling a stirring in his heart. Certainly he will see "God has descended in me." Avatar means descendance, God coming down.

Mahavira went up. For Meera, God came down.

But God never comes down, never goes up. God is where he is. But your experience will be different. If you try hard to achieve God, you will go higher and higher and higher; naturally you will feel the God hidden inside you is arising, rising up, reaching to the zenith. But if you surrender, nothing is arising in you. You are where you are, you simply wait in deep prayer, in deep love, in deep trust, and one day you find God is descending in you, coming from above. These are the experiences of two types of seekers. It has nothing to do with God. It has something to do with the seeker and his way: will or surrender, effort or prayer, yoga or *bhakti*.

So the religions which believe in *bhakti*, in devotion.... Christianity says Christ comes from God. That is the meaning of saying that he is God's son – he comes from above, he has been sent. And that is the meaning of Mohammed – he is a prophet, a messenger, *paigambara*. *Paigambara* means a messenger who comes from above, brings the message. He does not belong to this world; he comes like a ray of light into the darkness. And so is the concept of the Hindus' avatar – Krishna, Ram – they come, they come into the world.

The Buddhist, the Jaina concept is just the reverse. They say there is no God to come, and God is not a father and he cannot have a son. These are all very childish concepts for them. And if you look through their eyes they are; these concepts are childish, very anthropomorphic, man-centered. You create God in your own image, as if God also has a family. He has a family – the Trinity: God the Father, Christ the Son, and the Holy Ghost. The Holy Ghost must be a woman; otherwise the family will not be exactly as it should be.

But why don't Christians call the Holy Ghost a woman? Male chauvinism. They cannot make a woman also part of the Trinity; it is difficult for them, very difficult for them. So to what have they reduced their God? It seems to be a homosexual family. All men, not a single woman there. It looks ugly. But my feeling is that the Holy Ghost must be a woman.

We create God in our own image.

Jainas and Buddhists say that there is no God and there is no God's family and nobody comes from there. Then what has one to do? One has to arise. God is in you like a seed, as a tree arises from the earth and goes higher and higher. God is not like rain falling, but a tree arising. Man has the seed. Man is potentially God. So when you work hard, you start growing.

These are the two concepts. That's why Meher Baba says, "...God descending in man (Avatar, Rasool, Christ) and man rising to be God (the Perfect master, Satguru, Qutub, Tirthankara)." But it has nothing to do with God.

*When I was a child I was inoculated against the measles. Can I still catch them now?*

Yes, every child has been inoculated. Every child has been destroyed. Every child has been conditioned in such a way that he cannot get the measles I am talking about.

You have been brought up as a Christian or a Hindu. That very upbringing closes your doors. Even if Christ comes to you, you will not be able to see him. The idea that Christianity has given to you about Christ is so false, it is so foolish. It is so inhuman, that if Christ comes to you, you will not be able to recognize him. You will not be able to get the measles even from Christ! And Buddhists have created the idea of Buddha so abstractly and they have so conditioned their children with that abstract idea, with that inoculation, that even if Buddha comes across you, you will not be able to recognize him. So it is not only that a Christian will not be able to recognize Buddha, Mahavira, Patanjali, he will not even be able to recognize Christ.

There is a beautiful story in one of Dostoevsky's novels, *The Brothers Karamazov*. After eighteen hundred years Christ thinks, "Now almost half the world is Christian. If I go again I will be welcomed." The last time, they had treated him very badly, and it was natural because there was not a single Christian, there were only Jews; they tortured Jesus badly and they killed him. He must have still been thinking about the torture that he had met, but now he thinks, "Half of the world is Christian. Half of the world belongs to me; if I go now then people will simply fall at my feet. They will recognize a Christ has come back and he has fulfilled his promise."

So he comes, he comes to the small town of Bethlehem. Must be some old attachment with the town, some nostalgia of those days, where he had played and worked and had been a carpenter, must have loved women, played with friends. And he was a man who knew how to celebrate. He was a man who knew how to give parties, how to dance and sing and how to love people. And he was a man who knew how to drink. He had loved the small joys of life. He was a real human being.

And he used to call himself son of man more than he used to call himself son of God.

So he comes to Bethlehem. Naturally he descends in front of the church. He stands there under a tree. Naturally he has chosen Sunday – all the Christians are together and it will be easier for them to recognize him, because Christians believe in the Sunday religion. Six days they don't bother at all. Six days who will look at him? But Sunday they will be free and they will be able to look at him, so he stands under a tree. People come out of the church. They see a young man, looks like a hippie – long hair. They come around; seems to be a stranger in the town. The closer they come, the more they are surprised – looks like Jesus Christ. Pretending well. Seems to be an actor. And they laugh and they say, "You did well, but escape before the priest comes out. Otherwise you are bound to get into trouble."

But Jesus says, "What do you mean, did well? I am Jesus Christ."

And they laugh and they say, "It is okay, but you just escape. You seem to be crazy. Jesus Christ, and you? Yes, he has promised to come, but he will come sitting on the clouds, angels dancing and singing around. Where are the angels and where is the cloud? And what proof have you got?" Proof – a passport, a visa. "Have you got any certificate from your father?"

Jesus had not thought about these practical things. He looks a little uneasy and nervous. And before he can escape, the high priest comes. People very, very respectfully give way to the high priest. The high priest comes, looks at this young man, and tells him to come down. He was standing under the tree on a platform. "Come down, you fool. What are you doing here?"

Jesus says, "Even you cannot recognize me!"

The priest says, "I recognize you very well." And he tells a few people, church attendants, "Take this man into the church. Seems to be dangerous, this man. Pretending that he is a Jesus Christ? This is sacrilege. This cannot be tolerated. This man has to be punished! You cannot take Jesus so nonseriously."

Jesus cannot believe it. He says, "But I am the real one."

The priest says, "You keep quiet."

Jesus is chained, put into a dark cell in the church. He starts thinking and brooding "There seems to be no difference at all. This is the same way the Jews had acted. But they could have been forgiven because they did not know me. But my people, Christians, they sing to me every day, they think of me every day, they wait for me every day, and I have come, and they can't even recognize me. They think I am a pretender?"

Now he feels even sorrier than he had felt on the cross, because those were alien people. If they had killed him it was understandable, but are these people going to kill him again?

In the middle of the night he cannot sleep. In the middle of the night comes the priest with a candle, opens the door, locks it again, comes close to Jesus, falls at the feet of Jesus. And Jesus feels relieved, "So, nothing to be worried about. A little late, but he has recognized me."

The priest says, "I know who you are, but I cannot recognize you in the marketplace. And mind you, you are not needed at all. We are doing perfectly well. And you are the old disturber. If you come you will destroy everything that we have done in eighteen hundred years. It has been a long struggle to establish Christianity – and you have always been against establishment. You are not establishment. We will pray to you, we will sing your name, we will praise you like anything, but please don't come. And if you insist on being recognized in the marketplace, then be ready: tomorrow morning you will be crucified. We cannot tolerate such things."

Now Jesus is even more puzzled. This man recognizes him; he says, "I know that you are the true one, but I cannot recognize you."

The old priest says, "Listen to me. I am old, older than you, I am more experienced. I know how people live, I know how people behave. Don't try to be foolish again. Simply escape before the morning – and never come back again."

This is a beautiful parable.

Yes, I know you are inoculated. That's why it is so difficult to catch the measles I am carrying here. It is so difficult to drop your resistance. You find a thousand and one rationalizations how not to surrender. Surrender does not mean anything else: it simply means a state of no resistance, a state of vulnerability, a state of opening. And let me repeat: God cannot be taught, it can only be caught. God is like measles.

You say, "When I was a child I was inoculated against the measles." Everybody has been inoculated. The society takes every care to make you closed. That's why the work of a master is so hard. To attain to God is not hard, but because of this inoculation…. First the inoculation has to be undone, and that is the really hard thing. The poison that has been put into you in the name of inoculation has to be driven out of your system. That's why so many techniques are needed, meditations are needed, so that the poison oozes out of your system. The day your system is free of inoculation, suddenly you find the measles have started happening. And blessed are those who can get these measles.

*I would like to be a world teacher, the second tirthankara of the "Tradition of the moon." Is it possible to expose this desire to the public?*

First, if you really want to be a teacher, become a disciple. Unless you are a really deep disciple, you will not be able to become a teacher. If your disciplehood is perfect, one day suddenly you will find the Perfect master has arisen in you. It comes only out of disciplehood. But disciplehood is difficult because the ego has to be dropped. Everybody would like to become a world teacher. It seems so beautiful, it seems such a beautiful ego trip. Who will not enjoy being in such a position where he can teach, where he can guide?

But to where are you going to guide people? You are in the ditch. Resist the temptation. Otherwise it happens that the blind people start leading the blind people, and they all fall into the dark ditch.

Yes, people are in need of guidance, so if you start exposing your desire to the public, you are bound to find disciples. There is no lack of disciples. If you expose yourself, that you are the world teacher, you will find suddenly that disciples have started to come. And their coming will help you to feel that maybe it seems you are really the world's teacher. Otherwise why are people coming? How can people be so foolish? By and by, looking into their eyes, feeling their confidence in you, you will start feeling confident about yourself.

I have heard about a man, of course a Jew, who opened the first bank in the world, and he became very rich and the business was beautiful. When he became very old somebody asked him, "How in the first place did you start a bank?" "Nobody, I wrote the name 'Bank' and put the sign on my door. I had no trust in it that it would work, but I had nothing to do. I was unemployed, so I thought why not try. And within a few hours a man came and deposited his money. I was surprised. I looked at the man; I thought this seems to be the greatest fool in the town. I may escape with his money. Then came another and another, and by the evening I had deposits of a lot of money. And looking into these people's eyes, I became so confident that I deposited my own money in the bank!"

That's how it works. If you just declare that you are a world teacher, you are bound to find disciples. And when the disciples come, certainly, you have to be truly a world teacher.

And sometimes it will happen that not only will disciples come, but something will start happening to the disciples. Then you will be really surprised. Somebody's *kundalini* arising. Somebody seeing visions. Just by touching your feet, somebody feeling great silence.

It happened.... Ramakrishna loved this story very much.

There was a master, his name was Tapobana, and Tapobana had a disciple who served him with irreproachable diligence. It was solely because of this diligence and the services he rendered that Tapobana kept him, for he found the disciple rather stupid.

One day, the rumor spread throughout the whole region that Tapobana's disciple had walked on water – that he had been seen crossing the river as one crosses the street.

Tapobana called his disciple and questioned him: "Is what people are saying about you possible? Is it really true that you crossed the river walking on the water?"

"What could be more natural?" answered his follower. "It is thanks to you, Blessed One, that I walked on water. At every step I repeated your saintly name, and that is what upheld me."

And Tapobana thought to himself, "If the disciple can walk on water, what can the master not do? If it is in my name that the miracle takes place, I must possess power I did not suspect and holiness of which I have not been sufficiently aware. After all, I have never tried to cross the river as if I were crossing the street."

And without more ado, he ran to the river bank. Without hesitation, he set his foot on the water, and with unshakable faith repeated, "Me, me, me...." And sank.

So you are carrying a very dangerous desire.

The question is from Premprabhu. I know you. The first thing that you have to do is to learn the secrets of discipleship; then one day the master will be born. It is on the way, but don't be in a hurry; otherwise you will miss being a master. If you try to become a master, you will miss being a master. The mastership arises only when you learn slowly, slowly to dissolve into existence. The day you are not, you will be the master, not before it. If you are, then still some work has to be done. You cannot be the master. Only when you are absent does the master become present in you.

Right now it will be good if you take a bath. To explain this to you, let me tell you this anecdote:

A sweet old lady visited a doctor and surprised him by saying, "Doctor, I think I am pregnant, and want you to verify it."

It was obvious to the doctor, because of her advanced age, that she was imagining things. But he spoke to her kindly, "What makes you think you are pregnant?"

"I know. I know it because I feel life," she said as she patted her stomach.

To humor her along, the doctor asked her to disrobe. After a brief examination, he advised her to go home and take a bath and forget about the pregnancy.

"But doctor," she insisted, "I tell you I feel life, and you tell me to go home and take a bath? And I am feeling life!" And she again patted her stomach.

"Yes, yes," said the doctor gently, "you have got a bug in your navel."

So go and take a bath.

*Why am I the way I am? I feel like the lotus who wants to be the rose.*

So what is the trouble? So you are the lotus who wants to be the rose – and be it.

Whatever you are, you are. And it is to be accepted in absolute humility. Even if you are feeling that you are a lotus and you want to be the rose, so you are the lotus who wants to be the rose. What is is, and what ain't ain't! Relax into it, accept it, welcome it, and suddenly you will see a great peace surrounding you and a great silence arising in you and a great joy overflowing in you. We are missing joy because we are always trying to be something else.

Now, I can understand your question. I have been telling you, "Don't try to be something else," and I had told you, "A lotus is a lotus and a rose is a rose, and the lotus should not try to be a rose and the rose should not try to be a lotus; otherwise they will go neurotic." That's why you have asked the question.

You say, "I feel like the lotus who wants to be the rose." So you are thinking you have asked a very relevant question, and I can understand why you feel that way, but listen to my answer: so you are the lotus who wants to be the rose – so be it. That's what I mean: don't try to be anything else. If this is you, then this is you. Now, you would like to try to remain the lotus and not to be the rose. But if that is coming naturally to you, you will create a tension in yourself. Whatsoever comes naturally is good, whatsoever comes of its own accord is good.

The question is from Shanti Sagar, and I can see the possibility of his deep acceptance of the fact. Accept it. If this is the way God wants you to be, then be this way. Then this is your destiny.

Once you start accepting things, tensions disappear, anxieties fall, anguish is felt no more. And to be in a state of no anguish, no anxiety, no tension is to be religious.

*No effort is required to be born.*
*No effort is required to die.*
*No effort is required to fall in love.*
*Why is such effort required to know God (through meditation)*
*when this seems to be the most natural thing?*
*Is God trying to test us in some way?*

First thing: no effort is required in meditation either. Meditation also comes on its own accord. Through effort it never comes. To whom has meditation happened through effort? It will be almost like making an effort to love somebody. How can you make any effort to love somebody? The more effort you make, the more the love will be false, pseudo, just a pretension. Love has to arise naturally. So arises meditation.

But all meditators are not spontaneously in it – and neither are all lovers spontaneously in it. In fact, psychologists say – a tremendous discovery – that if love is not talked about, ninety-nine per cent of people will never know anything about it. If love is not talked about, if poets don't go on praising it, and if traditional literature is not available about love, ninety-nine per cent of people will never be aware that anything like love exists. They will know about sex, but not about love. But because of the poets and because of the novelists and because of the films and the TV, love is talked so much about that everybody starts thinking that he is in love. That love is also false.

And the same is the case with meditation. Ninety-nine per cent of people start meditating because meditation is talked about. There are times when it becomes fashionable. America is passing through such a phase. Meditation is talked about; everybody is doing meditation. If you are not doing it you must be missing something. You don't feel any need for it, it has not arisen in your being, you have not come to that point of evolution where meditation happens on its own accord; but everybody is doing it and everybody is going to the masters and everybody is sitting silently. Somebody is doing zazen and somebody is doing TM and somebody is doing Dynamic. You must be missing something. So greed arises; out of greed you start making effort.

That effort is not for meditation. That effort is to gain something which you think will be gained out of meditation.

These phases come and go. These cults arise and disappear. These are just like fashions. The real meditator has not come to meditate because others are meditating, but a deep need has arisen in him, has become a knocking in his heart, a continuous knocking. The whole world seems to be meaningless; he wants to go in. He wants to know who he is. Not because others have known! If there is nobody propagating meditation and no books are available and all books are destroyed and all masters go and hide in the caves in the Himalayas, then too there will be a few people who will meditate, who will find out how to meditate on their own accord. Those will be the real meditators. And for them meditation will be just as easy as anything. It will be just like breathing.

When such a man comes, then any technique functions for him. I observe it every day. If somebody whose time has come to meditate....

It is just like sexual maturity. A boy of three years has no idea about sex, and even if the boy of three years comes to see a man making love to a woman, he will not understand what is happening. At the most, he will think the man is trying to kill the woman; they are fighting or something. He will not have any idea what is happening. By the age of fourteen, suddenly something explodes in his biology. He is not aware of what it is, but something is happening. He is the same no more.

And then follows a time, a period, of very much embarrassment because the boy does not know what exactly is happening. But something is happening, something very much unknown, something which is creating trouble, something which is hovering around; and he does not know what it is and how to tackle it and how to figure it out. It is a natural phenomenon; now sex has become mature; the sex gland is secreting.

If life goes naturally, beautifully, if there are no life-negative teachers, if there are no politicians and priests to distract you – then near about the age of forty-two, exactly as sex maturity comes, comes meditation maturity. Near about the age of forty-two, one starts feeling to fall withinwards. Near the age of fourteen, one starts falling towards the other, becomes extrovert. Love is extroversion; relationship is to think of the other. Meditation is introversion; meditation is to think of one's own self, of one's own center.

Between the age of fourteen and the age of forty-two there comes a change. By and by one lives life, knows what love is, knows its fulfillment and its frustration, knows its joy and its sadness, knows its beauty and its ugliness, knows that there are moments of great ecstasy and then great valleys of darkness. Then one starts by and by moving towards his own self, because to depend on the other can never be really ecstatic. If your joy depends on the other, that joy can never have the quality of freedom in it. And a joy which does not have the quality of freedom is not much joy. If you are dependent on the other, then there is a limitation.

And the joy that comes through love is momentary. You can meet with the other only for moments, and then again you are separate and you fall apart. Just in the middle of it you fall apart. Just for a moment you become joined together. Then one starts thinking, "Is there a way to become one with existence and never to fall apart again?" That's what meditation is. Love is joining with existence through another person for only moments. Meditation is getting joined together with existence eternally. "Yoga" means "to join together".

This has to happen somewhere in the deepest core. And then there is joy and then there is freedom. And then there is bliss and there is no dark valley following it. Then happiness is eternal, then celebration is eternal. But that moment comes. That too comes, remember.

So you say, "No effort is required to be born. No effort is required to die. No effort is required to fall in love." I would like to tell you, "No effort is required to fall into meditation either."

But if there are hindrances.... For example, in a primitive community, when the child is born there is no effort – neither on the side of the child nor on the side of the mother. But that is not the case in a civilized society; effort is needed, the doctor's help is needed. Much effort is needed to help the child to be born, and the mother feels so much pain. And you don't know how much pain the child feels. If you want to know you can ask the primal therapists how much trauma he passes through. That small tube, the small passage, from the mother's womb to the world is very painful. And the child wants to get out of it, and he thrusts hard to get out of it. And the mother feels pain because the passage is small and the child is big.

And she wants to hold back, unconsciously. She cannot hold back – in the nature of things the child has to come out – but there is a struggle. The mother-and-the-child conflict has started. The child wants to get out and the mother is afraid and she is holding, she is controlling.

This is true about the civilized person, not true about the uncivilized. The uncivilized mother simply goes with it. And the uncivilized person has no need for primal therapy, because he never passes through any trauma; the mother is helpful. The child simply floats and comes out. In fact, you will be surprised to know that primitive women know such pleasure and ecstasy in childbirth that the ecstasy that comes through sexual orgasm is nothing compared to it.

What is the ecstasy in sexual orgasm? A man is thrusting into the woman and her sexual energies start becoming vibrated, start becoming stirred. That is her sexual orgasm. That pulsation spreads all over the body. But it cannot be compared with the child thrusting and starting to come out. It is the same passage. And the child is far bigger than any male organ. Naturally the whole being pulsates and the body goes through a great orgasm.

But only a primitive woman knows that, that it is great ecstasy to give birth to a child; it is not painful at all, it is joy. But when it is natural, then it is joy.

You say no effort is required to be born...? Not for the civilized. The civilized person needs much effort to be born. Maybe the mother has been given tranquilizers, sedatives, she has been put into unconsciousness so she does not pass through great pain, or even the birth may be a Caesarian, the mother may have to be operated on. The doctor is needed, the nurse is needed, the midwife is needed. Why? To undo the wrong that the society has done.

You say no effort is required to die? You are wrong again. You can go and look in the American hospitals. Many old people are ready to die, and they want to die; they are not allowed to die. The question of euthanasia has become one of the most important questions for the future because medical science has really evolved and it can help a person to live for two hundred years or even more. He may not have much of a life, but he can hang on; he can hang on in a hospital. He will not be able to move or to talk or to love, but he can be just there vegetating. It will be tremendous misery and hell.

Now, if he wants to die, no society allows him to die. They say, "It is illegal; you cannot commit suicide." A person who has become one hundred thirty or one hundred forty years of age wants to die because his existence is simply torture. The society seems to be very sadistic...they say, "You are not allowed to die; you will have to live." And the doctors will continue to help you to live because they have much compassion for you. Because of the compassion, you will have to live. Now, his wife is dead, his children are dead, his relations are dead, his friends are gone, and he is hanging on, for no purpose. He does not know what is going to happen tomorrow. Just hanging on and hanging on and hanging on.... Can you think of the misery that he will feel...? Then there will be the need to commit suicide. He will have to find ways and means. Maybe he will have to bribe the doctor to cut the connection from the oxygen tank, or not to give him any more medicines. He may have to bribe someone; effort will be needed.

Natural death is natural, but man is not natural anymore! So nothing is natural – not even death. If you die naturally, that will be a totally different thing. But you don't live naturally; how can you die naturally? Death has to be the culmination of whatsoever you have done in your life. If you have lived unnaturally, you will die unnaturally. A natural death is possible only if the life has been natural.

So the questioner says, "No effort is required to die." You are true. In a very primitive society no effort is required, but because of the compassion of the missionaries, primitives have disappeared. They have all become educated people now. Now effort is needed to die.

Why do so many people commit suicide? And the suicide rate goes on growing every year. Why? Isn't natural death enough...? Suicide means death with effort.

And the suicide rate will go higher and higher if the

governments are too adamant to relax and they don't allow people to die and they force them into nursing homes and into hospitals and force them to live against their wishes. Then more and more suicides will be there.

Man has disturbed all that is natural.

And you say no effort is required to fall in love? That too is not true. That too is not true. Looking at the TV continuously, looking at and watching films, reading poetry and novels, they all help you to fall in love. They give you the ideas; they nourish your so-called love. It is not natural.

The natural has disappeared. All that is nature has disappeared; everything is false and plastic. Hence meditation also has to be false and plastic. But real meditation never happens through effort.

Then what does one have to do? You have to do some effort in the beginning; otherwise you will never come close to any meditation technique, close to any meditation school. You will have to go through effort because you have become unnatural beings. Making effort will help you to understand what meditation is. It will not lead you into meditation; it will simply help you to understand what meditation is. It will help you to understand whether you can fall into that space called meditation easily or not.

If you feel that it comes very easily to you, that you can fall in that space and you can reach that space, effort will disappear by itself. There will be no need. You can simply sit with closed eyes and it is there. It is so natural. But only once it happens, then it is very natural. And unless it has happened you will not be able to know whether you are a natural meditator or not; so effort will be needed.

Man has been made so artificial that everything will have to be made through effort. But by making effort you will come to feel and see whether you can easily float into it or not.

And you ask, "Why is such effort required to know God when this seems to be the most natural thing?" If it is the most natural thing, then it must have happened to the questioner. It has not happened; otherwise you would not be here. What is a God-realized man doing here...? There is no point. Your seeking has stopped if you have known. Yes, once you know, it is very simple and easy, but until you know it, effort will be needed.

And remember, effort is not needed for meditation. Effort is needed to undo what the society has done to you. A dehypnosis is needed. The society has hypnotized you. The society has conditioned you; an unconditioning is needed. The society has made you dirty; a cleansing is needed. A good shower – that's what your effort is. Once you have started feeling that meditation is your innermost quality, you can go into it anytime. It is so easy, as breathing. Then all effort disappears.

And you ask, "Is God trying to test us in some way?" No. There is no God in the first place to test you. And even if there is a God, he is not in any way interested in testing and examining you. What is the point? And he is not a sadist to torture you.

Teachers are sadists; examiners are sadists. You can ask the psychologists. They say people who want to torture others, they become teachers. Some tendency to torture. And you cannot find more beautiful opportunities than small children. Torture them, test them, examine them – and for their own good! And nobody can prevent you, because you are doing it for their own good.

God is not in any way interested in testing you. The problem is not arising because of God. The problem is arising because of your society, your politics, your priesthood. They have made you in such a way that you cannot meditate. They have made such simple things impossible.

It is just like in the ancient days in China they used to put small shoes, iron shoes, on women's feet because that was the sign – a smaller foot was the sign that the woman comes from a royal family. If the woman cannot walk rightly, she is royal! So no rich women were able to walk; they had small feet. And if you encase the feet in iron shoes, what are you doing? Great pain was suffered just to have small feet. Those feet cannot be beautiful. Those feet are ugly because the growth has not happened. How can something retarded be beautiful? But that was thought of for thousands of years as beautiful, and women suffered it – and they enjoyed it, that they had small feet.

Now that has disappeared. Now, if a royal woman, a rich

woman in ancient China was to learn running, jogging, it would have been very difficult. Much effort would have been needed because she did not have the feet for it. Not that God is testing her – just because the society is foolish and the society has conditioned her feet in such a way that she cannot run.

And the same is true about a thousand and one things. Your society conditions you in a certain way; then you cannot do certain things. When you want to do them, much effort is needed to undo what the society has done.

The society has taught you to think, and to think continuously, and to think skillfully and cleverly. It has not allowed you to know that there are spaces of no-thought, because the society is afraid. Those spaces of no-thought are very dangerous. Those spaces of no-thought are very crazy. Those spaces of no-thought will give you great joy, but will make you so rebellious. Those great spaces will make you very, very happy, but a happy person becomes free. He cannot be easily forced to do foolish things.

You cannot send him to the army. He will say, "Nonsense. I am so happy, why should I go and kill others and be killed?" You cannot send him to the military; he will simply say no. You cannot force him to do foolish things for his whole life like a machine. He will say, "Why? I will do things that I like and that I love." An ecstatic person is a rebellion in the world. You cannot tell him to just be a clerk in an office and go on filing things, putting files upon files his whole life. He will say, "I will go and become a farmer because I love trees. If I am not going to be rich, it is okay. My richness will be of the inner." "I am going to become a fisherman. I will be on the open sea. I don't want to become a clerk."

But then things will be difficult for the society. Society needs clerks, society needs soldiers. Society needs very repressed people whose energies are boiling inside and have no way to go anywhere – so that they can be put into any work. Society arranges things in such a way that you can become slaves.

The society is not here to make you free people, because with freedom politics will disappear, states will disappear. In a free world there will be no nation and there will be no need for nations and there will be no need for armies. Millions of people just wasting their life – doing parade. Left turn! Right turn! Turn about! Millions of people – doing it very happily and thinking they are doing great things, great service to humanity.

Who would like it? Free people would like to become singers or dancers. Good if you dance. But "turn about," "left turn," "right turn"? Have you ever seen any bird doing right turn, left turn? Have you seen any animal? They dance, yes, they dance, but dance is a totally different thing. People will dance and people will sing and people will go into the forest and chop wood, and they will go to the sea and fish and they will go to the mountains, they will do farming, gardening, they will be carpenters, weavers, spinners. But people will do something that they like to do.

Right now you are doing something that the government wants you to do. And subtle is the trick. The university, the school, the college – subtle is the trick to force you into something which you never wanted to do. Then of course if you remain miserable it is just understandable. How can you be happy?

It is very rare that you come across a celebrating being because it is very difficult to escape from the prisons the society has created around you. In a natural world things will be just the reverse. It will be very difficult to find a miserable man. Why? There seems to be no need to be miserable. Buddhas will be just common. Rarely will you find a man who is not a buddha, if things go naturally. But things are not natural.

That's why you even have to learn how to meditate, and you have to learn how to love, and you have to learn how to be happy, and you have to learn how to know God.

*Why are all the religions against sex? And why are you not against sex?*

All the religions are against sex because that is the only way to make you miserable. That is the only way to make you feel guilty. That is the only way to reduce you to being sinners.

Sex is one of the most fundamental truths of life, so fundamental that if somebody says it is wrong, he is putting you in trouble. You cannot get rid of it. Unless you become really enlightened you cannot get rid of it. And to become enlightened there is no need to get rid of it. In fact, if you go deeper into it, enlightenment will be easier because a man who has gone deep in love will be capable of going deep in meditation – because in the deepest moments of love there are a few glimpses of meditation.

That's how meditation has been discovered. That's how *samadhi*, satori have been discovered. Because in a deep love affair, sometimes, suddenly, your mind disappears. There are no thoughts, no time, no space. You become one with the whole. People have carried those glimpses in their memories and they want to attain to those glimpses more naturally, more in their aloneness, because to depend on the other is not very good, and then it happens only for a moment. How to attain to that glimpse permanently, so it remains there, it becomes your nature?

Religions are against sex because down the centuries they have come to know that sex is the most enjoyable thing for man. So poison his joy. Once you poison his joy and you put this idea in his mind that something is wrong in sex – it is sin – then he will never be able to enjoy it, and if he cannot enjoy it, then his energies will start moving in other directions. He will become more ambitious.

A really sexual person will not be ambitious. Why? He will not hanker to become the prime minister or the president. Why? The energy that becomes ambition is repressed sex. A sexually free person will not try to become anybody. Whatsoever he is, he is beautifully happy. Why should he bother to hoard money...? When you cannot love, you hoard money; money is a substitute. You will never find a money hoarder a loving person, and you will never find a loving person a money hoarder. It is very difficult. Money is a substitute; it is a pseudo love affair. You are afraid to make love to a woman or a man, so you make love to dollars, rupees, pounds.

Have you not seen when a miser comes across money? Have you seen the light that comes to his eyes, and how the face becomes luminous, as if he is looking at a beautiful woman or a beautiful man...? Just give him a hundred-dollar note, a greenback, and see how he touches it, how he feels it. Saliva starts flowing. It is a love affair. Just look when he opens his money box and looks into it. He is facing God. Money is his God, his beloved.

And when an ambitious person is trying to become the prime minister or the president.... Ambition is sex energy diverted, and the society diverts you. You say, "Why are all the religions against sex?" They are against sex because that is the only way to make you unhappy, guilty, afraid. Once you are afraid, you can be manipulated. Remember this fundamental rule: make a person afraid if you want to dominate him. First make him afraid. If he is afraid, you can dominate him. If he is not afraid, why and how can you dominate him? How will he allow you to be the dominator? He will say, "Be gone. Who are you to dominate me?" First make him afraid.

And there are two things which make people very much afraid. One is death, so religions have exploited that. That you are going to die, that you are going to die, that you are going to die – they persist, so they, they create a trembling. So you say, "What, what am I to do now? How should I behave? How should I live?" And then they say there is hell and there is heaven. Greed and profit, punishment and reward.

So one is death. But death is not yet, so you can postpone it. It is not much of a problem; you say, "Okay, when we will die we will see. And I am not going to die right now. I am going to live fifty years more, at least, so why bother?" And man does not have a very distant-seeing vision; he does not have radar. He cannot see fifty years ahead. Yes, if you say to him, "Tomorrow you are going to die," he may become afraid, but fifty years? He will say, "Wait, there is no hurry. Let me do my things first." He may even start doing them faster because "Only fifty years are left? So let me do whatsoever I want to do. Eat, drink, be merry."

So the second thing, which is more fear-creating, is sex. Sex is already the problem. Death *will* be the problem; it is in the future. Sex has the problem in the present; it is already there. Religions contaminate your sex energy. They start making you afraid that it is wrong, it is ugly, it is sin, it will drag you to hell. They want to dominate you; that's why they are against sex.

I have no idea to dominate you, I am here to make you

absolutely free. And there are only two things needed to make you free. One is that sex is not a sin. It is a God-given gift, it is a grace. And second, there is no death. You will be forever, because whatsoever is remains. Nothing ever disappears. Forms change, names change, but the reality continues.

So I take away all fear. I don't want to make you in any way feel guilty, afraid. I want to take all fears from you so that you can live naturally, without any domination, so that you can live according to your own spontaneity. And that spontaneity will bring enlightenment. Then sex disappears, and then death disappears.

It has disappeared to me, so I know it will disappear to you also. So why be worried...? And it disappears more easily if you have known it rightly. Knowledge of anything takes you beyond; you are finished with it. If you have not lived rightly, you will be as other religious people who have not lived rightly: they hanker, they desire, they dream, but they repress, so they remain clinging to their repressions – they are never free of sex.

A beautiful story. Meditate over it:

The time is the not too distant future. We have finally destroyed ourselves by means of a nuclear holocaust. Everyone is waiting restlessly in a seemingly endless line leading up to the gates of heaven. At the head of the line, Peter is deciding which souls shall enter and which shall be turned away.

Some distance from the gates, an American stands in line wringing his hands in apprehension. Suddenly he hears a murmur beginning at the front of the line, and growing into a joyful rush of sound as it builds in volume moving down the line toward his place. He can make out sounds of celebration in many languages. He hears shouts of "Bravo," "Bravissimo," "Bis," "Encore," and "Hip, Hip, Hooray."

"What is it? What is it all about?" he implores of those up ahead of him in the line. At last someone closer to the gates shouts back to him, "Peter just told us: 'Screwing don't count!'..."

Get it? Sex has nothing to do with your enlightenment. Love

has nothing to do with your enlightenment. It is in fact going to help you because it will make you more natural. Be natural and don't cultivate any abnormalities, and you will be closer to God.

Hence I am not against sex, I am not against anything. I am only against unnatural attitudes, perverted attitudes. Be natural and normal, and allow God to flow through you. He will take you. His river is already moving towards the sea. Don't try to swim upstream, don't try to push the river. Go with the river. That's what surrender is, and that's what sannyas is.

## Chapter 5

# Beyond the Prism of the Mind

> Hakuju served as a distinguished lecturer at the Tendai-sect college. As he was lecturing with his customary zeal on the Chinese classics one hot summer's afternoon, he noticed that a few of the students were dozing off. He stopped his lecturing in midsentence and said, "It is a hot afternoon, isn't it? Can't blame you for going to sleep. Mind if I join you?"
>
> With this, Hakuju shut his textbook, and leaning well back in his chair, fell asleep.
>
> The class was dumbfounded, and those who had been dozing were awakened by his snores. All sat up in their seats and waited for the master to awaken.

The first principle, the principle that cannot be said – but we can still try. The first principle is that *samsara* is nirvana, that the ordinary is the extraordinary, that this world is the other world, that matter is mind, that there is no distinction between the holy and the unholy, that the profane is the sacred. This is the first principle. Yes, it cannot be said, and I am not saying it, but it can be indicated.

The indivisible is the first principle. The moment we divide reality, it becomes the second principle. The second is a shadow; the first is the original.

This is one of the greatest contributions of Zen to the world. Zen says the world is God, there is no other God. The creation is the creator, there is no other creator. The very creativity is divine. It is not like a painter who is different from his painting. It is like a dancer who is one with his dance. God is one with his existence. God is his existence. In fact, to say "God is" is tautological, it is a repetition, because "God" means the same thing that "is" means. God is isness. All that is divine.

It is very difficult for the so-called religious to understand it because his whole trip depends on the distinction: this is good, this is bad, this has to be done and this has to be avoided. The marketplace has to be condemned, and one has to move into the Himalayas or into the monasteries.

The ordinary religious mind depends on condemnation, it is an ego trip, so when you become ordinarily religious, you start having the feeling of "holier than thou". Because you live in a certain way – you eat certain things and you don't eat certain things, and you have a certain style to your life – you start feeling you are holier than others. A Catholic monk or a Jaina monk thinks he is very holy because he is doing certain things and he is avoiding certain things. His holiness consists of doing.

The insistence of Zen is that doing is not important at all, what is important is being. You are not what you do. You are what you are. And by doing, you never change, but if your being changes, certainly your doing changes. It becomes totally different; it becomes suffused with a new light. A new quality, a new dimension opens to it. You can do the same thing without your being having gone through any transformation, and then it will be second, secondhand, then it will not be real.

For example, Mahavira became naked. His nudeness comes out of the first principle; it is a flow from his innermost core. It is an innocence that has come to his life. You can become nude – there are thousands of Jaina monks down the centuries who have become nude – but it is an action. For Mahavira it was not an action; basically it was a change in his being. He became so childlike that there was no need for any clothes. There was nothing to hide. He became so open, so simple. From the interiormost flowed this nudeness. Then it had a different quality: the quality of innocence, of childlike simplicity. But those who followed him, and became naked as followers, were cunning people, clever people. It was a mathematical conclusion, a logical conclusion. They pondered over it. They thought Mahavira became Mahavira by becoming nude; "If we become nude, we will become Mahavira." Action is first for them.

Mahavira became nonviolent. He became so careful about every kind of life, even the life of the trees. He would not walk on grass; it may hurt the grass. He became so loving, so compassionate, because his being changed. Then his followers have been trying the same, from the other extreme, from the other end: they have been trying it as a cultivated behavior. They try not to kill, they try to avoid any violence, but it is just an action.

Action cannot change your being. The periphery cannot change your center. Only when the center changes, the periphery changes. Let this be one of the most fundamental rules.

The Zen people say *this samsara*, *this* world, is the other world too. There is no other world, so don't look for the hereafter; there is none. This moment is all! If you start looking for some other world, you have divided existence in two – and existence is indivisible. It is not that there comes a boundary to the world and then comes the boundary of God. God is not a neighbor! God is in the world. He is not transcendental; he is immanent. He is one with existence. So don't divide. The moment you divide, you are falling into the shadowy world of the secondhand.

If you can look with an undivided eye you come across the first principle.

You must have heard about the third eye. You have two eyes: two eyes means duality. And all those who have looked inwards, they say there comes a moment when the third eye opens. The third eye is one, single. There is no third eye physiologically in your body; it is a metaphor. When two eyes disappear and become one, when you don't look into existence with a dividing mind, you look into existence with absolute, undivided consciousness, then you are one.

Jesus says to his disciples, "If you become of one eye, then you will know my kingdom of God. If you attain to one eye, then all bliss will be yours and all benediction." He is talking about the third eye, and the third eye gives you the glimpse into the first principle.

The first principle is that *samsara* is nirvana, that the ordinary is the extraordinary. So please, don't think that something is spiritual and something is non-spiritual. You can do everything in a spiritual way and you can do everything in an unspiritual way. If you divide, you are unspiritual. If a man says this is good and that is bad, he is unspiritual. If a man says, "This has to be desired and this has to be not desired," he is spiritual no more.

Spirituality has no shoulds, no should-nots. Spirituality has a deep acceptance of whatsoever is – that which is. Buddhists call it *tathata*, suchness – such is the case. Whatsoever is the case is the case: one has to accept and relax into it. In that relaxation is the dimension of the spiritual. If you can do ordinary actions in a relaxed way, with no tension in the mind, with no hankering in the mind to be successful or to be winners, then you are doing a spiritual thing. Then it can be anything.

Zen people sip tea, and they call it a tea ceremony. Sipping tea can become spiritual. How does it become spiritual? To those people who have not looked into reality in any way it looks simply absurd. Sipping tea? How can it become religious? Yes, if you are chanting God's name, maybe it is religious. If you are praying, fasting, maybe it is spiritual, but sipping tea? How can it be religious or spiritual? The Zen people say if you can sip tea with an absolutely undivided mind, so that the tea and the sipper of the tea are no more divided, it becomes one energy, there is so much silence, one is relaxed – and if you cannot be relaxed while sipping tea, where else can you be relaxed? – a cup of tea can become a cup of prayer.

Then anything can become spiritual. Digging in the garden, looking after the trees can become spiritual. Anything whatsoever can have the spiritual quality because the whole existence is God. You just have to become aware of it. A relaxed awareness makes everything spiritual.

So this dictum that *samsara* is nirvana, is one of the greatest dictums ever uttered by any man on this earth. The founder of Zen, Bodhidharma, uttered it. It is a thunderbolt. It is one of the most revolutionary sayings. It destroys all distinction, and it brings to light that all other so-called religions are just philosophies, not really religions, because they go on dividing – the devil and God, hell and heaven, they go on dividing. Division is their work, and division is of the mind.

Mind functions like a prism. A ray of light enters into a prism and is divided into seven colors. Entering, it was of one color, it was pure white, it was undivided. Getting out of the prism, it is no more one; it is seven, seven colors, the whole rainbow. The world is divided because of the prism of the mind. That which enters in the mind is one; that which comes out of the mind is seven.

If you want to know the first principle you will have to get beyond the prism. You will have to come to that point where the ray is one.

Now, there are two ways to seek the truth. One is the goal-oriented way, and the second is the source-oriented way. The first is wrong and the second is right. When I say the first is wrong, I am not condemning it. I am not saying it is bad. What I am saying by "wrong" is not a condemnation; it is just an indication that it leads nowhere, that it leads into a cul-de-sac, that you can go into it, but you will never arrive. You can go on going and going, but you will never arrive. It is a false way. It appears like a way, but it is not a way. It has the appearance, but only the appearance.

Let us first understand the false way because if you can understand the false as the false, half the journey is over. Then it is very simple to understand the true as the true. To know the false as the false, you have already come to an understanding of what is or what can be the true. So always start by understanding the false first. False eliminated, the true remains. So first the false way.

Everybody is prone to getting into the trap of the false because it is very alluring; it functions almost like a magnet. The mind feels very much attracted to it. The mind has a tendency to be attracted to the false. Why? Because the mind itself is the false. It feeds on the false. So wherever your mind feels attracted, beware: something false, something illusory, something of the world of dreams is attracting you. Mind lives in dreams; it is made of dream stuff. In the day you call those dreams thoughts, in the night you call those thoughts dreams, but it is all the same, the same flow, the same energy. The mind goes on spinning dreams, sometimes verbally, sometimes through images, but the whole production of the mind is dream.

The mind feels very much attracted to the goal-oriented way because the mind is always attracted to the future. The mind is afraid of the present; it does not want to be in the present.

Have you ever observed a very, very significant fact that the mind cannot be in the present? – cannot be in the present at all? When you are in the present, the mind is not. The present is so small that there is no space for thoughts to move. It is so small that thoughts cannot exist. They need a little space to play around, to jog around. The present moment cannot contain any thoughts, so mind cannot exist in the present; it exists in the future or in the past. It is an expert about the past and an expert about the future – and both are not: the past is no more, and the future has not yet happened. So mind lives in the false: either that which is no more or that which is not yet. Both are false, both are unreal. So mind either runs backwards or forwards, but the mind is never now, never here.

And the whole art of meditation is to be herenow. To be herenow means you have slipped out of the mind. And even to slip out for a single moment is of tremendous beauty and tremendous significance because then you see what reality is. Then you see that which is. Then you see God, or truth. Then you see existence in its authentic color, quality, sound.

The moment mind starts working, the future has entered, or the past. Either you are imagining or you are remembering. So the mind feels very happy with the goal-oriented way. It gives enough space for the mind to fool around, to go on thinking thoughts, dreaming dreams. There is enough space. Future is an opening for the mind.

But the moment mind starts working, you are closed to the present – and the present is all that is true. The present means the eternal. The future and past are part of time; the present is part of eternity. Through the present you slip into God: you slip out of the mind and into God. You slip out of the ego, and into your innermost core, which is also the innermost core of the whole existence.

Your center is not your center alone. It is my center too. It is the center of the trees too. It is the center of the stars too. We are different on the periphery; we are one at the center. On the periphery you are separate from me. At the center there is no

I, there is no you; there is only we. And the "we" includes trees and rocks and stars and everything; it includes all. The "I" is a mind product. The "we" is a totally different direction, totally different dimension.

The goal-oriented seeker thinks, "What is the ultimate end of existence? To what meaning is existence moving? Where are we going?" The goal-oriented seeker thinks, "What are we going to become? What *have* we to become?" He never looks into being; he looks into becoming: "What am I to become? A saint? What am I going to become? What is my destiny in the future? What is the goal my life is striving to attain?" He looks into the future. The future is not. It is very dark there, very silent there, so you can easily imagine whatsoever you like. And the future cannot say you are wrong, because the future is not, so whatsoever you imagine never struggles, collides with reality. There is no reality; it is simply your projection. You can go on imagining, and there is nobody who will say you are wrong. You are always right, in the future.

In the present the reality is too much, and the reality will destroy the dream, but in the future there is no reality. You are alone. The world of the future gives you a freedom, gives you a freedom from reality – a bondage to dreams and freedom from reality.

The goal-oriented person starts thinking. "How should I be so that the goal can be attained?" He starts changing his behavior, his character, his style, his actions. He becomes a perfectionist. The goal-oriented person is always a perfectionist. He has some idea of perfection – how man should be – and he starts managing his own being according to that idea. Christians have one idea, Hindus have another, Jainas have another, but all have ideas how man should be. Christians may think man should be like Jesus; then that is the idea, and everybody has to fit with the idea. If you don't fit you are wrong; if you fit you are right.

Now the misery is: if you fit you are false. If you don't fit you are wrong, you may be real. So reality starts becoming wrong and unreality becomes right. Let me explain it to you.

Nobody else can fit with Jesus exactly, because God never

creates anybody the same way again. God does not have an assembly line; he is not making men as cars are manufactured. You can have as many cars similar to each other as you want. There is a mold, and the car is produced according to the mold, so you can have one Ford, another Ford, another Ford, millions of Fords, exactly similar. But God has no mold. God has no factory. He does not create according to molds. God is creativity; he never repeats. He is very innovative. Never again is the same person repeated, each is unique, so there is only one Jesus; there is never again. So the problem is if you try to fit with the idea of Jesus: how Jesus is, you should be, because that is the idea of the Christian; or the goal of the Buddhist – Buddha – one should fit with Buddha; or the goal of the Jaina – one should fit with Mahavira. Now, these are all false ways to approach reality.

If you fit with Jesus you will be false because you have not been made to fit with Jesus. You can be only yourself, nobody else, never anybody else. The only real way for you is to be yourself, whatsoever you are. And you cannot find any similar being in the past, and you cannot find any similar being in the present or in the future. You are alone, and this aloneness is beautiful. This is the way God respects you, by making you absolutely anew, unique, and alone.

If you fit with Jesus you are false, but Christians will say you are right. Now see how false becomes right! If you don't fit with Jesus you may be right, but then you are wrong. If you don't fit with Jesus you may be real, authentically yourself, but then you don't fit, so no Christian will appreciate you: you are wrong. Real becomes wrong, the false becomes right.

Whenever you have any idea, fixed idea, fixed ideology, you are creating neurosis in man. And there is great anxiety, naturally. If you cannot fit with the idea and you have been brought up as a Christian or a Hindu, you cannot fit with the idea, great anxiety arises: you are going wrong. Your life is the life of sin. You start feeling guilty. You feel nervous, you lose confidence, you lose courage, you become very much afraid. You become a coward, because whatsoever you do seems to be wrong. It is not fitting with Jesus or Buddha or Mahavira or Krishna, so you must be wrong. How can Buddha be wrong? And when you start feeling, "I am wrong," naturally, you tremble with fear.

Soren Kierkegaard has said that man is a trembling, but I would like to say man is not a trembling, man has been *forced* to become a trembling – forced by the so-called religions, who give you ideologies. "How you should be" – once you start thinking in that way, you are bound to be trapped into some trouble, misery, neurosis.

The first thing to become authentically yours, authentically yourself, is to get rid of any idea whatsoever that you are carrying.

Zen has no idea how you should be. That's why Zen people say if you meet Buddha on the way, kill him immediately. That is just a way of saying don't allow any idea to settle into your consciousness. Kill that idea immediately. Don't be an ideologist. Don't have any ideals, and don't be a perfectionist.

A perfectionist is a person who goes on trying to make himself according to the idea. One day you can succeed. That possibility is there – that dangerous possibility is there – you can succeed, but then you become pseudo. That's what hypocrisy is all about. You become a hypocrite. If you really become the idea that you have been carrying, you become a hypocrite. Go and look into your mahatmas, into your saints, and you will find them hypocrites, untrue to themselves. True to some idea, but untrue to themselves. And if you are untrue to yourself, you are untrue to God.

Then, the perfectionist has so many shoulds and should-nots. The whole life is without joy. He cannot enjoy, he cannot celebrate, he cannot be happy, he cannot delight. He cannot lose himself in any moment, he cannot abandon himself in any moment, because those shoulds and should-nots are continuously haunting him: "You should not do this, you should do this, you should not be like that, you should be like that...." He cannot relax. How can he relax?

Now, people come to me, and they want to relax, and they say, "We cannot relax." How can you relax by being a Christian or a Hindu or a Mohammedan? It is impossible to relax; they won't allow you to relax. They want you to be tense; they create your tensions.

Relaxation means you don't have any shoulds. You are simply living moment to moment, not according to some future idea of yourself, but according to your reality that is herenow. To live with the reality, moment to moment, is to be sane. To live with the idea is to be insane. The whole earth has become almost a madhouse because of these perfectionists. Perfectionism is a sort of madness; only mad people try to be perfectionists. Sane people never try to be perfectionists.

Sane people are humble people. They know their limitations, they don't try the impossible, so they enjoy the possible. If you try the impossible you cannot enjoy the possible, and in trying the impossible you miss the possible too. And from the other end, sane people enjoy the possible and they don't hanker for the impossible, and enjoying the possible, one day suddenly they stumble upon the impossible too.

Their joy becomes so much by and by, moment to moment, they go on being blissful. In ordinary things they are blissful. They don't ask for great things, they don't ask for paradise, to be blissful, they don't ask for God, they don't ask for nirvana. Small things. Playing with your own child, loving your wife, eating your food, taking a shower, or going for a morning walk, is more than enough. Just running on the beach is more than enough. What more do you want to be happy? The touch of the cool sand, and the warm rays of the sun showering on you, and the wild roar of the sea playing around you...what more do you need to be happy? Playing with a child, the laughter of the child...what more do you need to be happy?

But there are neurotic people. They will say, "What is there? Unless we achieve God we cannot be happy." And let me tell you, these people will not be happy even if they can achieve God. They cannot be. They will find faults; they are fault finders. Even God will not be able to fit in their idea of perfection. They will find faults with God. They will not be able to see any limitations, they will not allow any frailty. These are impossible people. And these impossible people destroy their own lives and destroy many others'. These people are the very source of madness on this earth.

The goal-oriented way is an ego trip: the ego always wants to be perfect. And the search cannot be fulfilled, because it is almost a blind man's search, a blind man groping in the dark, a blind man groping in the dark night with no light for a black cat which is not there.

The future is not yet. There is no goal in existence. Let this sink into your heart. There is no goal in existence, the existence is not moving towards any purpose. There is not any purpose; it is sheer joy. It is not a business; it is a play. Of course, I understand you cannot even play without the business mind.

Just a few days before, a young man came to me, and he was very tense, and I asked him – because I could see from his face too much goal orientation – I asked him one thing, "Do you play anything?" He said, "Yes, I am interested in games. I play many games. I play chess." And I asked him, "What happens when you don't win?" He said, "I feel very much frustrated; I cannot sleep. I feel good only when I am the winner." Even in play, you know it is a game, just a make-believe – even in play, if you are not the winner, you become tense. You have to be the winner, even in play.

Such a type of person, if you tell him, "I went to the cricket match," he will ask, "Who was the winner?" He will not ask whether the players enjoyed, whether it was a beautiful game, no; he will ask, "Who was the winner?" This is a wrong person.

If you meet a person who really knows how to enjoy, he will ask, "Did the players enjoy it?"

If you are playing chess and you enjoy it, it does not matter who wins and who is defeated, because that is secondary, that is not the purpose of the game. The purpose is to enjoy. The goal is not the purpose; the purpose is the way. If you can enjoy the way, the trees and the birds singing on the way, who bothers about the goal? In fact, the existence has no goal. It is just a way.

That is the beauty of the Chinese word *Tao*; it means the "way". They don't talk about God, because the moment you talk about God, it appears as if God is the goal. They say, "There is no God. There is *Tao*, the way."

You must have heard about one Japanese religion Shinto. The original was not Shinto; the original was *Shintao*. That is very beautiful; it means "the way of the gods". *Shin* means gods, and tao means the way. Shintao: the way of the gods. Everything is a god, and existence is the way. Gods moving on the way. You are not going to become gods. You are.

The goal-oriented idea is driving you mad. Drop that idea, and suddenly you will see sanity explodes into your being. You start laughing again. You start dancing again. You start singing again. You start playing again. And you have become religious. That is the idea of real religion, that you start dancing again, that you start loving again, that your life energy starts flowing, that your juice is stuck no more, is not stale, again flows, that you start sharing.

We are not going anywhere! We are here! And we have been here for the whole of eternity and we are going to be here for the whole of eternity. Now it is up to you to enjoy or not to enjoy. We are here and we are going to be here. There is no way to escape. Now it is for you to choose whether to enjoy or just to cry and weep for the goal.

The goal is not; there is no goal. The world is not moving towards some goal so that once achieved, it is finished. Then what will you do? Have you ever thought about it? Once the goal is achieved, what will you do? You will have to commit suicide. What will you do? If the whole existence achieves the goal, then? Then there is nowhere to go, nowhere to move; the goal has been achieved. Then the whole existence will dry up, will become dead, the juice will flow no more, the love will not be there, and the laughter will not be there, and trees will not bloom and birds will not sing and rivers will not flow. All has stopped. No, the world has no goal.

If the world has any goal, it would have achieved it by now. How long it has existed! The very fact that it has not achieved it yet is proof enough that it has no goal to achieve. It simply goes on; it is an ongoing affair. It is not a film that comes to an end, it is not a novel that comes to an end. We are always in the middle, never in the beginning and never at the end. We are always in the middle. And that is the way things are.

So the goal-oriented person misses all that is beautiful in life. The goal he cannot achieve because there is no goal, and on the way he misses all things. Have you watched? Sometimes you are rushing towards the market, to your shop or to your office, you pass through the same street where you go for a morning walk, or sometimes in the moonlit night you go for a stroll – the same road, the same trees – but when you are going to the office you have a goal in mind; then you don't see the greenery and then you don't listen to the birds. You are not interested in the way; you are interested in the goal. You want to finish it any way. The faster you can go, the better. You will not like to walk to the office. You go in a car or in a bus.

And if someday science manages to materialize and dematerialize man, you will simply stand in a machine in your house and dematerialize there and materialize in the office – so no need for the way. One day it is going to happen. There is no need to go. Immediately, from one place to another place you can have a quantum leap, a quantum jump. In the middle you will not be. Speed. Because you are not interested in the way.

But, the same way, in the morning when you go for a walk, has a totally different quality. You enjoy it. Each breeze passing through the trees and each bird flying around. You enjoy it because you are not going anywhere in particular. You are just going for a morning walk. It is playful. You can turn back from any point. There is no goal in your mind. You are non-tense, you are relaxed. There is joy, there is poetry. You start singing a song.

You can treat yourself on the way of life in these two ways. If you are goal-oriented – God, heaven, *moksha*, nirvana, whatsoever you call it – then you cannot enjoy, you cannot celebrate on the way. Zen says the way is the goal. That is the meaning when they say the *samsara* is nirvana. The way is the goal, so don't miss anything. Enjoy. Each moment has to be tasted; each moment is delicious. Each moment brings something to you, a blessing, a benediction. Don't miss it.

This is the first way, the false way, that is very attractive to the mind.

On this false way masochists feel very good, masochists become mahatmas. A masochist is a person who likes to torture himself. The greater the self-torture, the greater the mahatma. If somebody fasts for months, the crowd of worshipers will become bigger and bigger. And who are these worshipers? These are sadists. They enjoy. This foolish man torturing himself, and they enjoy – and they bring flowers in respect. What are they saying? They are saying, "We would like to torture you, but we cannot do so because of the law and a thousand and one things, and you are so kind that you save us the trouble and you are doing it on your own, and we are really happy." Masochists become mahatmas and sadists become followers, worshipers. They say, "Look at our mahatma. For three months he has not eaten anything," or "For years he has lived only on fruit juice," or "For years he has not slept," or "He is sleeping on a bed of thorns. Look at our mahatma. He has lived a life of celibacy; he has never enjoyed any relationship with anybody. He has never loved a woman. He has never tasted love; he has denied himself all the beauty that love can give."

These deniers, these life-negative people are worshiped tremendously. Who are these worshipers? And why should they worship these people?

I went to one town, and a few people came to me, and they said, "In our town there is a great mahatma. For ten years he has been standing, and people come from faraway places for his *darshan*. So I said, "But what else has he done?" They said, "What else? He is just standing." I insisted, "But still something?" They were puzzled; they said, "Why do you insist? He has done such a great thing. What else is needed? He is just standing for ten years."

I went to see the man because I wanted to see – that man must be mad. And he was mad! He was standing...his feet, his legs had become so thick. His whole body's blood had gone into the legs. Ten years of just standing, he had become just legs. The whole body had shrunk. He had elephant legs. Now even if he wanted to sit he could not. The flexibility of the body is there no more; the elasticity is lost. And I looked into his eyes; I have never seen such an idiotic person. Such dull eyes. And bound to be, doing such an idiotic thing, just standing. He was holding himself on crutches, he was holding ropes with his hands; and the whole night disciples would do *kirtan* and singing so he kept awake. Or if sometimes he would fall asleep standing, then a few people would support him so he didn't fall. These are sadists. Hmm? They should have helped him to go to sleep, but they were helping him not to fall. Now, these people have killed this man's whole life.

And why is he standing? He is enjoying in a way. Thousands of people come to see him. He has nothing. His ego is feeling very much fulfilled; he thinks he is a great mahatma. Money is being poured at his feet. Flowers and respect.

But nothing of the creative. He has not written a poem. If you respect a man who has written a beautiful poem, it seems meaningful. He has made the world a little more beautiful. If somebody has painted a picture or somebody has danced a beautiful dance, he has made the world a little more beautiful. He has to be appreciated. But nobody will appreciate him.

A man standing just doing nothing – dying. It is a long, slow suicide. And the man must be really interested in self-torture. This is great torture, but people call it *tapascharya*, they call it austerity, asceticism. Asceticism is part of the goal-oriented mind.

And the world is divided between masochists and sadists. Masochists become leaders, mahatmas. And sadists become followers; they say, "We cannot do it; we want to do these things to people, but we cannot do them." But there are a few people who are doing it on their own, so they appreciate.

Avoid this false way. Know it is false.

And on this false way many illusions exist. Now, a man standing for ten years will become hallucinatory, he will have hallucinations. Whenever he will close his eyes he will have dreams. And those dreams will become very, very real because he has deprived himself of sleep. You just try it for a few days. Don't eat, don't sleep. Within three weeks your hallucination will be perfect. You may start talking to God, you may start seeing God. Deprive yourself of your ordinary necessities, and the mind starts becoming hallucinatory. The mind goes berserk, and you can start seeing things which are not.

I have heard, a real story:

Fred P. Shields, 73, spotted a nest of copperheads one day in the eighty-foot well on his farm in Cheshire, Ohio, so he enlisted his forty-two-year-old son Fred D. and his eighteen-year-old grandson James to help kill them....

Now the son and the grandson didn't bother about whether those snakes were there or not.

...They attached a hose to the exhaust pipe of their pickup truck, stuck the hose into the well, and filled it with carbon monoxide. After a while, Shields lowered himself into the well to see if the snakes were really dead. When he failed to come out again, his son went in after him. When the second man failed to come out, the grandson went in. Rescuers from the sheriff's office retrieved the three men, all dead, apparently of carbon monoxide poisoning, but they found no sign of any snakes in the well.

You can see things which are not. Always remember that the mind is capable of seeing things which are not. And by seeing things which are not, you will miss seeing things which are. So the hallucinatory effort has to be avoided. Don't deprive – don't deprive your body either of food or of sleep or of rest. Don't deprive your body of anything. Let your body function as healthily as possible, as normally as possible. Don't torture the body, because your mind is part of the body. If you torture the body, the mind goes berserk and starts seeing things.

And once you start seeing things you are trapped. Then you want to avoid them or kill them, or, if they are beautiful things, you want to attain more of them.

That which is needs no deprivation. You need not lie down on a thorn bed and you need not go on a fast and you need not torture your body by not sleeping. In fact, the more healthy and normal you are, the more is the possibility for the truth to be seen.

The people who are goal-oriented, they don't look into life.

They look in books, because they can find the goal only in books. In life there is no goal. If you look around there is no goal. Life is there, every part of existence is full of joy, celebrating, the children are turning and dancing, and the birds are dancing, and the peacocks are dancing, and the stars are turning and dancing. The whole existence is turning in a dance. If you look into life there is dance, but there is no God. Where to find the God? Where to find the perfection? You have to look in the books. It exists only in the books, in the imaginations of those people who have written books.

I have heard:

A Japanese academic who wished to understand Zen more fully went to a monastery to submit himself to the koans. He was asked, "What is mu?" – to define, that is, a word which has no meaning in Japanese....

It is just like "hoo". "Hoo" is a Sufi word; it means nothing; it is just a sound. Exactly is the word "mu"; it means nothing; it is just a sound. In English there is one word coined by a new logician; that word is "po". Yes means yes, no means no. Po is just between the two; it neither means yes nor means no. Learn this word; it is a very significant word. If somebody asks, "Is there a God?" say "Po", because if you say yes, it is wrong – you don't know; if you say no, it is wrong, because you don't know. So po. Po does not make you committed to any ideology. It makes no sense; it is simply a nonsense sound. So is mu. If you ask a Zen master, "Has a dog buddhanature?" he will say, "Mu". It means neither no nor yes. If you ask, "Do buddhas exist after they have left the body?" he will say, "Mu". Or my disciples can use the word "hoo". This word "mu" has no meaning.

...As a good scholar, he proceeded to look up the syllable in Japanese and other Oriental dictionaries to determine a potential root meaning and habitual usage....

When the master gave him mu to meditate on, he went to the dictionary. Naturally, a scholar goes that way. He must have gone to the library. The master has said, "Meditate on mu": the master has said, "Meditate on something nonsensical, so that you can get out of your mind." The mind can manage the sensible, the mind can manage the rational, but the mind cannot manage the nonsensical. The nonsensical takes you out of the mind.

So if you meditate on mu, what will happen? Nothing can happen, because mu means nothing. If I say, "Meditate on 'dog'," much will happen. You may start thinking about a dog you had in your childhood, you may start thinking about dogs that you were always afraid of, the neighbors' dogs, or you may start thinking of a dog your girlfriend had, and then about the girlfriend and then all the girlfriends that you had, and so on and so forth. You can move from "dog" and the mind can function, the law of association. And infinite are the possibilities. You may think about "dog", you may read it in the reverse order; it becomes "god", and you may start thinking about theologies and religions....

The word "mu" means nothing; you cannot go anywhere with it. You have to remain stuck: mu. Now where to go? It does not remind you of anything; it makes no sense, so there is no association with it. If you go on meditating on mu, there will come a point of frustration, boredom. Exhausted, your mind will start rebelling. Your mind will say, "Drop this. Enough of it! And I cannot think anything about it." The mind is ready to think, but what to think about mu? There is no door opening anywhere, it leads nowhere, so one time comes, one moment comes, when the mind simply, fed up with the whole thing, drops itself, disappears. And in that moment there is a vision of reality.

That is the way of a koan. A koan is a nonsensical thing, you cannot figure it out; but the scholar went to the library.

...He proceeded to look up the syllable in Japanese and other oriental dictionaries to determine a potential root meaning and habitual usage. He presented his findings to the master, who repulsed him and immediately sent him away. Our scholar next thought the question to be more subtle and tried to analyze the tonal component of the syllable in every language of the

Chinese group. He again presented his findings and research to the master, who now thought it was time to convince this poor scholar of the seriousness of his situation, that it was not a question of another academic excursion. "I will give you one more chance," he said, "and if you do not solve the riddle, I will cut off your leg."

Now, even in the most extreme arguments or thesis examinations of the academic world, things usually don't become this tough and this rough....

The scholar could not believe what type of master he is. "He will cut off my leg! At the most you can fail, you can say that 'You have failed,' but cutting off the leg? This is too much, this is too rude."

...But the threat did frighten the scholar out of his wits, so to speak. He completely concentrated upon the syllable itself, *now*....

Because it was dangerous. This man can do something, and he looked dangerous. Zen masters look dangerous.

I have heard about one Zen seeker who was working and working upon his koan and was not able to solve it and was becoming very much afraid to go to his master because the master would beat him, throw him, jump upon him, and would do anything, whatsoever happened in that moment. So he was becoming so afraid, so much afraid that he was avoiding going to him. And that night he received a message that "Tomorrow morning you have to come," so he was very much afraid. He tried hard on his koan so that some answer would come that appealed to him, to this madman, "...otherwise he will beat me again." He could not sleep. He meditated, meditated, and he was feeling very tired and exhausted.

So, sitting in meditation, just for a moment he fell asleep, and in sleep, it is said, he saw in a dream Bodhidharma, the archpriest, the patriarch, the original patriarch, the master of all Zen masters. And Bodhidharma is really dangerous looking; his eyes are so big. And Bodhidharma looked into the face of this young seeker, and he became so afraid of Bodhidharma's eyes that, the story says, he awoke out of fear – and not only out of the ordinary sleep, but from the sleep of lives together. He awoke. Out of fear he became enlightened. The face of Bodhidharma and his eyes!

So this scholar was very much frightened; out of his wits he was.

...He completely concentrated upon the syllable itself, trying to puzzle out the meaning, and in the process of concentration itself achieved the result. The question had a nonanalytic effect, and a nonverbal result as well.

Those who are not privy to the extreme concentration brought about by the Zen master's exercise, or the scholar's reply, might not realize that many of the most important and compelling questions that face us cannot be looked up in an encyclopedia or dictionary. There is no place where the meaning of one's life is written up.

There is no book, no scripture, no bible which has the answer for your life. There is nobody who can give you the answer. In fact there is no answer; there is only an understanding. By understanding, the question disappears. There is no answer.

And the goal-oriented man seeks the answer, so he will come upon many answers and will hang around one answer for a few days, few months, few years, sometimes a few lives, and then will get fed up and will move to another answer. But that is a long procession; one can go on ad infinitum, from one answer to another answer.

The real path is not of finding an answer, but of finding an understanding. In the light of understanding, the question disappears. And suddenly *you* are the answer! Suddenly life itself is the answer! The way is the goal, the *samsara* is nirvana.

I have heard a very beautiful anecdote. You may have heard it. It has many versions, but this version I don't think you will have heard before:

Six blind medical students sat by the gate of a great city as an elephant was led slowly past. Inspired by scientific curiosity of the highest degree, the six blind students rushed forward to palpate the great beast and to determine the nature of his being. The first man's hands fell upon the elephant's tusks. "Ah," said he, "this creature is a thing of bones; they even protrude through his skin." Later on, years having past, this man became an orthopedist.

At the same time the second blind medical student seized the elephant's trunk and identified its function. "What a nose!" he exclaimed. "Surely this is the most important part of the animal." Accordingly, he became a rhinologist.

The third man chanced upon the elephant's great flapping ear and came to a similar conclusion: for him the ear was everything, so he, in time, became an otologist.

The fourth rested his hands on the huge chest and abdomen of the elephant. "The contents of this barrel must be enormous," he thought, "and the pathological derangements infinite in number and variety." Nothing would do but that he would become an internist.

One of the blind men caught hold of the elephant's tail. "This," he said, "would appear to be a useless appendage. It might even be a source of trouble. Better take it off." The blind man became a surgeon.

But the last of the six did not depend upon the sense of touch. Instead he only listened. He had heard the elephant approaching, the rattle of the chains, and the shouts of the keepers. It may be that he heard the elephant heaving a great sigh as he trudged along. "Where is the creature going?" he asked. No one answered. "Where did he come from?" he asked. No one knew. Then this man fell into a deep reverie. What was in the elephant's mind, he wondered, in having left wherever he was and having come to this great city? Why does he submit to the indignities of our curiosity and the slavery of chains? And while he was wondering how to find out the answers to these questions the elephant was gone.

This man became a psychiatrist.

The other students were disgusted at this impracticality. They turned their backs upon their visionary companion. What difference does it make, said they, what the elephant's purpose may be? And his chains – they constitute a legal not a medical problem. The important thing is to recognize the animal's structure.

Then they fell to quarreling among themselves as to whether the elephant's structure was primarily that of a nose or that of an ear or that of a tail. And although they all differed flatly from one another on these points, they all agreed that the psychiatrist was a fool.

People look into books, find out fragments, make philosophies out of fragments. That's how all the religions have evolved, and all the theologies and all the philosophies. They are all fragmentary.

The whole vision cannot be contained in any book, and the whole vision cannot be contained in any creed. Then where to find the whole vision? The whole vision can be found only when you drop the mind and look into the reality of things without thinking about them. It is not a question of contemplation, not a question of thinking, not a question of logical thinking. It is not a question of any syllogism. You have to just look silently, innocently, into that which is already herenow. That is revelation.

And not that you come upon a truth. Suddenly you find the seeker is the sought and the observer is the observed, that the objective and the subjective are not two, that they were looking like two because the mind was standing in between and was making a boundary. Now the mind has disappeared, the boundary has disappeared; there is only oneness, one whole.

Now the second way. The second way is the way I call source-oriented. The source is already here, the goal is not. The source is within you, the goal is without. The goal will be somewhere in the future, the source is already nourishing you. It is hidden in you; otherwise you would not be alive. It is flowing in you. The source is present, the goal is absent. To look for the absent is to look in a wrong way. To look into the present and for the present is to look in the right way.

The source-oriented person is never a perfectionist, cannot be. The source-oriented person is a holist, a totalist. He has no idea of perfection. He simply lives moment to moment in its totality. He lives a very unpredictable life. He lives a life of wonder and surprise. You cannot predict him. Even he himself cannot predict what he is going to do the next moment. Who knows? The next moment will come and we will see. The next moment will bring its own reality, and the next moment will create its own response. He lives responsively, responding. He is always alert to respond to every situation, whatsoever, but he has no prefixed idea how to react, how to respond, what to do. He is alert. The situation arises; he responds. He responds out of his alertness, but he never responds out of any answers that he has gathered in the past. His each moment is total.

Remember, I am not saying "perfect". His each moment is *total*. What is the difference? A perfect man, maybe, will never be angry. That is the idea of a perfect man: he will never be angry. But a total man can be angry. You can only be promised one thing, that he will be totally angry. It cannot be said he will not be angry. Only one thing can be said, that he will be totally angry; if ever he is angry he will be totally angry.

It happened a scholar came to Raman Maharshi, and he was arguing and arguing and arguing; and nobody had seen Raman Maharshi ever being angry. Raman was saying again and again, "I am not a philosopher, and I don't believe in proofs and arguments, and I don't know any logic. I say 'God is' because I have experienced it so." But the scholar wouldn't listen. Then suddenly the disciples saw something they could not believe. Raman Maharshi jumped, with his staff in his hand, and rushed after that scholar. And the scholar ran away; he also could not believe that this man would do such a thing. He chased him out, came back laughing, sat on his couch, and forgot all about it.

Now, this is a whole man. He is not perfect according to your idea of perfection, but he is whole. Yes, sometimes anger may be needed: that may be the right response. So one never knows. Even he himself would have been surprised by it. When he came back after chasing the man out he must have been laughing at himself too. "So this is possible," he must have laughed. He must have enjoyed the whole thing; he must have chuckled.

A whole man lives moment to moment, not knowing what is going to happen. His life has no script. His life is not a drama; he has no script. Nothing is decided beforehand. Each moment opens a door, and he responds accordingly. He responds with the totality of his being. I can see Raman *totally* angry in that moment. And that is the beauty of it, that is the innocence of it.

The whole man is spontaneous, natural. He is not a hypocrite, he is not pretending anything. He is open, vulnerable, available. He is childlike, simple, and tremendously beautiful.

This is the way of Zen. It is the most unique phenomenon in the whole world of religions. Zen is the highest peak that religion has attained yet. It is the sanest religion.

Now this beautiful anecdote. It is simple, but now you will be able to understand.

> Hakuju served as a distinguished lecturer at the tendai-sect college.

Hakuju was a great Zen master, but a Zen master continues to live his ordinary life. Somebody once asked Bokuju, another great Zen master, "What did you use to do before you became enlightened?" He said, "I used to cut wood for my master, and carry water from the well." Now he himself had become the master. And the inquirer asked, "And now? Now what do you do?" He said, "I chop wood, and carry water for myself." And the man asked, "Then what is the difference? Before also you used to chop wood and carry water, and now also you do the same, so what is the difference?" Bokuju said, "Before, I used to do it unconsciously. Now I do it consciously." The quality of being has changed; action remains the same.

*Hakuju served as a distinguished lecturer at the Tendai-sect college.* And remember that Bokuju was in a simple situation. To chop wood is easy, even after enlightenment it is easy, but to lecture in a college is more difficult. It is more difficult than chopping wood. But Hakuju continued; he became enlightened, but he continued the way he was doing. He became famous all over the country, but he continued, he remained a lecturer.

Zen believes that the ordinary life has not to be renounced. The ordinary life has to be transformed by your inner understanding.

Another great Zen saying. Another great Zen master has said, "Before I came to my master, rivers were rivers and mountains were mountains. Then my master confused me utterly; then rivers were no more rivers and mountains were no more mountains. Then living in the presence of my master, by and by the confusion disappeared, the smoke disappeared, and one day again rivers were rivers and mountains were mountains."

Now, what is the difference, because rivers were rivers before and mountains were mountains before? Now they are mountains and they are rivers again, so what is the difference? The difference is not in the outside. The difference is in the inside. Before, they were just ordinary mountains, rivers; now they have an extraordinary quality. That quality you give to them, you pour into them. Your luminosity makes your whole existence luminous.

A man is not what he does; a man is what he is. So the emphasis of Zen is never to change your actions; just transform your understanding, transform your consciousness. Bring a new consciousness into existence.

> As he was lecturing with his customary zeal on the Chinese classics one hot summer's afternoon, he noticed that a few of the students were dozing off. He stopped lecturing in midsentence and said, "It is a hot afternoon, isn't it? Can't blame you for going to sleep. Mind if I join you?"

Now, a perfectionist will not be able to do it at all. How can a perfectionist fall asleep before his students? Howsoever hot the summer is, and he may be feeling sleepy, because the body is the body.... Whether it belongs to an enlightened person or to an unenlightened person doesn't make any difference: the body follows its own laws. He must have been feeling sleepy; it was really hot. But a perfectionist will try to pretend. A holist, a totalist will not pretend. The moment he felt sleep was coming to him he stopped in midsentence. He would not complete even the sentence; he lives moment to moment. Even to wait to complete the sentence is false. Why wait? He stopped in midsentence and asked the students, *"It is a hot afternoon, isn't it? Can't blame you for going to sleep."*

And see the point. A perfectionist will always be blaming everybody, that "You are wrong," that "You are not doing this," that "This should be done this way." A perfectionist is continuously condemning everybody; that is his joy. He is trying to put everything right in the world.

It is said a man, must have been a perfectionist, came to a Zen master, Rinzai, and the man, who was a Christian, said to Rinzai, "In our scripture it is written that God created the world in six days, and then on the seventh day he rested. But what sort of world? I have been asking my Christian missionaries, but they can't answer, so I have come to you, master. What sort of world? Such an ugly world, so full of pain and misery. Full of imperfections! What a world God created. And he took six days!" Rinzai looked at the man, and he said, "Do you think you can improve upon it?" The man was a little puzzled, but still he said, "Yes, I think I can." So Rinzai shouted, "Then what are you doing here? Why are you waiting and wasting time? Improve! How many days will you take?"

The perfectionist will find fault even with God. "Why did he create this world? Why did he create tuberculosis and cancer? And why did he create poverty and richness, and why did he create this and that? Why?" A perfectionist continuously condemns; that is his joy.

If this master Hakuju was a perfectionist, he would have shouted at the students, "What are you doing? For what have you come here? You are falling asleep? This is not the way of a seeker, not the way of a disciple, not the way of a student." But rather than saying this, he says, *"It is a hot afternoon, isn't it? Can't blame you for going to sleep."* He understands. The total man understands. He understands his limitations; he understands everybody else's limitations. He never asks the impossible.

*"Mind if I join you?"* Really beautiful. Just superb, a master stroke. *"Mind if I join you?"* He is asking their permission, because a few of them may be perfectionists! And they were.

*With this, Hakuju shut his textbook, and leaning well back in his chair, fell asleep.*

And not only that, when a really total man falls asleep, he snores too:

*The class was dumbfounded, and those who had been dozing were awakened by his snores.*

Must have been a man of childlike qualities. It is very difficult to fall asleep so easily, and to snore. And to snore before one's own students? Must have been a very egoless person.

*The class was dumbfounded....* They could not believe it, because the man was known as an enlightened master, all over the country. Even the emperor used to come to see him. And this enlightened man has fallen asleep, cannot keep himself awake, is as ordinary as any ordinary person? They were dumbfounded.
And when they heard him snoring, it was unbelievable. Who has ever heard of a buddha snoring? But a real buddha will not be worried. If he wants to snore, he will snore. If he feels like snoring, he will snore. He will not bother what you say about him.

*...and those who had been dozing were awakened by his snores. All sat up in their seats....*

Now their sleep disappeared.

*...and waited for the master to awaken.*

This you can find only in the Zen literature, this possibility of being so human, of being so imperfect and yet unworried about it. A tremendous acceptance of all that is, of sleep, of snoring. No effort to hide yourself behind any facade.

Once there was a famous Buddhist layman named Busol. He was a deeply enlightened man; his wife too was enlightened, and so were his son and daughter. A man came up to Busol one day and asked, "Is Zen difficult or not?" Busol said, "Oh, it is very difficult. It is like taking a stick and trying to hit the moon."

The man was puzzled and began to think. "If Zen is so difficult, how did Busol's wife attain enlightenment?" So he went and asked her the same question. She said, "It is the easiest thing in the world. It is just like touching your nose when you wash your face in the morning."

By now the man was thoroughly confused. "I don't understand. Is Zen easy? Is it difficult? Who is right?" So he asked their son. The son said, "Zen is not difficult and not easy. On the tips of a hundred blades of grass is the Buddha's meaning."

"Not difficult? Not easy? What is it then?" So the man went to the daughter and asked her. "Your father, your mother, and your brother all gave me different answers. Who is right?" She said, "If you make it difficult, it is difficult. If you make it easy, it is easy. But if you don't think, the truth is just as it is."

If you make it difficult, it is difficult. If you make it easy, it is easy. But if you don't think, the truth is just as it is. *The truth is just as it is.* This suchness, this total acceptance, this total surrender to truth – no pretensions, no hypocrisies, no effort to hide yourself behind screens, no effort to show yourself as more than the life-size – this authenticity is Zen. And this authenticity is the door to the first principle.

Be spontaneous, be natural, and you have already arrived.

I was reading a few lines of Ogden Nash:

The centipede was happy quite, Until a toad in fun Said: "Pray, which leg goes after which?" This worked his mind to such a pitch, He lay distracted in a ditch, Considering how to run.

If you ask a centipede.... A centipede has a hundred legs.

The centipede was happy quite, Until a toad in fun Said: "Pray, which leg goes after which?" This worked his mind to such a pitch, He lay distracted in a ditch, Considering how to run.

Now it becomes impossible. The moment you think, things become impossible. If you don't think, the truth is as it is.

The last parable:

The Buddha sprang from the right side of his mother and took seven steps in each of the four directions. He then looked once each way, pointed one finger to the sky, and touched the ground with his other hand. He said, "In the sky above and the sky below, only I am holy."

This is a very beautiful story. When Buddha was born, the mother was standing under a tree. He was born while the mother was standing, and he was born in a very miraculous way. He suddenly sprang from his mother's side, stood on the ground, walked seven feet, put one hand towards the sky and touched the earth with the other hand, and said, "In the sky above and the sky below, only I am holy."

Zen people have laughed about this story very much. If they were Christian they would have tried to prove it, that it has to be real, historical. But they don't take things seriously.

One Zen master, Un-mun, said....

Somebody asked Un-mun, "What do you say about this nonsense story?" He said, "On the Buddha's birthday, I was there, present." Un-mun present? The inquirer was surprised.

Un-mun said, "As he sprang from the side of his mother, I hit him and killed him, and fed him to a hungry dog. The whole world was at peace."

The inquirer was very much puzzled, so he went to another master, saying, "What do you say? The story is nonsense, and Un-mun's answer is even more nonsense; he says, 'I was present. Not only present, I killed Buddha then and there, and fed him to a hungry dog, and the whole world has been at peace since then.'"

Otherwise Buddha would have created trouble for people. Zen masters say, "Buddha, why were you born? You created so much trouble for people, because everybody is trying to meditate since you came. Had you not come, the world would have been at peace. Nobody would have been meditating, nobody would have been into this trip of nirvana. Why did you come?" That is the meaning of Un-mun when he says, "I killed him and fed him to a hungry dog, and since then the world has been at peace."

The inquirer went to another master, Lin-chi.

"What the Buddha said on his birthday is wrong," said Lin-chi, "so I will hit him thirty times. And what Zen master Un-mun said is also wrong, so I will hit him thirty times. And what I just said is wrong, so I will hit myself thirty times."

In fact, the moment you say something about the first principle, you go wrong. Nothing can be said about the first principle. Yes, it can be experienced. Drop the mind, and experience it.

## Chapter 6

# The Irrational Rationalist

*Dr. Abraham Kovoor has attacked you in an article published by the "Weekly Current". What do you have to say about it?*

I enjoyed it. It was sheer delight. It was delicious. It was simply far out. I enjoyed it because nobody else has complimented me so highly as he has done. I could not believe that somebody would praise me so highly. Listen to his compliments.

First compliment: he says Osho is crazy. True, sir. I agree absolutely. In fact, there is no way to God unless you are utterly crazy. Only those who are courageous enough to go beyond the boundaries of so-called sanity attain. Only those who are ready to put their minds aside, only those who are ready to cut their heads off completely, they attain. I am crazy. So was Buddha, so was Jesus.

There are books written against Jesus in which people have tried to prove that he was mad. And of course when Mahavira was walking on the streets, naked, ecstatic, people must have thought him mad. He was driven out of towns, cities; shelter was not given to him. Down the centuries the man of God has always been thought of as mad. The reason is simple: if he is sane then you are all insane, then the majority is insane. The majority cannot accept the fact. It is easier, more comfortable to call him insane.

But remember something George Bernard Shaw once said. Somebody was saying, "Millions of people believe this. How can they be wrong?" And George Bernard Shaw said, "If millions of people believe it, how can they be right?" Millions of people and being in the right? – impossible. The greater the crowd, the less is the possibility of truth.

Truth has been available to only a few individuals. Why? Because only a few dare to enter into that madness. Only a few dare to put their reasoning, cunningness, argument aside. Life is not logic; it goes beyond it.

And not only the mystics say so; now even the physicists – who are not mystics at all – what they are saying is incredible. Let me quote a few things. The physicists are now saying the same old nonsense as the mystics used to in the ancient days. The so-called rationalists have always called those mystics mad. Certainly whatsoever they say does not follow ordinary reason; it is something beyond. Now listen to what physicists are saying; they speak of a universe which is finite but unconfined. They say the universe is expanding, but expanding into nothing. They also tell us that electrons are capable of passing through space without taking any time to do it. They are now even proposing to make use of the term "quark" to describe a particle of which the essential property is that when three of them combine, their collective weight is less than that of any of them by itself, although nothing has been lost by their conjunction.

It is absurd. It cannot be so according to ordinary logic. But if you ask the physicist he says, "What can we do? We are helpless. It is so. We cannot change the reality. Just to adjust to your logic, we cannot change the reality. And the reality does not believe in your Aristotles. It does not suffer from Aristotle-itis. It does not bother about what your logic says; it goes on its own way." So the physicists say, "What can we do? Change your logic. If it looks mad, maybe the universe is mad."

It looks mad, but the mystics have always said so. In the Upanishads it is said, "Take the whole out of the whole, and the whole remains behind." Now, Dr. Abraham Kovoor will call this man mad. If you take the whole out of the whole, nothing remains behind! This is ordinary mathematics and logic. But the Upanishads say, "You take the whole out of the whole, and the whole still remains behind. You go on taking as many wholes as you want, and still the whole remains behind." The mystics have also stumbled upon the illogicalness of reality.

Now, what do you say about this "quark"? It fits absolutely with the Upanishadic idea. It does not fit with Aristotle. Bad for poor Aristotle! And bad for poor Dr. Abraham Kovoor!

I am crazy. I have seen the reality which does not fit with the mind. In fact, the mind is the only barrier to reality. It does not allow you to see the reality. The more you are confined in the mind, the less is the possibility of knowing. And if you insist that you will know only through the mind, then you will never know.

The mind is very ordinary. It is good for day-to-day use, but to penetrate the infinite, to penetrate the eternal, to penetrate that which is – the ultimate mystery – the mind is just as futile as if you are trying to empty the ocean with a teaspoon. It is just irrelevant.

The reality is irrational, the reality is nonsensical, the reality is absurd.

Now, Abraham Kovoor can be against the mystics, but what will he do against the physicist? And why have they both come to the same conclusion? Science has penetrated into reality from a different door, but the reality is the same. So have done the mystics: they have entered from a different door, but they have entered into the same space.

Now scientists say the universe is expanding. Into what? Because when we say "the universe," we include everything that is. When we say "universe" we mean the whole, the total. Now you say the universe is expanding. Into what? There cannot be anything outside the universe. We have included, by the very definition of the word "universe," that all is in it. So nothing is outside it. Into what is the universe expanding? Even if you say "into nothingness," then the nothingness is outside the universe. Then the nothingness is very real into which the universe can expand. Then the nothingness is not just nothingness. Then you have not decided rightly what the universe is.

This concept of an expanding universe is crazy, but that is what mystics have been saying down the ages. Hindus have chosen the word "Brahman"; Brahman means "that which goes on expanding".

Now, Abraham Kovoor says that he believes only in something which is proved objectively. God is not proved objectively. What is proved objectively? The electron is proved? The neutron is proved? The proton is proved? What is proved objectively? Nobody has yet seen electrons, nobody has yet seen neutrons, nobody has yet seen protons, but the scientists say they are. If nobody has seen them, nobody has looked at them, nobody has observed them as objects, then why do you say they are? Scientists say, "Because we can see the effect. We cannot see them, but we can see their effect." The same say the mystics: "God is not observed objectively, but we can see the effect."

Can't you see the universe running so intelligently? Can't you see tremendous intelligence permeating the whole?

And it is not only the mystics who say the universe is full of intelligence. Just the other day I was reading and I came across one of Albert Einstein's quotes. He says, "The scientist's religious feeling takes the form of a rapturous amazement at the harmony of the natural law which reveals an intelligence of such superiority that compared with it, all the systematic thinking and acting of human beings is an utterly insignificant reflection."

"Intelligence of such superiority"! And this is not Jakob Bohme, Ramakrishna, or Osho. This is Albert Einstein saying so. Intelligence of such superiority that human intelligence is reduced to utterly insignificant status! The world is running in such a deep harmony; that harmony shows that there is a unity in it, that it is not a dead universe, that it is not a "stupid" universe, that it is intelligent.

Physics has become metaphysics again. Physicists even talk about atoms having free will. Albert Einstein has said that no event can be postulated without the presence of a witnessing observer. And Eddington says: "Religion first became possible for a reasonable scientific man about the year 1927." But Dr. Kovoor seems to have not lived since then! Eddington also says: "We begin to suspect that the stuff of the world is mind-stuff. The universe looks more like a thought than like a thing." And that is what I mean when I say that there is intelligence, great intelligence in existence or God. Recently a new branch of science, molecular biology, has conclusively proved that the "matter" of organic life, our very flesh, really is mind-stuff. Eddington, Jeans, Einstein, Schrodinger all agree in this. But the problem with the learned Dr. Kovoor is that he goes on fighting against out-of-date religion with the aid of his out-of-date, so-called science!

You can ask what is the purpose of this intelligent universe. The scientist David Foster says: "To become more intelligent." I love this answer. This is what the mystics have always been propounding. From unawareness to awareness...from unintelligence to intelligence...there is the way and there is the goal. The Upanishads say: *"Tamsoma jyotirgamay"* – "O master of the Universe, take me from darkness to light."

What do we mean when we say "God is"? We only mean that the world is intelligent, nothing else.

Now, Dr. Kovoor has a very childish idea of God, and he goes on demolishing that idea – and without ever bothering about the fact that that is not *my* idea. It seems he has not read anything of whatsoever I have been saying. Through his article I could not gather that he has read anything. What type of rationalist is he? He is ready to condemn me and criticize me, and without ever having read anything. At the most, it seems that he has read a few reports of journalists in the newspapers – and that too it seems was many years ago because for years I have not been conducting meditation sessions and he says I conduct meditation sessions and I hypnotize people! He is not aware of what I am doing here. This is not a rationalistic approach.

And he says he believes only that which is proved objectively. In the article, he mentions that fifty years ago, his wife conceived a son from him, and now that son is still alive and still healthy and "still growing and proliferating independently as Dr. Aries Kovoor". Now, he says he believes only in the objective truth. The mother knows; the father only believes. The son is never an objective fact for the father. Dr. Kovoor's wife may know to whom the son belongs, but not Dr. Kovoor. Dr. Kovoor, you may be misguided by your wife! And women are very strange creatures. What objective proof have you that this is your son? There is no possibility of any objective proof. You trust, you believe.

God cannot be proved objectively, that's true. Nobody is trying to prove him objectively. In fact, if God is proved objectively, he will be no longer God. Then he will become a thing. Then you can dissect God in your lab, you can dissect God in the scientist's laboratory. You can analyze; then it will not be God at all.

We are not saying that God exists as a person; at least, I have never said so.

Now, he goes on saying that "Osho holds the foolish view that through meditation man can 'feel the very core of existence'." If this is the foolish view, then Buddha is a fool and so is Krishna and so is Christ, so is Lao Tzu, so is Chuang Tzu, so is Zarathustra, and so is Mohammed, because they all hold the view that through meditation you can come to the very core of existence – because through meditation you come to your innermost core of intelligence. Through meditation you become so silent that your own intelligence is revealed to you. In that very revelation, God is revealed.

If I am intelligent in my innermost core, then the existence cannot be unintelligent, because I am born out of this existence. I am a by-product of this existence. If I am intelligent, then the universe has to be intelligent; otherwise from where will my intelligence come? Dr. Kovoor is an intelligent man. And that is enough proof that there is God. Otherwise from where comes this intelligence?

He goes on saying that life is nothing but chemicals; life is "sustained by the oxidatory chemical action (oxidization).... This chemical action is maintained by my breathing and blood circulation. It is not in any way different from the production of heat and light energies during the combustion of the hydrocarbon in a burning candle." But a burning candle has no intelligence. He says there is no difference in any way between a man's life and a burning candle. The burning candle is not intelligent.

I tried because I thought "maybe" – so I criticized a burning candle last night. But I could not provoke her. I succeeded with Dr. Kovoor. I "pushed his button"; he is very angry. Can you push the button of a burning candle, and will the burning candle criticize you? There seems to be a little difference, Dr. Kovoor. It can't be just a burning candle. You got hurt; you jumped to defend yourself. You have been arguing against me;

you have been calling me names – all the names that can be called. He says Osho is an "ignoramus," Osho is a "fool," Osho is "crazy," Osho is "mad," Osho is "absurd," Osho – so on, so forth. He has exhausted the whole vocabulary.

Now, I tried hard with a burning candle. Nothing happened. The burning candle continued to burn. There is some difference. The difference is that of intelligence.

And if you say that life is born out of chemicals, then too you will have to accept that somehow the chemicals are carrying a latent intelligence. Otherwise from where will this intelligence come in? Out of the blue? From where?

He says life is nothing but oxidization, breath – breathing in, breathing out. But can't you become a witness to your breath? Can't you sit silently? The Buddhists have been doing so down the ages. Can't you see the breath coming in, going out? You breathe in; you can watch. You breathe out; you can watch. Between the two there is a gap; you can watch that gap too. Certainly somebody else is there hidden behind the breathing process: a witnessing intelligence.

That's what meditation is all about: to know the witness, to know the *sakshin*, to know the observer.

Even if life comes out of chemicals, out of oxidization, even if life is prolonged by oxidization, one thing is certain: that life is far superior to these things. There is intelligence, there is awareness. This awareness cannot be objectively proved, because I cannot put this awareness on the table for your examination. This awareness is subjectivity. When a scientist is trying to analyze something, there are two things: the thing that he is analyzing and the person who is hidden behind and is analyzing it. The analyzed is not the analyzer; and the analyzer is not the analyzed. The observer, the subjectivity, is there standing behind.

The object confronts you. That's why we call it "object" that which confronts you. How can I confront myself? I will always remain the subjective. Things can confront me; I will always be the one who confronts things. I cannot be a thing. Man cannot be reduced to being an object.

And if man's consciousness cannot be reduced to being an object, what to say about the total consciousness of existence? That's what God is.

He says, "I am an atheist because I do not believe in Gods, and I do not believe in Gods because it is not rational to believe something for which there is no objective evidence." There is no objective evidence for the subjectivity. That's why we call it "subjectivity." By the very nature of it there is no objective evidence, but inference is possible. A candle is a candle. A candle is not Kovoor. And there *is* a difference! And it is not a slight difference. The difference is great because the difference is that of subjectivity. The candle has no subjectivity; it has no interiority. The candle has no intention. It is burning there; it has no innermost core. If Kovoor is standing there, he has an intention, an interiority. That interiority, that intention, that subjectivity cannot be objectified, and if we cannot objectify a single man's consciousness, how can we objectify the consciousness of the total? But the total is full of intelligence.

Watch the trees, the birds, the life growing, evolving. Watch the stars moving.... In such absolute harmony, with such rhythm – it cannot be just accidental.

There are only two possibilities. Either the existence is just accidental or it has something running in it which joins it together. We call that thread God which runs into everything and joins and keeps the whole existence together. God is not a person, is not a thing. God is just the intelligence of the existence.

He says, "Unlike Osho, I am not a fool to believe in a creator of the cosmos that was not created. Universe is matter and energy in space and time. Matter, energy, space, and time have neither beginning nor end." Now, I have never said that God created the universe. That's why I say he has never read anything I have said. He goes on projecting his own ideas and arguing against them! I have never said that God has created the universe. I have again and again said that the creation is the creator, that the world is God, that there is no separation, that it is not like a painter and the painting – that it is like a dancer and the dance. God *is* existence. There is no separation. Not that God has created it; God has become it. You cannot find God anywhere else other than in his existence, and you cannot separate them.

Can you find the dance when the dancer has gone? Or can you call a person a "dancer" when he is not dancing? They are always together; the dance and the dancer are together. They are two aspects of one energy. Creation and creator are together.

In fact, my own choice is that I don't like calling God a "creator". I call God "creativity". It is an ongoing process. Not that one day God created the world. The creation continues. It is moment to moment, moving, it is a process, it is dynamic, it is riverlike. And God is not separate.

But then he will say, "Then why bring God in? Why can we not simply say that 'existence' is enough?" There is a reason. If you don't like the word "God," there is no problem with me. You can drop the word "God". I bring the word "God" in only to indicate that existence is not just material, it has intelligence; that the existence is not just the outer periphery, it has an interiority; that there is a great intention moving, that it is not without a soul.

If you want some other word you can use one, Dr. Kovoor. I am not a fanatic about words; any word will do. You can call it "X energy". If you are so obsessed with the idea of being anti-God, drop that word; that doesn't matter. Buddha never used it, Mahavira never used it. There is no need; it can be dropped. If you accept that the existence is intelligent, drop the word "God". We are not worried about it. But if you accept intelligence in existence, you have accepted God. That's all we mean by "God". It is a way of saying that things have not just happened accidentally.

What do I mean when I say there is "intention"? If I give you a wristwatch and you open it, you will immediately say, "Somebody has done a beautiful job." If I say to you, "Nobody has done this. It is just out of existence, out of millions of years of existence, just accidents. Things got together; somehow it turned out to be a watch," you will laugh at me. You have already laughed! You will not even believe a small wristwatch can turn out without anybody making it, without any intelligence functioning behind it. That will be a great miracle. You cannot believe even a small wristwatch can come out of accidents, and you can believe that the whole existence – so delicate, so subtle, so complex that we have not yet been able to know its mystery – has come just out of accidents?

It is as if you give a typewriter to a monkey and he goes on typing at random, and one day suddenly a great book like the Bible happens. Out of accidents. The monkey goes on typing, goes on typing. Something will happen. And you see the Sermon on the Mount is being typed! Just accidentally? It is not probable. It is impossible. No possibility of it ever happening.

That's what I mean when I say "intelligence", "intention". The existence is functioning so together, so beautifully, and the evolution is moving to higher peaks. All this shows that existence is full of intelligence.

To remain confined to your intelligence is to remain confined in an imprisonment. To get out of this limitation and to look into the intelligence of the universal, of the universal intelligence, to have a feel for it, that's what religion is. But one needs to go crazy over it.

Dr. Kovoor says, "Life must have originated on different planets at different times by chemical evolution first and then by biological evolution…." But it makes no difference. If it started on some other planet, how did it start? Whether it started here on the earth or on some other planet, how did it start? The atheist, the materialist has to agree with one thing: that it started suddenly for no reason at all; it was not there and it started. It was not hidden, it was not latent, it was not in a seed form. If you say it was hidden, it was latent, it was in a seed form, that's what religions say. They say, "God is hidden and is getting more and more expressed."

Man is yet the highest expression of that intelligence. The tree is a lower expression; the rock a still lower expression. But all are expressions of the same intelligence. Man, as far as we know on this earth, is the highest expression of that intelligence. There are higher possibilities, because man is not the end. And the highest possibility that we have seen is what we call "enlightenment". A man comes to such a peak that all thoughts disappear and only pure awareness remains – no clouds, only pure sky of being; no smoke of thoughts, only the flame burning bright, of pure life and awareness, of pure energy.

## The Irrational Rationalist

We have seen in Buddha the ultimate expression of that intelligence. That's why we call Buddha "Bhagwan," because he comes closest to the ultimate intelligence. Maybe there are higher possibilities. One can never be closed to the possibility; maybe there are higher possibilities. It is impossible to conceive of, but maybe. It is impossible to conceive of it because when all thoughts have been dropped there is no longer anything contaminating consciousness, so what more can be possible? That's why we have called Buddha "Bhagwan". "Bhagwan" simply means that he has become the vehicle of the intelligence, and now the vehicle does not interfere at all.

When I say "God is" I do not mean God is the creator. I mean God is the hidden energy of existence. Matter is visible God, and soul is invisible God.

He does not believe in God, but he believes in four gods instead. Those four gods are matter, energy, space, and time. Now, he seems to be completely unaware. Since he left school – he is eighty, so he must have left school somewhere sixty years back – it seems since he left school he has not been in touch with what has been happening in science, in the world of science. Dr. Kovoor, much water has flowed down the Ganges. Now matter exists not! And you talk about maker. Friedrich Nietzsche declared, "God is dead," and God is not dead. He is still alive and kicking. But matter, on the contrary, is dead. Matter has been found not to exist.

When the physicists went deeper into the constituents of matter, they found there is no matter at all; there is only energy. Then what is the "matter" we see in a rock? It is just condensed energy. Matter is appearance. It only appears. There is no solidity. Solidity is just an appearance. Hindus have the right word for it; they call it "maya". Maya means that which only appears and is not. Matter has been proved maya! And that's what Shankara has been saying in India and Buddha has been saying and Nagarjuna has been saying: that matter is illusory. Science has absolutely proved it, that matter is illusory.

When you go deeper into matter and when you come to the electrons, matter is not. Those are nonmaterial energy phenomena. But the energy moves so fast that it creates the illusion of stability, solidity. It is as if you run an electric fan very fast, so fast that you cannot see the blades separately and you cannot see the gaps between two blades. Now scientists say if the fan runs with the same speed as electrons run, you can sit on the fan and you will not feel the blades moving. They will be moving so fast. Sunrays move, in one second, 186,000 miles – in one second – and that is the speed of electric energy. That is the speed of electrons. Now, in a small space the electron is moving with such great speed that you cannot see the gaps. That's why the wall seems to be solid and you cannot pass through it. In fact, it is not solid. In fact, the wall can be reduced to such a small size that it will become invisible – it has much space in it.

The scientists say the whole earth can be reduced to the size of one orange. It is very porous. The whole of existence – all the matter that exists in the whole of existence – can be reduced to such a small size that you can carry it in your suitcase. All is porous; much space exists.

And those small elements that go on running are not material either. They are just "electrons" – electric energy. Now, Kovoor goes on talking about matter. Matter exists not, Doctor. You'd better start looking into modern science again.

And the second thing. He goes on talking about space and time, and Albert Einstein has proved that they are not two. Time also does not exist separately from space; it is a dimension of space. So Einstein uses "spaciotime"; he never says "space and time".

Now matter has disappeared. Time has disappeared as a separate entity; it has become a dimension of space. So there are two things: energy and space.

Now, Albert Einstein also says to keep this energy and space together, intelligence is needed. Great intelligence is needed; otherwise they will fall apart. Who will keep them together? How will they be kept together? That intelligence is God.

So three things: space, intelligence, energy. Three things.

That is the Christian trinity, the very idea of the three: God the Father, Christ the Son, and the Holy Ghost. And that is the idea of the Hindu Trimurti: Brahma, Vishnu, Mahesh. Three faces of one reality. These are metaphors, because mystics are not talking about mathematics. Mystics are talking in poetry; the same truth is being expressed in poetry. This is the whole idea of the three *gunas* of the Sankhyas: *sattva, rajas, tamas*. Three gunas, three attributes, are there, but they are faces of one reality. That reality is God.

You can call it X, Y, Z, whatsoever name you like. It doesn't matter. A rose is a rose is a rose. By what name you call it makes no difference.

But he goes on talking as if matter, energy, space, and time are four things. He is not aware of modern science.

David Foster, the cybernetic scientist, says: "Nothing whatsoever is known about the following rather basic phenomena: mass, electricity, magnetism, spaciotime, et cetera, et cetera.... Existence remains a mystery, it is not available to knowledge...essentially it is unknowable." I call this unknowable element God.

What is matter? Physics says there is no matter as such. What we know as matter is made of waves or quanta. The quantum is a mysterious phenomenon. It is a point and a line simultaneously! Absurd. Illogical. Bizarre. And if you ask what sort of waves are these, the answer is: "waves of probability". Not even waves of "anything"! The modern understanding of science is mystery and magic.

If we think deeply into anything, we are bound to stumble upon God because God is the depth of existence. If you go deep into the rock you will come upon God. If you go deep into yourself you will come upon God. God is the depth. If we think hard enough in any single direction we always arrive at the unthinkable. If we ask enough questions along a given line of inquiry, we come in the end to an unanswerable question. That unanswerable question is "Who am I?" That unanswerable question is the koan of the Zen people. That unanswerable question is what meditation is all about.

Second compliment: he says Osho is an ignoramus. Perfectly true, sir. I don't claim any knowledge. I only claim ignorance, utter ignorance...but that's what the Upanishads have been saying: those who say that they know, know not. That's what Socrates has been saying: "I know only one thing: that I know nothing." These are all ignoramuses, and I am happy with this company – the Upanishads, the Taoists, the Zen people, the Sufis. I am tremendously happy with this company.

In fact, to know reality, to know yourself, you have to unlearn. Knowledge is good, but good only for the practical world, good only for the objective world. It is not good for knowing yourself. You need not know anything to know yourself. What you need is to go within. You can enter into your being. There is no need to know anything beforehand. Knowledge has to be dropped.

A German philosopher came to Raman Maharshi and said to him, "master, I have come to learn from you, and I have traveled long and I have been desiring and desiring to come, and now I am happy that I have come." And Raman said, "Please, the first principle is that you will have to unlearn. I am not here to help you to learn! You already know too much! If you want more learning, go somewhere else. Here the whole work is of unlearning, unconditioning. I am ignorant, and I help people to become ignorant again, so that they can become innocent, childlike."

And yes, Jesus is right. Only those who are childlike will be able to enter into the kingdom of God. That quality of innocence has to be attained.

Third compliment: Osho is a fool. Good. True. If I was not a fool, why should I be seeking and searching for God? Only fools do that. Clever people seek money, power, prestige. Cunning people seek something of the world. Only fools try to seek the ultimate.

In Hindi we have the same word for "fool" as for the "enlightened one". We call a fool *buddhu*; it is derived from "Buddha". People must have thought Buddha a fool. He looks foolish. He had everything that one can desire – the palace, the beautiful woman, the kingdom – all comforts – and suddenly he renounced. The masses must have called him *buddhu*, a fool. These are the things one desires, and he is renouncing them. And what is he going to seek and search for? What more is there than this? St. Francis was thought to be a fool.

Dr. Kovoor has put me in the great company of the greatest people who have walked on the earth. I am thankful.

Fourth compliment: Osho is dangerous. I am. Those who come to me are going to be destroyed by me, because that is the only way to give them rebirth. If you come to me, I am going to destroy you because only through that destruction is resurrection. A master has to be a death to the disciple. You will never be the same again. The danger is there. I will take all that you have away. All the illusions have to be taken away. I will leave you naked and nude, empty. But in that emptiness happens that which is real, happens that which is eternal. I am dangerous.

And the fifth compliment: Osho is a voyeur. Beautiful. Psychologists say that there are two types of people: voyeurs and exhibitionists. Man is a voyeur, woman is an exhibitionist. And out of the voyeurism of man, all that has happened has happened. It is voyeurism to inquire into truth. It is voyeurism to penetrate into reality, into the mystery of reality. It is voyeurism to go to Everest and to see what is there. It is voyeurism to go to the moon. Women have not been very creative in that way because they are not voyeurs; they are exhibitionists. They are satisfied to exhibit themselves. Finished. Their work is finished. Man is a voyeur.

And the mystics are the voyeurs par excellence. They penetrate to the very mystery of God.

You can ask Sigmund Freud. He says that the male energy starts seeking the female energy. That is natural. That's why the woman waits and the man takes the initiative. Even small children will play the game of doctor. And the woman will be the patient and the boy will be the doctor – the voyeur! He wants to see how this girl clicks, what makes her click, what is inside her. Now the scientist is born – and the mystic too.

Out of this sexual curiosity, all curiosity is born. All curiosity basically is sexual. But nothing is wrong. I love to see a beautiful woman as much as I love to see a beautiful rose. I love to see a beautiful face as much as I like to see a beautiful sunrise. I love to see a beautiful body as much as I love to see a beautiful bird on the wing. I love beauty. I am a voyeur. And I love beauty so much that I want to find out how this whole existence clicks. In that very search, one stumbles upon God.

And I want to know how I click, what is this intelligence in me. And only because of that search does one come to one's own being.

Nothing is wrong in being a voyeur. And I would have thought that Dr. Kovoor was a voyeur. His name fits with the sound of "voyeur" – "Kovoor". It must be accidental, because he believes in accidents. But it rhymes well. But according to himself, it seems that he is an exhibitionist. That's not very good. You are in bad shape, Dr. Voyeur. I had always thought you were a man! Now you have created suspicion in me.

The quality of voyeurism is the quality of inquiry. Nothing is wrong in it. Everybody should be a voyeur. And I would like even women to become voyeurs; only then will they be able to become more creative; only then will they be able to penetrate into the mysteries of life. We should try to know what it is! The very curiosity helps you to grow towards higher peaks of intelligence.

The sixth compliment: Osho is a sexual pervert. That is wonderful. To go beyond sex is certainly a perversion. It is not natural. So it is a perversion! It is not part of unconscious evolution. It is conscious revolution. It happens only through transforming the unconscious into the conscious. When not even a trace of unconsciousness remains one is free from all desire. This is real *brahmacharya*. But to have eyes in the valley of the blind is certainly a perversion. Dr. Kovoor, who is not a voyeur, simply shows his obsession with sex. Just a nice old dirty man!

And the last compliment: Osho is absurd. I am really at a loss how to thank Dr. Voyeur. These are the words I love! I am the genius of the absurd, and that is the highest that one can attain. Tertullian, a mystic, a Christian mystic, is reported to have said, "I believe in God because God is absurd." I also believe in God because God is absurd. I believe in existence because this existence is really absurd. It is incredible. It is so beautiful. It is so wonderful. It is so fantastic. It is so psychedelic. And it comprehends all contradictions. It is so tremendously in harmony that even contradictions don't contradict! The night and the day, and the summer and the winter, and life and death – what more contradictions can you find and what more absurdities? But somehow everything fits together. The absurdity makes life more fun.

If God was just an Aristotelian, life would have been without fun. It would have been too serious – and dull and boring. God is not dull, not boring. Life is full of joy and delight. There is love and there is song and there is celebration.

I am absurd.

You will think that Dr. Kovoor uses all these terms in a very condemnatory sense. That is his business – that is his problem. I am a religious man. If I can find a rose flower, I don't bother about the thorns. If I can see that the black cloud has a white, silver lining, I dance for the silver lining; and I feel thankful for the black cloud also because without it the silver lining cannot exist. I look through religious eyes. Even the negative turns positive. So maybe he has tried to condemn me, but that is *his* problem. Why should I take it as a condemnation? I take it as praise; he has complimented me. And these are my words that I like, that I enjoy.

Now, a few things that I am sorry to say that I cannot agree on with Dr. Kovoor.

The first thing: he says that man has no soul. That means man has no interiority, no intention. That means man has no meaning.

He goes on throwing theories upon me which I have never propounded, and then he condemns them. He is fighting with ghosts – and he himself has created them. I have never said that man has an individual soul. We have individual bodies, but our soul is universal. On the periphery we are different; at the center we are one.

Now, he goes on condemning and criticizing, "How is it possible? When the body dies, where can the soul go? Nobody has ever seen the soul going." I have never said that the soul goes anywhere. There is nowhere to go! In fact, the body is nothing but the visible aspect of the soul, and the soul is nothing but the invisible aspect of the body. Man is an ensouled body and an embodied soul. These are two aspects of some energy: X or God. One aspect is the body, another aspect is the soul. When a man dies it is not that the soul goes somewhere. When the man dies the soul moves into the unmanifested.

Now, he says one man, a certain Peter, has been revived seven times. He dies of a heart attack; through artificial techniques he is revived again. Again after a few days or a few hours he dies; again he is revived. In all, seven times. So Dr. Kovoor asks what I say about it. Does the soul go and come back again, go and come back again? No. There is nowhere to go. The soul becomes unmanifest when the situations to manifest it are no more there. When the situations are there again, it becomes manifest.

It is just like the seed. Where has the tree gone? You cannot find it in the seed. It has disappeared in the seed. It has become unmanifest in the seed. Put the seed in the soil, and again the tree is there. And again the tree will die one day and will leave many seeds.

The manifest becomes the unmanifest, the unmanifest becomes the manifest. These are the two wings of reality. Nobody goes anywhere. There is nobody to go and nowhere to go.

I don't believe in individual souls. I believe in the universal ocean of consciousness. A wave arises; then the wave disappears. Where has it gone? It has gone to the same source from where it had arisen in the first place. It had risen out of the ocean; now it has gone back to the ocean.

There is a beautiful story about Junnaid, a Sufi mystic. He was passing through a small village. It was evening, and a small boy was carrying a small candle. He was going to the mosque to put the candle there. The mosque was dark and it was a dark night, and the night was descending. Junnaid just laughingly, jokingly asked the small child, "Have you yourself lighted this candle?" And the boy said, "Yes, sir." And Junnaid said, "Then tell me one thing. From where has this flame come? From where? And you say you yourself have lighted the candle, so you must have seen from where this flame has come." The boy must have been a genius. He laughed and blew the candle out, and he said, "Right now it has gone.

Where? You have seen it! Where has it gone?"

The coming and going is not from somewhere to somewhere. We arise out of the cosmic consciousness; we fall back into the cosmic consciousness. We arise again; we fall back again.

My concept of the soul is exactly the same as that of Gautam the Buddha. There is no individual soul, there is no ego. That's why I insist so much: drop the ego. Then you will start living a life – a cosmic life, a divine life. Then you will live like God – because God will live through you. You will not be there.

Second thing: he calls me a fraud. I would have loved it if I could have agreed with him. I could not. I am sorry. He calls me a fraud because he says I claim miraculous powers. I was simply amazed. I have never claimed any. With whom is he fighting? With Satya Sai Baba? I have never claimed any miraculous powers, and he says I claim miraculous powers. That's why I am a fraud, because there are no miraculous powers. My whole emphasis is that the whole existence is miraculous! There are no miraculous powers, but the whole of life is miraculous. And I don't claim any power. I am the most ordinary man. I don't claim anything. I have no claim.

When I say that I am the most ordinary, I mean it exactly. I am not special; I am not "holier than thou". Then what am I doing here with people? I am just helping them to come back to their reality, to their ordinariness, to their first principle. If you start living and enjoying your ordinariness you are divine, because the ordinary is the divine.

He projects something, then he demolishes it, and he thinks he has demolished me.

And the third thing. Because I say that without God there will be no meaning and I had asked Dr. Kovoor, "What meaning will your life have if there is no God?" he has answered that his life has an aim, and that aim is to impart whatsoever he has learned to other human beings. But that seems to be very irrelevant. One candle imparting to other candles! What is the meaning of it? There is no difference. And why do you say "human beings"? And what is the point? Even if you make a candle very much informed – you talk and talk and talk – what is the point? A candle is a candle – there is no difference, sir. And this is your whole aim of life! Whatsoever you have learned in life, you have to teach others. This does not seem to be much of an aim. It seems more like a duty – and a mechanical one at that.

And why help these candles – these chemicals, oxidization processes – why help? If they remain ignorant, if the candles are ignorant, what is lost? And he says, "My aim in life is to help people so that they become aware and nobody can exploit them." But what is the point if one candle exploits another candle? A little wax goes from here to there – what is the point? It does not seem very meaningful.

And then, finally, he says, "Except for creating mental derangements and hallucinations...there is absolutely no beneficial value in meditation...meditation is a...technique of inducing self-hypnosis." Now, he says meditation only creates "mental derangement," "hallucination," and only "religious maniacs" do meditation, and people who are "mentally sick". That means all the Vedas were written by mentally sick people. And the Bible and the Koran and the Dhammapada and the Tao Te Ching and the Zend-Avesta all were written by mentally ill people. Then all that has been of any value on this earth was illness! Then Buddha has no health; then Buddha has no well-being. Then who else can have well-being? Then Nagarjuna and Shankara and Vasubandhu and Bodhidharma and Bokuju and Lin Chi, all are "religious maniacs". Then Jalaluddin and Bahauddin and Junnaid and Mansoor are all mentally ill people.

If these are ill people, then who is healthy? Adolf Hitler? Mao Zedong? Genghis Khan? Tamerlane? Nadir Shah? Who is healthy?

He says meditation only creates derangement. He does not know even the ABCD of meditation. He has not even read about it. Experience is not the question at all; he has not even read about it. Or whatsoever he has read must have come from some people who are just like him. Maybe he has been reading Karl Marx on meditation! Or Bertrand Russell on meditation.

If you want to know about meditation, ask the meditators. If you want to know about meditation, the real, rational way is to go into meditation and see what happens because the proof of the pudding is in its tasting.

He has no idea what meditation is. He calls it a technique of hypnosis. It is just the opposite, let me tell you. Hypnosis means sleep, induced sleep. The word *hypnos* means "sleep". Hypnosis means "suggesting to you to fall asleep". Meditation means *awareness*. Meditation means helping you to become more aware. Meditation is not hypnosis. Meditation is a process of *de*hypnosis; it is a dehypnotization. You are hypnotized already by the society, by the schools, by the priests and the politicians. Meditation is a way to dehypnotize you, to uncondition you, so that you can attain to your childhood innocence again. And the difference is so vital and so clear and so distinct that unless one is absolutely closed to understanding there is no way to miss it.

Hypnosis is sleep; when you hypnotize a person he falls asleep, he loses consciousness. When a person meditates he becomes conscious – he attains consciousness. He becomes *more* conscious. In fact a meditator by and by starts feeling that he needs less sleep than before; and with less sleep he feels more vital. If he was sleeping for eight or ten hours before, now he feels five or six or even four or three hours are enough; that gives him enough rest. And a meditator by and by comes to know that even in sleep something remains aware in him.

But these are experiences, Dr. Kovoor. I cannot invite you into my sleep. I am helpless. Otherwise I would have invited you into my sleep to see what is happening. The only way to know is to meditate.

And I am not saying something for the first time. Down the ages thousands of mystics have said the same thing. Krishna says in Gita, "When everybody is fast asleep, the yogi is awake." Buddha's disciple Ananda asked Buddha, "I have a feeling that in your sleep you remain alert." Buddha said, "You are right. Body goes to sleep, mind goes to sleep; I remain aware." In fact modern psychology says that a layer of your consciousness is there which is always alert, always awake.

Have you not watched? A mother is sleeping. There are thundering clouds in the sky, or airplanes are passing by, and her sleep will not be disturbed. But her small child – just a small movement or the child starts crying – and she is fully awake. What happened? She was not disturbed by the airplane passing, she was not disturbed by the thundering in the clouds. What happened? Just a small noise from the child, and she is fully alert. A part of her being is aware and keeps caring for the child. She closes herself against the thundering clouds, but she cannot close her awareness from the child. She is alert.

If you fall asleep here and I come and I suddenly call a name, "Is Ram here?" nobody will listen, but the man whose name is Ram will say, "Who is disturbing my sleep? Yes, I am here what do you want?" Everybody heard it, but nobody responded; only Ram responded. A part of his mind – even in sleep – knows this is the name, somebody has called him.

Even in sleep you go on chasing the mosquitoes. If an insect crawls on you, you throw it away, and sleep is not disturbed. Something keeps alert, surrounds you.

This is in ordinary life. When you become a meditator, this awareness becomes deeper, more crystallized. A point comes when you can sleep and yet remain awake.

I would like to invite Kovoor into my sleep, but my sleep is subjective. I know it, but I cannot put it in front of you, Dr. Kovoor, so that you can examine it objectively.

But there is a way: you can learn meditation. You can meditate, and you can see what the difference between hypnosis and meditation is. They are diametrically opposite!

And he says "There is absolutely no beneficial value in meditation." Now, this is going too far. So many universities are experimenting, and there is now solid proof from medical colleges, medical research, psychiatric research that meditation is of tremendous benefit. He seems to be completely unaware of what is happening in the world.

I invite you, Dr. Kovoor. You should come here. We have thousands of books here – the latest ones. It seems you have not seen books for sixty years.

And whatsoever he says in his article is just elementary biology, high-school biology. When I was reading I thought, "My God, what knowledge!"

Now there is absolute proof that a meditator is less prone to ulcers, less prone to heart attacks, less prone to high blood pressure. A meditator is less prone to many illnesses that happen ordinarily to everybody. A meditator is less prone to madness, to insanity, to neurosis, psychosis. And a meditator is certainly more quiet, calm, and collected. A meditator is more responsible. A meditator is more loving. And there is definite proof that a meditator lives longer than a non-meditator. A meditator has a higher IQ, more intelligence, than a non-meditator, more vitality, more creativity.

Meditation is therapeutic. In fact, "meditation" and "medicine" come from the same root. Meditation is a healing force, because it relaxes you and allows nature to heal you. But that is not the primary benefit of meditation. It is just a side effect. The basic benefit is the entry into the divine. Self-realization. God-realization. Oh! the ecstasy of it, the blessing and the benediction.

And these are not assertions of mystics. Now scientific labs are producing papers, research work, theses, dissertations. Through scientific equipment, measurement, ways and means, now it is almost a certain fact that mind can exist in many wavelengths and meditation changes the wavelength. Meditation creates more "alpha" waves – and alpha waves release joy, happiness, bliss, benediction. Forget what the mystics say, but you can listen to the scientists.

In the end, I pray for the old man. Please, you also pray for him. His days cannot be many and I would not like him to die believing that he is nothing but a chemical process and oxidization! Poor thing!

And finally Dr. Kovoor requests the government to prevent my work. This is great! What type of argument is this? This is nerve failure, Dr. Kovoor! Can you not argue yourself, so now you need the support of the state?

And he thinks he is a rational man and he has a scientific outlook. I don't see rationality or scientific outlook. I simply see a dogmatic, closed attitude, as if he has decided once and for all what is truth and is adamant not to listen to anything which can disturb his dogmatic ideas, ideologies.

Now, a few non serious questions.

*Life is beautiful, but I am unhappy. You are giving much love, but I cannot take it. What you say is true, but I cannot follow it. I want to be transformed, but what is preventing me?*

I will just tell you one anecdote:

After passing a group of women talking near his church, the minister decided to preach a sermon on gossip.

"Members of the congregation," he began, "as I entered the church the other day prior to one of your Ladies' Aid meetings, in one group someone was saying, 'Mrs. Wilson is a wonderful woman, but....' At another group I heard, 'Miss Brown is really a nice woman, but....' At still another group someone was saying, 'The Arnolds seem to be a lovely couple, but....' And I am telling you right now, that if you are not careful, you are going to slide right into hell on your *buts*!"

*I am always afraid of wasting time. Time is valuable, and I want to use it rightly. Can you guide me as to what I should do so that no mistake is committed?*

First, time is not valuable. There have been people who have been saying "time is money." They are neurotic people. They have created much neurosis in the world. Time is not valuable, because eternity is available. There is no end to time and there is no beginning to time. So don't be worried about it. The more you worry, the more you waste. Only an unworried person knows how to live joyously, moment to moment. Time consciousness is a great disease...and the whole West is suffering from it. And the disease is spreading to the East too. It has even spread to the animals. I was reading one anecdote....

An old lady kept a parrot which was always swearing. Every Sunday she kept a lid over the cage, removing it on Monday morning, thus preventing the bird from swearing on the Sabbath. On a Monday she saw the minister coming towards the house; so she again placed the cover on the cage. As the priest was about to step into the parlor, the parrot remarked, "This has been a damned short week!"

You have enough time. And don't be so afraid of committing mistakes! That is the only mistake one has to avoid – the only mistake, I say, that a man can commit in life – and that is: becoming afraid of committing mistakes. Then you never grow, then you never go anywhere, then you never do anything. Then by and by you will slip into dullness and deadness. You will become stuck, stagnant. Commit mistakes. What is wrong in committing mistakes?

Just remember one thing: don't commit the same mistake again. Commit new mistakes every day. Be inventive. Innovate. A man only learns when he commits many, many mistakes. Go astray as far as you can go. God is everywhere. Where can you go? And the further astray you go, the deeper is your understanding of coming home; and when you come home, you understand what you were missing.

Nothing is wrong. You are too afraid and too cowardly. Drop this fear and drop this cowardliness.

*Osho, please help me.*

I cannot do that. I am not your enemy. I am not a do-gooder. I don't "help," because the help, the very desire to be helped, is a desire to continue as you are. You want some props, some supports. You want consolation, comfort. No, I am the last person to give you any consolation. I am going to withdraw all props, so you fall flat on the ground. From there starts a new life, a new beginning.

Henry Thoreau once observed that if he knew for certain that a man was on his way to see him with the single purpose of trying to help him, he would run for his life.

That should be the attitude towards helpers. If somebody is coming to help you, escape! Your life is in danger. Avoid the do-gooders, the so-called saints and mahatmas.

I am not here to console you, to comfort you, to make you

secure. I am here to destroy you utterly, because only then is the new born – the new man, the new consciousness. If I help, the old will continue. All help goes to help the old. All help keeps the old surviving; it nourishes it. No, I am not going to help in any way.

I know you want help. You don't want resurrection. You want help. You don't want death, you don't want a new life. But if you are around me long enough, by and by I will withdraw all your supports. I will even take the earth beneath your feet away, so you fall into the bottomless abyss of existence. You disappear into that abyss...and in that very disappearance, God appears to you. When you are utterly helpless, God's help becomes available.

I am not going to help you. I am going to make you utterly helpless so that in your helplessness a prayer arises, so that in your helplessness, surrender becomes possible, and then comes God's help. Only God can help. And all other help is a barrier to God's help.

One beautiful story that I always love.... Krishna has just sat down to take his lunch and in the middle of the lunch he rushes towards the door, and his wife, Rukmini, says, "Where are you going?" But he is in such a hurry that he doesn't answer. At the door he suddenly stops, then comes back slowly, a little sad, sits back, starts eating. Rukmini asks, "What is the matter? What happened? Where were you going so suddenly, as if there was some emergency? And now suddenly you turn back from the door and you are sad. What happened?"

Krishna says, "One of my lovers, one of my devotees, is passing through a capital and people are throwing stones at him and blood is flowing from his head and he has wounds, but he remains utterly helpless – not a condemnatory word on his lips, not even in his mind. His surrender is total. I had to rush to help him. He was so helpless!"

Then Rukmini is even more surprised. "Then why did you come back?"

Krishna says, "By the time I reached the door, he had taken a stone in his own hand. Now he is ready to answer himself. Now I am not needed. Now he is no more helpless."

Remember, all human help becomes a barrier to divine help.

My purpose here is to make you *really* helpless, utterly helpless, so God rushes towards you and fills your emptiness. That will be the day of real rejoicing, ecstasy.

Don't ask for my help. Ask that I destroy all that you have arranged around yourself as help, comfort, consolation. Ask that I kill you. Ask that I behead you. The moment your head has rolled down on the earth, you will grow a new head, and that head will be the divine. That will be God's head.

## Chapter 7

# The Song of Sound and Silence

*A puzzled monk once said to Fuketsu, "You say truth can be expressed without speaking, and without keeping silent. How can this be?" Fuketsu answered, "In southern China, in the spring, when I was only a lad, Ah! How the birds sang among the blossoms."*

God is. Truth is. Love is. There is no way to say it, and there is no way to hide it. There is no word which can express it, and there is no methodology of how to keep it unexpressed. That is the dilemma of the mystic. He has to say it, and it cannot be said. He cannot keep quiet about it, he cannot keep silent. It overfloods him; it starts overflowing; it is beyond him to keep silent. He has to say it, and nobody has ever been able to say it.

God is not a word, neither is truth a word, nor is love a word. And they are not just silences either, because their isness is a singing isness; they are songs. It is not just dull and dead there. It is full of joy, it is overflowing joy. It is celebration, it is ecstasy, it is orgasm, because it is a meeting of the opposites, because it is a meeting of the polarities, because it is a marriage, a marriage of yin and yang, day and night, summer and winter, life and death, sound and silence.

So when it happens, you cannot say it, but you have to sing it, and that is the beauty of the song. It has something of the word and something of silence in it. That is the beauty of poetry, the beauty of dance. Something is visible, something is invisible; the manifest and the unmanifest meet there, embrace each other, are fulfilled in each other.

If you simply say and use words and there is no silence in those words, your words will be like dead stones. They can hit somebody's head, you can argue with them, but you cannot convert. They don't have that quality of silence which becomes conversion. When a word has a silence at its innermost core, when a word is luminous with silence, it brings conversion. Then it is a gospel, then it is good news. Then somebody, who is saying something with silence in it, is not throwing a dead rock at you, but is throwing a flower. It will also hit you, but it will also caress you, and it will go deeper because you can be vulnerable to it and it will reach to your very heart. Because how can you protect yourself against it? You will be non-defensive.

So remember, all the mystics have been singing and dancing, celebrating. They go on saying, "We cannot say it," and they go on saying all the same.

There is a difference in saying and saying. When you say without knowing it, without realizing it, it is just gibberish, just words and words and words, without any soul in them; it is a corpse; there is no aliveness in it. Those words stink – they stink of death. There is no heartbeat of life. When you know, when you have experienced, when you have fallen into that abyss called God, when you are transformed by that surrender, when you are totally immersed in it, when your every cell is bathed in it, then you say; but your words are not mere words. They carry silence. They are vehicles of silence; they are gestures of silence. We have a special name for it in the East: *mahamudra* – the great gesture.

Look at my hand. If it is empty, if there is nobody behind it who has experienced, then it is an ordinary gesture. But if there is somebody behind it who has known, who has lived, who has experienced, then raising this hand is a great gesture, *mahamudra*. Then the ordinary hand becomes extraordinary. Then ordinary words are no more ordinary words. You cannot go to the dictionary to find their meaning. When a word is full of silence, you will have to go within yourself to find its meaning, not to a dictionary, not to a library. You will have to go within yourself. The meaning will be found in your experience.

The word of a man who knows is loaded, loaded with great fragrance. You will have to decode it in your innermost core of being, into the innermost shrine of your being.

Truth is a transcendence, transcendence of all duality. So

those who say truth cannot be said, only say a half-truth; and those who say that truth can be said only in silence, they also say a half-truth.

Zen brings the whole truth to the world. Zen is a great blessing to the world; it brings the whole truth.

The whole truth is: Truth cannot be said, and yet can be said. If not said, then showed, indicated. The ordinary duality is transcended. We are always moving from one pole of the duality to the other. Sometimes we say, "Yes, it can be said"; this is one pole. Then we become aware, "How can it be said?" – the other pole. Then we keep silent, but then again we become aware that there is something left: "Yes, it can be said." This way it goes on moving, it swings.

Zen says truth is a transcendence, transcendence of all duality. The duality between the word and the silence is also to be transcended.

The Bible says in the beginning there was the word. The Vedas say in the beginning there was silence, eternal silence, and the silence brooded over the sea, and it was dark. And the Bible says there was the word. The first thing that happened in existence was the word. God said let there be light, and there was light. Both are half-truths.

If you ask the Zen people...They have not written any Bible or any Veda yet, and they will never try, because they don't believe in scriptures. They say it is beyond the scriptures; it is a transmission beyond the scriptures. But if they ever write a Bible, or if they are forced to, like Lao Tzu was once forced to write the Tao Te Ching because the king wouldn't allow him to leave the country unless he wrote his experiences....

Lao Tzu wanted to go to the Himalayas, to die there; certainly there cannot be any more beautiful a place to die. Those eternal peaks, those snow-covered virgin peaks, where can you find a better place to disappear in God? What better moment? He wanted to go – he was very old and he wanted to go to the Himalayas to rest and disappear there, nobody ever knowing about him. He wanted to disappear absolutely alone. He wanted his death to be private.

And death is a private thing. Nobody else can be with you when you die; it is absolutely internal. So he wanted to escape and go away from the crowds. He was afraid too many people will surround him and his death will become a public affair.

But the king insisted, "First you write whatsoever you have known." And he ordered the guards on the boundary saying that "This man is not to be allowed to go out." So he was caught at a guard post, and for three days he sat in the guards' room and wrote down the Tao Te Ching.

If somebody forces a Zen master to write down a Bible, a Veda, then they will say there was song in the beginning. Neither word nor silence, but song. There was song in the beginning, and God sang and danced. Not "Let there be light": God sang and danced. And that dance became the beginning of creation.

That dance continues. That dance is what existence is.

The song has a mystery about it because it is a meeting, a marriage of opposites. In the song there is sound and silence. The song says something, but says in such a way that you cannot grasp it. Not that it doesn't say anything. It makes much available, but you cannot grasp it, you cannot just possess it. If you try to possess, you will kill it. You cannot have a song in your fist; otherwise the song will be killed. It is too delicate; you cannot be that rough with it. A song has to be preserved in the heart, not in the fist. About a song you have to be receptive, not aggressive. You can keep an argument in the fist; it is hard, rocklike, it will not die. You can keep and possess an argument, you can become the possessor of an argument. That's why the ego enjoys very much to have arguments, proofs, logic, philosophies. The ego feels very much fulfilled: "I know so much."

The song cannot be possessed that way; the ego cannot be its possessor. The song can penetrate your being, but the ego has to give way. If the ego comes in between, the song will be shattered. You may get fragments of it, and you may start interpreting those fragments, but you will miss the unity of it. And it was in the unity.

A song has not to be thought about. If you start thinking, about a song, you are already missing it. When you listen to music, how do you listen? Do you bring your mind in? If you bring your mind in, where is the music? Music and the mind both cannot exist together. That is the mystery of music: you have to put your mind aside. You cannot argue with music; you cannot nod your head in agreement or disagreement. You cannot say, "Yes, I agree," or "No, I don't agree." There is no question of agreement or no agreement. With music you simply become one. If you want to feel it you have to put your head aside. The heart has to open towards it. It goes directly to the heart, it showers on the heart. It helps the flower of the heart to open and bloom. It is a nourishment for the inner lotus.

The Zen people will say, "There was song in the beginning, and then God sang and God danced, and that's what he has been doing since then." Each moment it is a dance. Look around. Can't you hear these birds? These are not birds; don't be deceived by them. These are not birds. It is God singing, the God of the beginnings – because it is always a beginning. Each moment is a beginning. Never think that the beginning was somewhere in the past. This is the beginning, and it is always the beginning and there is no end. It is God singing.

Can't you hear the silence of the trees? It is God, silent.

In the birds he is singing, in the trees he is silent. Birds cannot exist without the trees, and, let me tell you, the trees cannot exist without the birds either. The birds sing for the trees, and the trees are silent for the birds, and there is a marriage. They are tied together. If trees disappear, birds will disappear. Kill all the birds of the world, and you will one day see the trees are disappearing. Everything is intertwined, everything is interlinked. This is what we mean by the word "ecology" – everything is together.

It is God singing, it is God silent.

Once you understand that God is both, then this highest possibility opens for you. This is the first principle, that you need not divide, all division is false, that you need not create any duality, because existence is non-dual, because existence is one.

And all our misery is because we are divided. Why do you feel so thrilled when you are in love? What happens? Is the thrill just chemical, hormonal? No, it is not. The thrill is existential. When you are in love, at least with one person you feel to be one, at least with one person you have dropped duality, at least with one person you are no more separate, at least with one person the boundaries are not there. You have removed the boundaries. Two spaces have come so close, they overlap. You feel so thrilled with love, so blissful with love, because it is an experience of God, a very limited experience of course.

And if it is so beautiful to be one with one person, how much more beautiful will it be to be one with the whole, to be one with all the persons, men and women, trees and birds and animals and the clouds and the mountains and the stars? How will it be? How much more beautiful? The beauty cannot be imagined, because the difference will not be only of quantity, it will be of quality. It will be utterly different.

Love can at the most be only a glimpse of a ray, not the ray itself, but only a glimpse in the lake. A ray of the sun playing on the lake, and you see the glimpse. That glimpse is love. When you find out the real ray, it becomes prayer. When you start moving through that ray, upwards, you start climbing on that ray and you start reaching towards the source of all light, then you are growing in spirituality. One day you are dissolved into that light. You yourself have become that light. That is the orgasm I talk about. That's ecstasy.

And Zen people say that when you know, you have to say, knowing well that it cannot be said. You have to sing it.

Zen masters have been very creative. Either they were singers, dancers, or painters, or in some sort of art, calligraphy, pottery. Whatsoever they could do they did. That became the gesture of their expression. They were not inactive people. Deep down they were not doers, and on the surface they were not inactive at all. Deep down they were just instrumental to the divine. No doer, no idea of doing anything – just being, but on the surface very creative. The world would have been far richer if every religion had developed such a school as Zen.

For example, Hindu monks have lived a very uncreative life. Jaina monks have lived a very uncreative life. Except Zen, even Buddhists have lived a very uncreative life. So has been the case with the Catholics.

Zen brings creativity. And remember, if you want to be one with the creator, you will have to learn some ways of creativity.

The only way to be one with the creator is to be in some moment of creativity, when you are lost. The potter is lost in making his pottery; the potter is lost while working on the wheel. The painter is lost while painting. The dancer is lost; there is no dancer, only the dance remains. Those are the peak moments, where you touch God, where God touches you.

Now, the scholar, the so-called scholar, becomes wordy. He goes on learning more words, more words, more information, more scriptures. He has no silence. That is a very lopsided phenomenon. Then against the scholar there are a few saints, who keep quiet; they don't even say a single word. That too is moving to the other extreme. They become uncreative. Of course, they are silent, better than the scholar – at least they will not throw their rubbish into other people's heads, at least they are not committing any crime – but in a higher sense they are also criminals because they are not benefiting existence. They are parasites. They are not making existence richer by their being here. They are not helping God in his dance, in his song.

Zen brings the highest synthesis. Don't be afraid of speaking, but don't go on speaking if you don't know. Don't be silent. Just being silent will not help.

It has to be understood because too many times this comes to your mind too: Why go on speaking? Why not keep quiet? But your silence will be *your* silence. The words will go on moving, revolving inside you. You will become a madhouse inside. You may look silent from the outside; you will not be silent inside. How can you simply drop those words, those old habits of many lives? The mind will go on chattering, the mind will go on saying things, repeating things. The mind is like an automaton; even if you don't want to talk the mind goes on. If you don't talk to others it goes on talking to itself. It creates both the parties: it talks from one side and answers from another side; it goes on playing the game. From the outside one can be easily silent, but from the inside?

And if you are silent from the inside, you will be surprised that your silence becomes so loaded with ecstasy that you have to sing. There is no other way. That you have to dance, that you have to share. When you have you have to share. If you have it at all you will have to share. If you don't have it you can keep quiet, but what is the point of keeping quiet if you don't have it?

There are two types of people: one who goes on talking without having it, and one who goes on keeping silent without having it. Both are in the same boat.

There is a third type of person, who has come to know it, who has really become silent and in the silence he has heard the soundless sound, in the silence God has delivered his message to him. God has spoken to him. He has had a dialogue with God himself. The silence has filled his heart with so much juice, with so much life, with life abundant, that he is bursting. He has to say it. There is no way to get rid of it.

And his saying will have a totally different significance because words will not be mere words. If such a person sits silently, even his silence will be a sharing. If such a person keeps completely silent, you will see his silence is singing all around him. You will feel the vibe. His silence is saying something. He is indicating from his silence too. If he speaks he speaks. If he is silent, then too he speaks.

If you don't sing it, remember, you don't have it. If it does not overflow in a thousand and one gestures, then it is not there. You cannot hold it if it is there. And you cannot possess it if it is there; it is not your property. You cannot become the owner of it. You cannot hoard it, you cannot be miserly about it. If it is there at all, it drowns you utterly. It possesses you. You cannot possess it; it possesses you. And then it leads you into a thousand and one gestures. In a thousand and one streams you start flowing, and whatsoever you do becomes an expression.

I have heard a very beautiful legend. The legend is, there was a great master in India, the twenty-seventh successor of Gautam the Buddha; his name was Hanyatara. A king in south India requested him to come to his court. The king himself came, bowed down to Hanyatara, touched his feet, and said, "Please, come to my court, to bless us. And this has been my desire, to listen to some sutras of Gautam the Buddha by a man who is a buddha himself, so I have been avoiding scholars, pundits, professors. I have been avoiding, I have been waiting, because those sutras that Buddha uttered are so pregnant that only a man who has attained to that consciousness will be able to give expression to them."

Hanyatara came to the court with an attendant. The king was thrilled; it was his dream for his whole life one day to have a Buddha in his court, in his palace. The whole palace was decorated, the whole town was decorated; the whole capital was celebrating. It was a great day of celebration. But the king was puzzled, a little bewildered: Hanyatara sat silently, not saying a single word, and the attendant recited the sutra. Now, this was not the purpose at all. The king could have found better people to recite the sutra than the attendant. He was just an attendant who looked after Hanyatara, just used to do small errands, a very ordinary man, not even a great scholar. His grammar was faulty, his pronunciation was not exactly as it should be. He was an ordinary man.

Just out of respect, the king kept silent. When the sutra was finished, he touched the feet of Hanyatara and said, "Sir, enlighten me about this; otherwise I will remain puzzled. Why did not *you* recite the sutra?"

And Hanyatara said, "What, I did not recite the sutra? Then what else was I doing the whole time here? You fool!"

The king was even more puzzled, because he had kept quiet, he had not said a single word. The king said, "Please, explain it to me. I don't understand. I am an ordinary, ignorant person. I may not know the ways of the buddhas."

And Hanyatara said, "I sat silently, breathing in, breathing out. That was my sutra. What else is there in life? Breathe in, breathe out. Be alert, aware. When I breathed in, I was aware; when I breathed out, I was aware. It was all awareness! What else is a sutra? Awareness. If you had listened to the rhythm of my breathing you would have understood. I have recited it! Words are one way to recite it. Breathing silently, but with full awareness, is another way to recite it – and far better a way. I have been very expressive today, as I have never been before. Thinking that you have been waiting for so long, I thought, 'Why not give the real thing?' "

The king was thrilled, seeing the compassion. Now he felt there was a certain rhythm in his silence. Now he became

aware, retrospectively of course, that this man was not silent in
the ordinary way. He had seen silent people; sometimes he
himself had sat in silence. This was a different silence. There
was a song, certainly there was a song. There was a fragrance
around this man. There was a vibe of a different quality; he
was vibrating. Strange it was, but now he remembered, yes,
it was there. And the way he was breathing was no ordinary
way. Not that he was doing anything special in the breathing:
his breathing was pure, natural, like a small baby.

When you breathe, your breathing is never natural. If you
are a little angry, your anger changes your breathing. If you are
full of passion, lust, your lust changes your breathing. If you are
greedy, your greed is reflected in your breathing. Continuously
your mind mood infiltrates breathing and changes it. You can
watch it. When you are angry, try not to disturb the breathing,
and you will be completely unable to be angry. Just try not to
change the breathing. Let the breathing remain as it was before
you became angry, and then try to be angry. It will be
impossible. The breathing has to change first. Through the
breathing the body changes; the mind first affects the breathing.
When you are in a moment of lust, watch, keep the breathing
natural, and you will suddenly find the lust has disappeared, the
moment came and passed.

By and by you will be able to see each mood is reflected in
your breathing, so your breathing is never natural, because there
is some mood or other. The natural breathing means there is no
mood: that means there is no mind – neither anger nor greed
nor lust nor jealousy nor love nor hate. No-mood means no-
mind. In that state of no-mind the breathing is natural. Then
there is a song to it, then there is a totally different quality to it.
Then it is pure life. Then the flame is without smoke.

Yes, the king remembered, there was something strange,
something was happening. He had missed it. He started crying.
He said, "I have missed it. Why didn't you tell me before?
Now I know there was something, and I had even felt it, but
my consciousness is not so developed, so I could not understand
what was happening.

"And I was too concerned about that foolish sutra. I was
continuously thinking about why you were not reciting the sutra

and why this attendant was reciting the sutra. I was so much concerned about the sutra that I missed.

"But I am grateful that you showed such compassion, that you showed your being so naked, so true, so authentic."

He presented a great diamond, the most valuable he had, to Hanyatara, and then he said to Hanyatara, "I have three sons. Sir, be kind enough. I will call them. Bless them."

Thinking that young people are young people, and the youngest was only seven, they may disturb the sutra reciting, he had not called them to participate before.

The three young princes came in.

Rather than blessing them, Hanyatara showed the diamond that the king had presented to him to the first prince, the eldest. He must have been somewhere near fifteen. The prince looked at the diamond and said, "A great diamond, of the finest water, purest water. Where could you get it? It is rare. It is no ordinary diamond."

Yes, his understanding about the diamond was perfectly true. It was a rare diamond, of the most perfect water. Even Hanyatara had never seen such a thing.

Then he called the second prince, who must have been near about ten, and the second prince looked at the diamond, and he said, "Not only the finest, not only the best, it is certain that it belongs to my father because in this kingdom nobody can have such a diamond. It is rare. Sir, it does not belong to you, it cannot. To protect this diamond you will need a great army, otherwise you cannot have it. Just this attendant won't do."

Yes, his understanding was also very correct.

And then the third son was called. He was only seven. He looked at the diamond, looked at Hanyatara, and laughed and said, "What? Do you want to befool me?" He was only seven, and he said, "Do you want to befool me? You cannot! Because the real diamonds are never of the outside. And what are you trying to show me? You have the real diamond within *you*. I can see it! This is just a stone that you have in your hand. Throw it, sir!"

And it is said that Hanyatara hugged this small boy.

This boy's name was Bodhitara, and Hanyatara changed his name to Bodhidharma. He became the twenty-eighth successor of Buddha; he was the first patriarch of Zen in China, this small boy Bodhitara, whose name Hanyatara changed to Bodhidharma.

Hanyatara said, "This boy has looked into the deepest reality anybody can look into. *Dharma* means 'the ultimate reality'. He has penetrated to the ultimate reality." He said to the king, "Even you could not see who I am. That's why you missed my sermon, my silent sermon. That's why you missed my silent song. I was singing here but you missed. But this boy, yes, I cannot befool him. This boy is going to be my successor."

And then he said to the king, "Sir, forgive me. I have not come for you and I have not come because you requested me to. I had to come because of this boy. I have been in search of this boy! This has been a promise from the past life, and this has been a decided gesture: in the past life I told this boy, 'I will seek you and find you and I will show you a diamond, and that will be the moment of your examination. If you can see my inner diamond and you are not befooled, you will be my successor.' "

The legend is of tremendous value. First, the silent sermon. Yes, sometimes a mystic can be silent – but he is not silent! His silence is a very telling silence. He may not do anything, he may not even move his eyes, he may not move any of his limbs, but still his presence goes on doing a thousand and one things. Just to be in his presence, just to breathe with him in the same rhythm, and something is transferred: his song, his silence, his dance. You will never be the same again.

Truth is not hidden, from the very beginning. Truth is unhidden; only your eyes are closed. Truth is being preached from every tree and from every bird and from every rock and from every star; just your eyes, your ears, your sensitivity is not there. You are deaf. Truth is not dumb; you are deaf. And truth is not hiding anywhere.

A man came to a Zen master and asked, "Sir, where should I go to find the truth?" And the Zen master said, "You just keep looking in front of your nose and go on, and you will find it.

It is just in front of your nose! Truth is just in front of you. In fact, wherever you look it is truth, you just need to know how to look for it. But you are looking for other things; that's why you go on missing.

That great king missed Hanyatara's sermon. It was a Zen sermon, the same as Buddha preached to the first Zen master, Mahakashyap, sitting silently, holding a flower in his hand. This second sermon, of Hanyatara to the king, was even more subtle. He was not even holding a flower in his hand. He was just breathing in and out, a natural breathing, an ordinary breathing, unaffected by the mind. And truth was there and the sutras were recited there through his breathing, but the king missed.

You may have come across a buddha in your life – or you may have come across many buddhas in your past lives – but you have missed because you were not sensitive enough to feel that vibe. That vibe is subtle. You were not aware enough to move to that height, to feel the presence.

Be a little more alert. The sermon is preached constantly. From everywhere God is speaking to you. Even when everything is silent he is speaking through silence. His song is eternal.

Zen says, "Truth is not hidden, from the very beginning, so you are not to uncover truth, you are only to uncover your eyes." You just have a curtain on your eyes. Just pull your earplugs out. Your ears are plugged; hence you cannot hear.

How to unplug the ears? How to open the eyes? How to drop barriers that don't allow you to become sensitive enough? What is the way? The way is *immediacy*. Be immediate, be in the moment.

Otherwise buddhas can go on shouting from the housetops, and you will not hear – or you will hear something which has not been said at all.

A few scenes. First scene:

Warden: "Can't you see the sign *'No fishing here'*?"
Angler: "Yes, and I don't agree. There is good fishing here! Just look at this lot I have landed today. Whoever put that sign up must be crazy."

The second scene:

The Dean of Women was lecturing to a class on the subject of sex morality. "In moments of temptation, ask yourself just one question: Is an hour of pleasure worth a lifetime of shame?"

One of the girls raised her hand naively and asked, "How do you make it last one hour?"

The third scene:

Ethel was shapely but shy, and visited a doctor for the first time. He ushered her into his private office and said, "Now, my dear, please get completely undressed."

Ethel blushed and replied, "Okay, Doctor, but you first."

Fourth scene:

The following ad appeared in the Personal column of a London paper: "My husband and I have four sons. Has anyone any suggestions as to how we may have a daughter?" Letters poured in from all over the world. An American wrote, "If at first you don't succeed, try, try, and try again." A Buddhist from Thailand suggested that they should seek the help of Buddha. A South African recommended a special diet. An Indian proposed yoga.

A Frenchman merely wrote, "May I be of service?"

And the last and the fifth scene:

A lion tamer had quit without notice, and the circus manager needed someone to replace him for the next night's show. He put an ad in the local paper, and the next morning two applicants showed up outside his office. One was a rather ordinary looking young man, and the other a ravishing redheaded beauty. Neither one of them looked very much like a lion trainer, but the manager was desperate. "All right," he said. "Here is a whip, a chair, and a gun. Let us see what you can do with the big Leo over there. We will let you have the first try, miss, but be careful. He is a mean one."

The ravishing redhead strode past the whip, the chair, and the gun, and empty-handed, fearlessly entered the cage. Big Leo rose, snarling, then came charging across the cage towards her with a ferocious roar. When the lion was almost upon her the girl threw open her coat. Underneath, she was stark naked. Leo skidded to a stop and crawled the rest of the way on his belly. He nuzzled the girl's feet with his nose, purred, and licked her trim ankles.

The astonished circus manager grinned happily and turned to the pop-eyed young man. "Well, young fella," he asked, "think you can top that?"

"Yeah," panted the applicant. "Just get that stupid lion out of there."

Truth is all around, but your interpretations are *your* interpretations. God is speaking all the time, but you hear not, or even if you hear, you hear something else. You hear according to you, your mind comes in, and hence you go on missing.

Unless the mind is dropped you will not be able to know what truth is. Truth cannot be discovered by mind; mind is the barrier. It is because of the mind that you have not been able to discover it. It is not a question of how to train the mind to know the truth. The more the mind is trained and becomes capable, the less is the possibility to know the truth. The more skilled a mind, the farther away you are from the truth.

Mind is the barrier. No-mind is the door.

How to attain to no-mind? The only way – the *only* way – is to be in the present. The only way is not to think of the past, not to think of the future. And you cannot think of the present. That is the whole secret: you cannot think of the present; there is not space enough for thought to move. Thought needs room to move. Can you think anything right now? If you think it, either it will be of the past or of the future.

This moment of silence. If you think, "Yes, this is a moment of silence," it is already past. Or you say, "How beautiful!" It is already past. Utter a word "beautiful," and it is already past. You cannot think. Thinking stops when you are in the present.

So that is the only key, and it is a master key; it unlocks all the doors of being. Immediacy, that is the whole insistence of Zen.

If you go to a Zen master and you ask something, it is unpredictable what he will do to you. He may hit you. Or he may not hit you; he may hit himself! Or he may say something absurd, totally irrelevant to what you have asked. Somebody asks, "How to attain Buddhahood?" and the master says, "The cypress tree in the courtyard." Now what? How are they related? They are not, but the master is indicating, "Please, drop all this nonsense. Look at this – *this* – cypress tree in the courtyard. What nonsense are you talking about? – Buddha, and how to become a buddha. You are talking about the past and the future. You have heard about Buddha in the past, so you have a greed, a desire. Now you want to become a buddha in the future, so you have come to me. All nonsense." He simply gives something immediate; he says, "Look! The cypress tree in the courtyard." It is not relevant if you think in terms of the mind. If you think in terms of no-mind it is the only thing relevant.

A man comes to a Zen master and asks, "What is the way?" And the master says, "Listen," and everything becomes silent, and just by the side of the master's hut flows a fountain, and the water is making the sound, the murmur. The sound of the water, the sound of the running water. For a moment everything is silent, the seeker, the questioner, is also. The master says, "Listen. Hear. This is the way." The sound of the running water? That's all he has heard. And the master says, "Hear! This is the way to become a buddha, to attain to enlightenment." He is bringing the mind to an immediacy, to a state of immediacy.

What is he saying? He is not saying anything about the sound of the running water. In that moment, when suddenly the master shocked the inquirer – because he was asking about the way to attain to nirvana, and the master says, "Listen" it is so out of context, it is so unrelated to his question, that for a moment, out of the shock of it, the sheer shock of it, everything becomes silent. And when the master says, "Hear. This is the way," he is not saying anything about the running water or its sound. He is indicating the silent moment that has penetrated into the consciousness of the inquirer. He says, "Hear. This is the way."

If you become immediate you attain. If you live moment to moment you attain.

Once a Western psychiatrist went to see a Zen master in Japan. "How do you deal with neurotics?" he asked.

The master replied, simply, "I trap them."

Trap them? The psychiatrist could not understand what he means by trapping them. How can you trap a neurotic? The neurotic will trap you!

"But how?" pressed the psychiatrist.

The master replied, "I get them to where they cannot ask any more questions."

Then they are trapped, if they cannot ask any more questions.

If the mind is allowed to ask questions, then the mind goes on and on, so the Zen master brings you down to the immediate facticity of life. Sometimes he may hit you. By hitting, suddenly you are herenow. It is great compassion.

You ask, "Has God created the world?" and the master hits you, sharply. For a moment you are puzzled, shocked. For a moment all thinking stops. The very shock of it, the unpredictableness of it. For a moment, certainly, certainly for a moment, everything stops. And the Master says, "This, this is how God created the world." This is how God goes on creating the world. This moment of pure silence, this moment of no-mind, is the door to all solutions, to salvation, to liberation.

This is unique; sometimes a Master will do something which you had not expected at all. And the Master can do that only if he is not following certain rules. He is not following any. If he simply repeats from old Masters, then disciples become acquainted with it. No, sometimes he will do something you cannot believe.

There was a Zen Master who used to talk about God or

Buddha, but whenever he would talk about God or Buddha or the ultimate reality he would raise his hand: one finger pointing towards the sky. This became a joke among his disciples. Whenever they would talk about such great things they would raise their fingers and point to God. A small young boy was the attendant of the master; he used to bring his tea and things like that. He became a perfect master in showing his finger, and he was always there and the master was always doing it to everybody, so he became very perfect; he could imitate it perfectly.

And the master was aware of it. Sometimes he would be standing by the side at the back and the master would raise his finger and he would also raise his finger and everybody would laugh – and the master was aware of what was happening.

One day the boy did that, and the master called him in front of him, took a sharp knife, and cut off his finger. The boy's finger was cut off. The pain was sharp; the boy shrieked. And the Master said, "Stop! Now do it. Now do it! Whatsoever you have been doing for so long – now do it without the finger!"

And when the Master shouted, "Stop!" all pain disappeared in that moment, there was silence. And the small young boy showed the finger which was not there anymore, blood was flowing. But it is said in that moment he became enlightened.

Now, it is possible. That very sharpness of it.

Another story. In a Zen Master's ashram there were five hundred monks, and there were two wings. Just in the middle was the master's hut; on one side was one wing, on the other side the other wing. There was a beautiful cat, and there was a great debate between these two sides as to whom it belonged. It almost became a quarrel, and things went to such a state that both the wings were ready to kill each other for the cat. To whom does it belong? The left wing was saying, "It belongs to us"; and the right wing was saying, "It belongs to us." It was a really beautiful cat.

The master heard it. He called the whole ashram, and the cat was brought, and he said, "Now, give me a true answer, any one of you, and the cat will belong to him. Stand up and show your understanding of reality, any one of you. And if you don't show within seconds, I will cut the cat in two, and one part will go to the left side and one part will go to the right side."

They were shocked. They could not find out how to respond to the master's demand. What to do so that the cat can be saved? What to do? They started thinking. In their very thinking they missed the moment because when you think, you cannot be immediate and you cannot show your understanding of reality. You cannot show the understanding of immediacy. Not a single monk out of those five hundred could show.

For seconds the Master waited, then took a sword, cut the cat in two; half the cat was given to each wing, and he disposed of it. He said, "Now go." They were all sorry.

By the evening, one monk, who had gone outside, came back. When he came in to see the Master, he was just taking his shoes off, and the Master said, "Where have you been? Were you not there when I cut the cat in two? I had told the other monks that if they can show some understanding of reality the cat can be saved. Where have you been?"

The young man, who had taken off one shoe and was going to take off the other shoe, took that shoe, put it on his head, walked back.

And the master called him, "Come, my son. Had you been here the cat would be alive still. The cat could have been saved if you were here."

That immediacy. Not that this is the answer, but the immediacy. That was the moment. He allowed it to happen. It was not done with the mind, with thinking. It was done without any thinking, it was done without any mind. He simply said that it is as foolish as me having my shoe on my head to cut the cat. It is as foolish. But it was not an answer from the mind. It was an immediate response. And the master said, "My boy, if you had been here, the cat would have been alive. But those fools could not show any understanding."

Now this small, beautiful anecdote:

*A puzzled monk once said to Fuketsu, "You say truth can be expressed without speaking, and without keeping silent.*

*How can this be?"*
*Fuketsu answered, "In southern China, in the spring, when I was only a lad, Ah! How the birds sang among the blossoms."*

A very simple anecdote, but with great significance. Meditate over it.

*A puzzled monk once said to Fuketsu....*

From where do you become puzzled? From the mind. The mind is always dividing things, and then cannot figure it out. Once you divide, there is conflict and confusion. How can it be? Once you divide – this is good, this is bad – then the question arises: "Why has God created a world where so much evil exists?" You divide, that this is good and this is bad, and once you divide, then the problem arises: "Why has God created such a world where so much evil exists, so much bad?"

Now, you call God "God" because you think he is good. God is both and neither. Division is yours. It is your problem; it is not God's problem. You say, "Why do so many people die? Why has God created a world where death happens?" You don't understand at all. First you divide life in two parts, life and death. It is undivided. For God death is as beautiful as birth; they are both parts of the same phenomenon. For the whole there is no distinction between birth and death. Birth is a death, and death is a birth. They both are the same: two polarities, two which can exist only in togetherness. Life cannot exist without death, and neither can death exist without life.

Have you ever observed the fact? All that you love in life is possible only because of death. You love a woman because today she is beautiful, tomorrow she may not be. Old age. Today she is here, tomorrow she may not be there. Death is possible. You love the woman. If you knew that the beauty is eternal, that always and always the woman will be beautiful and that nobody is going to die, will there be joy in life? It will be sheer boredom. And if it was impossible even to commit suicide, you cannot conceive of a more miserable life – just people living and living and doing the same thing again and again and again and nothing ever changes and everything is eternal, nobody ever dies. Just think if all the people that have lived on the earth were living now – there will not be any space even to stand – and everybody was eternal.... Life will lose all beauty. The beauty is in its momentariness.

That's why I go on insisting: Celebrate the temporal. By celebrating it you will know that this is the way the eternal functions. The temporal is a function of the eternal.

Celebrate the temporal. Celebrate the momentary. In the momentary is the eternal, hiding. Don't throw it away. If you throw the momentary you are throwing the baby with the bath water. The eternal is hidden there. The eternal comes in the momentary, penetrates the moment.

*A puzzled monk once said to Fuketsu...*

What was his bewilderment? What was his confusion? Why was he so puzzled? The puzzle was there because he says the master has said... *"You say truth can be expressed without speaking, and without keeping silent."*

Now, this is impossible; this is very contradictory. If you say, "Truth can be expressed by words," okay. If you say, "Truth cannot be expressed by words," then it naturally means, "Truth can be expressed by silence." But the master says, "Truth cannot be expressed by words, and truth cannot be expressed by silence." And the master says, "Truth can be expressed by words too, and it can be expressed by silence too." Now, it is confusing. Now, it is illogical, it is absurd.

How can this be that truth can be expressed without speaking and without keeping silent? One can do only one; either one can speak it or one can keep silent. You deny both? Then what is the possibility?

*Fuketsu answered, "In southern China, in the spring, when I was only a lad, Ah! How the birds sang among the blossoms."*

Now, this is very irrelevant. What the disciple is asking and what the master is saying is not related at all, but it is related in a non-mind way. Meditate over it, how it is related in a non-mind way.

He has said many things. First, he says *"...in the spring"*. First, he says, "When the spring came, *How the birds sang among the blossoms.*" They were expressing truth, but they were silent when the spring was not there; and when the spring came they sang, they burst forth into celebration. So the first thing is "when the spring is there". What does he mean? He means when you have the spring in your heart, when the light has dawned upon you, when the right maturity has happened, when the right climate has happened, when your fruit is ripe, when the spring has come – that is what satori is, the spring of the inner heart – when the *samadhi* has come, then you need not bother: the birds don't go to schools to learn how to sing. The spring has come. They don't seek teachers. They don't go in to anybody, they don't ask the elders, "How to sing? The spring has come." When the spring comes the spring starts singing in them.

What the master means is that when *samadhi* is there, you will know. How to say it without saying it and without keeping silent – you will know it. It is not a question.

Many people go on asking foolish questions. The question was foolish. People come to me, they say, "If we become enlightened, what will happen to our family?" You please first become enlightened. "If we become enlightened what will become of our business?" You first become enlightened. Right now you are asking it as if it will create some problem. It has never created any problem. Whenever somebody becomes enlightened, he knows what to do. If an enlightened person does not know what to do, then who will know?

If you come to me and you ask me, "When truth has happened, how are we going to express it?"...When it happens when the spring comes – the birds know how to sing. In fact, there is no "how" to it. The very presence of the spring, and the birds are thrilled. Something goes berserk in their hearts. Something simply starts pulsating their being, something simply starts singing in their being. It is not that they sing. It is spring that sings in them. It is satori, it is Samadhi, that is expressed by you. It is not a question of *you* expressing it.

That's why the master says, "It cannot be expressed through words, and it cannot be expressed through silence." The very question that can be expressed through words is foolish, the very question that can be expressed through silence is foolish, because nobody knows – when the spring comes the cuckoo will sing in its own way, and the parrots will fly in their own way, and there will be a thousand and one songs, different, unique.

The cuckoo cannot screech the way parrots do, and the parrots cannot imitate the cuckoos. And there is no need. The cuckoo is beautiful, so is the parrot.

When satori has happened, nobody knows. Meera dances; Buddha never danced. The cuckoo and the parrot...

Listen....

Chaitanya sang, took his drum and danced all over Bengal. Mahavira remained in silence, never spoke a single word. Now, you will be puzzled. Then how do the Jaina sutras exist? How? It is a beautiful story.

Jainas say Mahavira never spoke, but those who were able to hear him, they heard, and they have collected the sayings. Listen again; you may have missed: Jainas say Mahavira never spoke, but those who could hear, they heard. In his silent presence they heard what he was saying, and they collected the sayings. The Jaina sutras start always, "We have heard." They don't start, "Mahavira said," no. The disciples say, "We have heard. That's true, on our part, we have heard. We don't know whether he has said it or not, but in a certain moment we heard it. A voiceless voice, a soundless sound."

Yes, a cuckoo is a cuckoo, a parrot is a parrot, and both are needed. If the world is only for cuckoos it will be ugly. Too many cuckoos, it will not be good. Existence needs variety, and existence is rich because of variety. Yes, it is good sometimes a Mahavira keeps silent, and it is good sometimes a Meera goes mad, dancing. It is good to have a Christ and a Krishna. It is good to have a Zarathustra and a Mohammed and a Lao Tzu. All are so different and so unique, and yet the message is the same.

Those who have eyes to see, they will see the same truth being expressed in millions of forms. And those who have ears to hear, they will hear the same song, sung in so many different languages.

It is the same rose; whether you call it "rose" or *gulab* does not make any difference. In India we call it *gulab*, in the West you call it "rose". Sometimes we can even quarrel and argue "What is it – *gulab* or rose?"

Zen masters say, "Don't quarrel, please. Bring a *gulab* or a rose, whatsoever you call it. Bring it here. Make it immediate, and then look." And then the quarrel ceases because when somebody brings a rose you will see – and he call it *gulab* – you will understand; you will say, "Okay, that's okay. Call it whatsoever you want to call it. It is the same thing I have been calling rose and you call *gulab*, and we have been quarreling."

Scholars quarrel, argue. Masters look at the thing called rose or *gulab*, or there can be a thousand names – there are so many languages, each language has a different name for it.

Each person who attains to *samadhi* gives expression in his own way. But the question is: Has the spring come?

So the master says, *"In southern China, in the spring, when I was only a lad, Ah! How the birds sang among the blossoms."* The second thing he says, "When I was only a boy when my eyes were innocent, when I was young and fresh and virgin, when I was not corrupted by the society, when I was uncorrupted, when my freshness had not gathered any dust of knowledge, experience – *Then*."

*"...in the spring, when I was only a lad, Ah! How the birds sang among the blossoms."* There were a great many flowers and a great many birds, and singing, the same song, the same spring, the same youth, the same life juice. What he is saying is, "Please, let the spring come first, and don't be worried about how it can be said neither in words nor in silence."

It can be said both in words and in silence. In fact, whenever it is said, there is word and silence together. But the word is not a mere word; that's why they say it cannot be said through words. And the silence is not a dead silence, it is not the silence of the cemetery; that's why the master says it cannot be said through silence, either. The word is not of the pundit, and the silence is not of the dead man; but there is a great marriage between word and silence. The word speaks through silence, the silence speaks through the word; and when silence and word meet there is song. Then there is celebration.

When the spring has come there is celebration. When the *samadhi* has happened there is celebration. In that celebration it is expressed, and it is expressed abundantly. In that celebration, in that blossoming, it is expressed. But it is expressed only for those who can understand, who can see, who can feel, who can love.

Chapter 8

# The Profound and the Trivial

*My experience of me is the most profound experience of my life. It is also the most trivial. Please clarify.*

The question is from Dhruva, and the question is really significant. The question has arisen out of an insight, almost a mini-satori.

That's how life is, profound and trivial at the same time, simultaneously. There is no contradiction, Dhruva, in the profundity of life and its trivialness. You have been taught that the sacred is far away and it is never the profane. You have been taught a distinction between the profane and the sacred, between the profound and the trivial. In fact, there is no distinction. The trivial is the profound, the ordinary is the extraordinary, and the temporal is the eternal.

So this is a great insight. Don't lose sight of it. More possibility is there that you will lose it, because it will go against the grain. Your whole training has been such that you are always dividing: into good and bad, into the pure and the impure, the perfect and the imperfect, into virtue and sin, the holy and the unholy. You have always been making these distinctions, and because of distinctions you have missed the reality of that which is.

This cuckoo singing there and Christ speaking to you are not different. A leaf falling from the tree and a word falling from the lips of Buddha are not different. The very dust is divine. The distinction is man-made, it is a mind trick.

And because of these distinctions, these categories, we are never together, we cannot be together. How can you be together if you make such an unbridgeable gap between the profound and the trivial? Then you will find your whole life is trivial. Eating, drinking, sleeping, walking, going to the office or to the farm – all is trivia.

Then where will you find the profound? In the church, in the temple, sometimes praying and meditating, sometimes listening to me? Then the profound will not be much in your life, and the profound will be, in a way, false. It will not permeate your whole life. It will not be there always with you. It will not surround you like a climate. Sometimes you will have to make an effort to have that quality of profundity, and again and again you will lose it. And you will become divided, schizophrenic; you will become two, split, and you will start condemning yourself.

Whenever you will see something trivial you will condemn yourself, that "I am just trivial, ordinary." And whenever you will see something profound you will start feeling holier than thou; you will start feeling very egoistic. Both are dangerous.

To feel that you are trivial is a condemnation. It creates an inferiority complex. It pulls you down into sadness. It forces you to remain depressed. And, naturally, you cannot love yourself: you are so trivial. You are so ordinary, how can you love yourself? You fall too short from the ideal of perfection. So a great condemnation arises in your being, and the moment you condemn yourself you are in hell. Then nobody can take you out of it. Even if somebody comes and says you are beautiful, you will not trust him. You will think he is trying to cheat you, bribe you. He is trying to exploit you. How can you be beautiful? You know yourself better than he knows you. You are not beautiful; you are ugly. You are the ugliest person in the world.

Because of this condemnation, love will not happen. How can you love anybody if you are feeling so condemned in yourself? And how can you allow somebody to love you if you are feeling so condemned? Love is impossible. When you live in self-condemnation you live in hell. Hell is not somewhere else: it is in your attitude; it is a condemning attitude.

When you accept yourself and you enjoy yourself, you are in heaven. Heaven is also an attitude.

And you can move from heaven and hell any moment you

decide! And you go on moving; you swing between heaven and hell. Just understand that it is your creation.

So if you feel condemned because of your trivia, you will be in hell. And then sometimes you will start feeling very holy because you have done something great. You have saved a life – somebody was drowning in the ocean and you saved him, and a child was caught in a house on fire and you jumped in and you risked your life, you have done something great – then you will feel very egoistic. Ego is again hell.

To feel superior is to be in hell, to feel inferior is to be in hell. To drop all superiority, inferiority, and just to be is to be in heaven.

The idea of condemnation is also ego-oriented. People have impossible ideals. Just the other night Vishnu came; he writes again and again that "I am not perfect. What should I do?" that "I am imperfect," that "Whatsoever I do is imperfect." He is torturing himself because he is imperfect. But who is not imperfect? The very idea that "I should be perfect," is very egoistic. The very effort is egoistic. Nobody is perfect.

In fact, perfection cannot exist, by its very nature. To be perfect means to be dead. Then there will be no evolution, when you are perfect. Then how can you survive? For what? If God is perfect then God is dead. If God is imperfect only then is he alive and can be alive.

I preach the imperfect God, and I preach the imperfect existence, and I preach the beauty of imperfection and the life of imperfection. The very idea that "I have to be perfect," that "No flaw should be there in my life" is egoistic. And certainly you will find a thousand and one flaws.

So on one hand you are on an ego trip, which creates trouble, makes you miserable, because you are not perfect; and on the other hand the same trip creates condemnation. You want to be superior and you know that you are inferior: both are two aspects of the same coin. You remain in hell.

Enjoy your imperfection. Enjoy the way you are.

And drop all distinctions between the holy and the unholy, sin and virtue, good and bad, God and devil. Destroy all those distinctions. Those are the traps you are caught in. Those are the traps which don't allow you to live, don't allow you freedom. You cannot dance: one foot is encaged in inferiority, another foot is encaged in superiority. You are chained. How can you dance? Drop all these chains.

That's what Zen people say: "A hair's distinction, and heaven and hell are set apart." That's what Tilopa says. A little distinction, a hair's distinction, and hell and heaven are set apart, and you are caught in the duality. No distinction, and you are free. No distinction, is freedom.

The profundity of the trivial and the trivialness of the profound, that's what I teach.

Eating is trivial if you look from the outside. If you look from the inside it is profound, it is a miracle – that you can eat bread and the bread is turned into blood, that it becomes your flesh, that it becomes your bones, that it even becomes your marrow. You eat bread, and the bread becomes your thoughts, dreams. It is a miracle. It is the profoundest thing that is happening. When you are eating, it is no ordinary thing. God is at work. It is creative. While chewing bread you are creating life, unknowingly, unconsciously. You are making a thousand and one things possible. Tomorrow you may paint and that bread that you had eaten has become painting. Tomorrow you may sing, or right now you may do something which would not be possible if the bread was not there.

The Christian prayer is beautiful; it says, "God, give us our daily bread." Looks very trivial! What does Jesus mean when he says, "Pray every day, 'Give us our daily bread'"? Couldn't he think of anything more profound? Bread? You just change the word "bread" and say every day in your prayer, "Lord, give us our daily tea," and you will see how foolish it looks. But the bread or tea or coffee – or Coca-Cola!...yes, Coca-Cola too is divine.

Everything is divine – because how can it be otherwise?

The prayer says, "Give us our daily bread." It is raising the trivial to the profound. It is a great statement. The Hindus have always been saying, *"Annam Brahma"* – "Food is God." Raising the trivial to the profound. Looking into the trivial so deeply that it changes into the profound.

You are taking a shower. It is trivia, everyday business, but it can become profound. Just look deep into it. Just standing under the shower, and the water goes on flowing, and the body feels fresh and young and alive, and the water is a blessing. Because we are made out of water. A man is almost eighty per cent water, and the first glimpse of life happened in the sea. The first thing that existed was the fish, and even now, in the mother's womb, the child floats in seawater, with almost the same ingredients, the same saltiness. That's why when a woman is pregnant she starts eating more salt; she needs more salt because the child needs seawater around him. The child is still a fish in the beginning, primary stage. Water is life, and when you are taking a shower life is showering on you – eighty per cent of life is showering on you, the most necessary element for life. No life is possible without water. These trees will not be there if the water is not, and these birds won't sing, and these animals won't be there and these men will not be there. All life will disappear if water disappears.

There is a profound experience when you are touched by water. You can make it so profound! It depends on you, how you go into it. It can become a meditation, a prayer. You can feel grateful, that God is great, that water is still available.

To breathe is so trivial, who bothers about it? But breath is your life. All languages have words for "life" which really mean "breath". Sanskrit has *prana* for "life"; it means "breath". The word "soul" means "breath"; the word "psyche" means "breath".

And the Bible says God made man and breathed life into him. Life started by breathing into man; otherwise man was just dust. "Adam" means "dust," "earth". God made Adam out of mud. "Adam" is the Hebrew word for "earth". Then he breathed life into him. And that's how life happens always. A child is born and the first thing we wait expectantly for is that he should cry. Why? Because only through crying will he start breathing. For two, three seconds even the doctor cannot breathe, the nurse cannot breathe. Whether the child is going to breathe or not, who knows? He may not breathe. If he is not going to breathe then there will be no life. If he breathes there will be life. Still the same happens as it happens with Adam: God breathes in the child, in each child.

God is the invisible force, the life energy that surrounds you.

It enters through breath in you, and the day you die you will die through exhalation. You start life with inhalation, you stop life with exhalation; then you will not breathe anymore. Again Adam is Adam, again dust is dust, dust unto dust.

Breath is life, but have you looked into it? Standing under the sun in the morning, breathe. It is God you breathe in. And then it becomes profound. It is your attitude.

The trivial and the profound are not two separate things. They are one, they are together, they are two aspects of one energy. Your life is trivia if you don't look deep. If you start looking deep your life is profound.

So Dhruva, it is a great insight. You say, "My experience of me is the most profound experience of my life. It is also the most trivial. Please clarify." Don't get confused. There is nothing to clarify. It is how life is: the trivial is the profound.

The question has arisen because Dhruva must have been thinking these are contradictions, the trivial and the profound. No, they are not contradictory; they are complementary. The trivial hides the profound. The trivial functions like a cover, like a crust; it protects the profound. It is almost like a seed. The seed is protecting the possibility of the tree. That possibility is very soft; the seed is hard. The hard seed, the hard crust of the seed, is protecting the softest possibility, of flowers, of a big tree. And the seed will protect it till the seed finds the right soil. Then the seed disappears, then the sheath disappears, then the hard crust dissolves into the earth and the soft life arises.

The profound is hidden in the trivial, so look deep. Wherever there is the trivial there is the profound. Don't escape from the trivial; otherwise you will be escaping from the profound. And don't seek the profound *against* the trivial; otherwise you will never find it.

> *A play question: if you were to come here now to this ashram as a young unenlightened man, how would you respond? Would you become part of the ashram? What work would you do? Where would you sit?*

The question is from Somendra. A beautiful question.

First, he asks, "If you were to come here now to this ashram as a young unenlightened man, how would you respond?"

Even if I was unenlightened I would not be so unenlightened to come to this ashram. That much is certain.

Mulla Nasruddin's wife was dying, and of course he was consoling her in every way, and the wife opened her eyes and said, "It seems almost certain that this night will be my last. I will not be able to see the sunrise again. Mulla, how will you react to my death?"

The Mulla said, "How will I react to your death? I will go mad!"

Even in that serious moment the wife started laughing: she said, "You cunning fellow. You will not go mad. I know within a week you will be remarried."

And Mulla said, "No. I will go mad – but I will not go *that* mad."

So even if I was unenlightened I would not be *that* unenlightened.

Second thing, you say, "Would you become part of the ashram?"

Even now I am not part of the ashram. I cannot be part of any institution or any organization, even my own. And if I had come as an unenlightened man, naturally, the ashram will not be mine, will be somebody else's. I cannot be a part even of my own organization, so how can I be a part of anybody else's organization? Impossible.

And then you ask, "What work would you do?"

I have never done any work. I am the laziest man in the world you can find.

And the last, you ask, "Where would you sit?"

I would escape immediately! I would see some organization, some ashram and I would run! You are asking, "Where will you sit?" I will not sit at all.

*Usually I am "this way" or "that way" but for some time I have experienced all kinds of contradictions, simultaneously. I see women as objects of worship, and at the same time I lust after them. I am content to let life flow, and I am afraid of the future. I crave to be alone, and I crave to be always with people. I feel bizarre because these contradictions all seem equally real and true. Is there anything to be understood or done about this?*

Whenever you come across a contradiction, watch very carefully. There is bound to be something of great significance. Never avoid contradictions, because life is contradictory. Life exists through the tension of contradiction. So whenever you come across a contradiction you are very close to the source of life. Let that be always remembered.

The ordinary reaction is whenever you come across a contradiction you start trying to solve it, start finding explanations for it, or start dropping it into the unconscious so you need not worry about it. You start doing something about it immediately the moment you feel some contradiction because you have been taught to live noncontradictorily. You have been taught a very dangerous thing. Nobody can live noncontradictorily. If you want to live you have to live through contradiction, *as* contradiction.

You have been taught to be consistent; that's why you have become false. This is the whole trick. How does such great hypocrisy exist in the world? Why? Why has the whole world turned out to be hypocritical? There is a trick to it, a great trick; a great technology is behind it. The technology is: teach people to be consistent, and they will become hypocrites. Because life exists through contradiction.

Life is inconsistent. One moment this, another moment that; life is that way. One moment you are feeling loving, another moment you hate the same person; life is like that. Now, you have been taught if you love, then love always. What happens? You cannot love always, so only one thing is possible: when hate comes you hide the hate, you repress the hate, and you go on pretending love. This is what hypocrisy is. When you don't love you pretend.

You are full of hate for your wife, but you come home and you hug her and you kiss her and you inquire, "How are you, honey?" and all that. And deep down you are hating her and you want to kill her. In fact, the whole day you have been fantasizing how to kill this woman. But you have been taught to be consistent. So, once, you had fallen in love, and you have said things in those love moments and you have promised that "I will love you forever and ever" – now you have to be consistent.

What will you do with your hate that is bound to arise? Each love object is bound to be the hate object too. If you want not to hate, then you will have to stop loving. If you really want not to hate anybody, then you will have to stop loving, but you cannot love consistently. The inconsistency will come up again and again.

It is as if somebody has told you, "If you see the day, don't see the night. That is inconsistent." So what will you do? In the day you keep your eyes open, in the night you keep your eyes closed and believe that it is day. But the night comes; it doesn't follow your ideas. It has to come. The night follows the day; the day follows the night.

You have been taught, "Be consistent." Your so-called character is nothing but an effort to be consistent.

A real man cannot have any character. A real man is bound to be characterless because to have a character means to have consistency. To be characterless means to be free.

I said something yesterday. Now, if I have a character, I will try to be consistent with my past; whatsoever I said yesterday, I have to say the same thing today. But then I have to repeat my past. I cannot live in the moment and I cannot live in the present.

In fact, a consistent man is one who goes on changing his past into his future, who goes on putting his past as his future, ahead of himself. That is the man of character, consistent man. An inconsistent man is one who never allows the past to become his future, who remains free for the future, who has no promises to keep, who has no commitment with the past. Whenever it was, he lived it totally; gone, it is gone.

A real man will love you and will hate you too. And sometimes he will say, "I will love you always"; and sometimes he will say, "I cannot love you again. Impossible." Sometimes he will be in a deep honeymoon with you and sometimes in a deep divorce, and both things will go like day and night. A real marriage is a continuous honeymoon and divorce, and honeymoon and divorce. Mini honeymoons, mini divorces; big honeymoons, big divorces. It continues like day and night.

So whenever you come across a contradiction, be watchful, be very alert. You are very close to life. And when you are consistent you are just false, a plastic thing, you are not real.

I don't teach consistency. I teach the freedom of being inconsistent. I teach the freedom of being contradictory. That's my whole approach towards life.

Of course, you are afraid of being contradictory because then you will not know who you are. With character there is something, something very secure: you know who you are. You have a label: a good man, a bad man, a saint, a sinner. You can believe in your identity when you are consistent – that you are a good husband, a good Christian, a churchgoer, and this and that. With the inconsistency your identity disappears; you don't know who you are. You become an opening, you are no more closed, you have an open future. You don't know what you are going to do the next moment; only the next moment will tell. To live in that insecurity needs courage.

Sannyas is what I propose. Sannyas means to remain in insecurity; sannyas means not to allow your past to influence your future, not to allow your past to project itself into the future. Let the dead bury the dead. The past is gone, gone. Don't cling to it, and don't help it to cling to you.

The moment something has passed it has passed. Be completely clean of it and be free and fresh again; then you will be real, authentically real, and there will be joy, and there will be celebration and song. I am not saying you will not ever be sad, no. You will be sad. The false man is never sad – because he is never happy. The false man just remains in the middle, never happy, never sad. He is simply so-so, lukewarm; he is never too cold and never too hot. He is just "okay". He somehow manages. He has a comfortable life, but no real life.

I am not saying that the real man will always be happy. I am saying the real man will always be real. When he is sad he will be really sad. He will sing a song – of sadness. He will accept his sadness as part of life, as part of growth. He will not reject it. If he feels like crying he will cry; he will not say, "What am I doing? This is not good. Only women cry, and I am a man." He will not say that. He will say, "If my eyes want to cry and the tears are rolling down, good. I have to be real. I am only whatsoever I am." He will cry. His tears will be true.

Your smiles are false, your tears are false. You manage to smile, and you manage to cry too. So you live an empty life. The real man's life will be full, sometimes full of joy and sometimes full of sadness.

And the real man one day becomes enlightened. The unreal man never becomes enlightened. When the real man becomes enlightened, then there is no joy and no sadness. Then his being is just a witness. Joy comes: he watches it. Sadness comes: he watches it.

Now, these are the three stages. The false man: his joy is just a show, a mask, his sadness too; he pretends. The real man, the second stage: he is natural, spontaneous; his joy is true, his sadness is true. You can trust him. When he is crying, his whole heart is crying; and when he smiles, his whole heart is smiling. And the second stage is a must to attain to the third, the enlightened man. The enlightened man is neither sad nor happy. He has attained to the witnessing soul; he simply watches. He knows the sadness has come, the happiness has come, but these are like climates that come and go and change, and he remains centered.

The false man cannot jump to the enlightened state; hence I teach the real man, but the real man is not the goal.

That's why my work goes beyond the Encounter ideology, Gestalt ideology. The Gestalt ideology or the Encounter ideology stops at the real man. Good. Better than the unreal. But not enough. Something has yet to happen. I use Encounter groups, Gestalt groups, and all the therapies that have become available in the West. They are perfectly beautiful; they bring you from the first, false state to the authentic, real state. But my work goes beyond them. But I can go beyond only if you have gone through the second stage. From the first there is no way, from the false there is no way, to enlightenment; only from the real is there a way.

You will have to go through the ecstasy of the real and the agony of the real. When you have lived deeply all the realities of life, the witness will arise. It arises naturally, out of being real.

So you say, "Usually I am 'this way' or 'that way'." That is not a good way. You get fixed with one thing, this way or that. Become more fluid, remain more fluid, because life is not solid; it is fluid, it is flow. And that's what is happening and is confusing you.

"But for some time I have experienced all kinds of contradictions, simultaneously." Good. You are blessed. This confusion is the beginning of a great journey, a great pilgrimage. If you become afraid you will go back to the false.

The false is secure. Let me remind you again and again: the false is comfortable. A good way to die is the false, but not a good way to live. Even your death will be false, because how can the death be real? When you have not lived really, how can you die really?

So many people die, but rarely does a real death happen. When a Buddha dies it is a real death, or when Lin Chi dies it is a real death. There are very few deaths which are real, because there are very few lives which are real. You only pretend to live, and then one day you pretend to die.

I have heard, a man met an old friend on the road, and the old friend was a very, very fanatical Christian Scientist. The old friend asked this man, "How is your father now?" and the man said, "He is very ill." The Christian Scientist, of course, to be consistent with his philosophy, said, "He is not ill. He only thinks he is ill."

That is the Christian Scientists' ideology, that you only think that you are ill, that's why you are ill. You are not really ill. He said, "He only thinks he is ill. He is not really ill."

After eight days, these two men met again, and the Christian Scientist asked again, "How is your father now?"

And the young man hesitated a little, and then he said, "Now he thinks he is dead" – to be consistent with this old man's ideology.

The father has died, but this is a reality.

You go on living in a fantasy world. Your life is nothing but your thinking, a pseudo thing; and so is your death. Your illness, your health, your happiness, your sadness are all so bogus that how can you die a real death? A real death has to be earned. One has to become worthy of real death. And one becomes worthy only by living truly.

Now you are very close to a great source of light. That's why you are feeling all sorts of contradictions simultaneously. That means your solidity is melting. Your hate and love are not categorized as two anymore. They are not put into boxes separately anymore; they are merging with each other. The profound and the trivial are coming together, and you are confused because now you cannot label what is what.

"I have experienced all kinds of contradictions, simultaneously. I see women as objects of worship, and at the same time I lust after them." That's what has happened down the ages. There are two things man has done with woman: either he has worshipped woman as a goddess or he has condemned woman as a witch. Either he has exploited the woman for his lust or he has touched her feet and said, "You are divine. Divine mother." Either the woman has been a prostitute or a divine mother. Man has not accepted woman just as human.

And woman is human, as human as you are. She is neither a divine mother nor is she a prostitute, but that's how the mind goes on. The mind makes things different, separate, puts them in categories. You have killed the real woman, because the real woman is both, the prostitute and the divine mother, together, simultaneously. If you fall in love with a prostitute you will find a divine mother. Even a prostitute will turn into a divine mother if you are in love with her; you will not find the prostitute. And fall in love with a divine mother and you will find the prostitute too.

What I am saying is that life is not so small as to be put into boxes – that this is a prostitute and this is a divine mother. Life is vast, so big. It contains contradictions. And that is the beauty of life and that is the richness of life.

Man has been changing between these polarities. Sometimes he calls the woman the divine mother. That too is inhuman, because then you put the woman on a pedestal and you don't allow her to be human. Watch. When you force a woman to be a divine mother, what are you doing? You are not allowing her to be human. And she will pretend that she is a divine mother, so if you want to make love to her she will be reluctantly ready. She will say no, and she will mean yes. She has to say no; she is the divine mother.

A good woman has to be a dead woman. Even while you are making love, she will lie down there like a corpse. A slight movement, and you will become afraid: so are you wrong, she is not so good, not so virtuous? If she starts enjoying your lovemaking, you will think that she is a bad woman. Only bad women enjoy lovemaking, not good women. Good women? They don't think of sex at all.

Look at the trick. You put the woman so high; then you don't allow her to be human. You have made her "superhuman". That is a way to make her *inhuman*. Or you force her to be a prostitute; that is again a way, to put her below the human, to make her again *inhuman*. Then you go to the prostitute, you give her the money, you make love to her – with no responsibility, with no love. It is simple, pure lust, but you know that that woman is a bad woman. How can you love her? You feel good, there is no problem. You can lust after this woman and you can use her as a thing. She is just a prostitute, not a human being; you don't relate to her. You just go and do things to her, pay the price, and you are finished. Next day in the marketplace, you will not even recognize her.

In both these ways you have turned the woman into inhuman beings. Both are ugly.

The woman is both: the divine mother and the prostitute. Just as you are both: God and animal.

Let me repeat: the profane is the sacred, the *samsara* is the nirvana.

Through these categories.... The reality is so complex and so deep it cannot be categorized, it cannot be demarked into definitions. No woman is just a prostitute and no woman is just a divine mother. And that is true about man, the same way.

Once you see this, you are freed from categories, logical boxes, pigeonholes, and you can see reality as it is.

A woman is a human being, as you are a human being. Yes sometimes she is a witch; just as sometimes you are mean, ugly, horrible, she is too. And sometimes she is ecstasy, pure ecstasy. Sometimes she is the most beautiful phenomenon on the earth, just as you are.

In India we have the right representation, the symbol of Kali. You must have seen the pictures of Kali or the statues of Kali. That is really a great understanding about women. Kali is painted as black, as black as the devil – "kali" means "black" – and yet she is the divine mother. And she is most beautiful. She is black, as black as the devil, but her form is that of the divine. She has a beautiful face, a beautiful body, absolutely in proportion; but she is black. And then, she is dancing on the chest of her husband, almost killing him. Shiva is her husband, and she is dancing on his chest and almost killing him. And she loves him too. She loves and kills together. All contradictions put together.

The mother gives you birth, the woman gives you birth, and by and by the woman kills you too. She brings your death closer; hence the attraction and the fear. You are attracted with the divine, and you are afraid with the devilish.

So you say, "I see women as objects of worship, and at the same time I lust after them." Both are complementaries. Accept them. That's how reality is. The woman is both, and you are both. And if you accept this contradictory reality, one day you will go beyond it, you will transcend it.

There is a transcendental element too, but that transcendental element can be understood only when you pass through contradictions. If you avoid contradictions you will never attain the transcendental. Go through the contradictory, and by and by you will become just a witness to them both.

How does it work? It works in a simple way. If you think you are good, you are identified with good. If you think you are bad, you are identified with the bad. But if you allow both good and bad together, you cannot get identified with either. You remain unidentified, and that is the fundamental, the radical change. You remain unidentified. You cannot figure out who you are, good or bad, day or night, life or death, beautiful or ugly. You cannot identify with anything, so you remain unidentified.

Good comes and passes, and you know you cannot be good, because the bad is coming. And the bad comes and passes, and you know you cannot be the bad either, because the good is coming. So you cannot be good and you cannot be bad; then who are you? You are a witness. A witness who watches everything come and go, a watcher on the hills.

"I am content to let life flow, and I am afraid of the future." The same. The same contradiction on so many levels.

"I crave to be alone, and I crave to be always with people." The same.

"I feel bizarre because these contradictions all seem equally real and true." They are. And when for the first time you recognize that they are true and real, one feels bizarre. That's what the Zen people say: first the rivers are rivers and the mountain are mountains, then the rivers are no more rivers and the mountains are no more mountains – bizarre, confusion, clouds, everything topsy-turvy, all disturbed – and then one day mountains are again mountains and rivers are again rivers, everything settled again, on a higher plane of course, on the transcendental plane of course.

You will have to go through this bizarreness. To be sane one has to pass through many insanities.

"Is there anything to be understood or done about this?" Just understood, nothing to be done about it. I don't teach doing. Nothing has to be done. You just watch. Watch more and more carefully, watch in detail. Watch the subtlest nuance of any change in you. Watch all – with no prejudice, with no judgement. And that watching will integrate you, will make you more and more aware.

And that is the whole purpose of life: to create more intelligence, to create more awareness.

*Is there anything I can give you back?*

Nothing, because that is what I give to you. I give you nothing, and only nothing can you give me back.

In fact, don't start thinking of giving me anything back, because I am not giving you anything. I am simply making you aware of things that you already have. You don't owe anything to me, not even a thank you. If you thank me, that is simply generous of you, you are just being polite and gentlemanly; otherwise there is nothing. You don't owe anything to me. I have not given anything to you and I am not going to give anything to you, and nothing can be given, in the very nature of things.

In fact, if you are not angry at me, I will be happy enough. Because I take away many things. I don't give anything to you. I take away your ego, and I don't give anything instead. I take away a thousand and one things. And when those thousand and one things have been taken away, suddenly you become aware of that which has always been there from the very beginning.

So let me say it in this way: I give you that which you already have, and I take away things which you don't have but you think you have. I take away that which is not there but you believe is there. I take away your illusions.

But I cannot give reality. Reality is that which cannot be given; it is already there. I eliminate the illusion, and the reality is there. I simply give you back to yourself.

There is no need to be worried – "Is there anything I can give you back.?" Just if you are not angry, that will be enough. If you can forgive me, that will be enough.

I know it is very difficult to forgive me. That is the greatest danger a master takes on his shoulders. It is very difficult for the disciples to forgive him, and they are always watching from the corner of their eyes to find some fault. They are always waiting to find some loophole so they can jump upon it and they can say, "So, I have found the reality. This man is nothing," and they can go and condemn. It is a very dangerous game.

The disciples are continuously watchful. They are like spies, spying on the master, if they can find something.

Just the other Question-Answer day, when I talked about Dr. Kovoor, two, three persons got almost mad about me. They have written letters that "Why did you do this? It is cheap!" And I go on telling you the cheap is the costly! And the trivial is the profound! And the world, the *samsara*, is nirvana! Do you hear me, or not? And they have demanded, almost it is a demand, that "You have to answer it, why you attacked him." I have not attacked him; I have attacked these three people who have written to me. What have I to do with Kovoor? He is not going to come here, I am not going to go there. We are not going to meet anyway. I have attacked these three persons, and I have got them, trapped them, they are trapped. I have attacked their idea of me.

One has written, "It is inconceivable that a man of your height should come so low." But who in the first place has told you that I am a man of height? You yourself project, and if your projections are destroyed, you are angry at me?

I go on repeating, just to be safe, that I am a very ordinary man. Otherwise you will hang me in the sky. You will say, "You are so high."

If you find me eating or if you find me taking a bath.... Do you know? In heaven there is no provision for God's bathroom. No provision. I have gone through all the scriptures.

Can you believe God farts? Impossible. So high, and farting? Belching? These things are good for human beings, not for gods.

Who has told you I am so high? But you project.

And I am not so foolish as to accept your projections. If you want to project such things, you will have to find some other people. You are not allowed to project anything on me. I will go on throwing it. I am not here to fulfill any of your expectations. That is the very trouble you have to tolerate with me. You would like me to be dead and sitting on a golden throne, and then you can worship me easily. But I am alive.

And I go on doing things that I like. I don't care what you think. If you are disturbed it is your problem; it is none of my business. Then you have to look into yourself and find ways not to be disturbed.

These things come again and again in your mind, and you don't see that they are *your* problems.

Somebody else has asked, "Why do we have to pay money here? I have no money," he says, "and I want to be here." But then who is going to pay for you? You will need money, you will need food, you will need a shelter, you will need clothes, sometimes you will be ill, you will need the hospital: who is going to pay for you? Now, he thinks that this ashram is money obsessed. If people who don't have money are allowed, then Laxmi will have to go even more money obsessed because for them also she will have to arrange. Just to avoid money obsession, money has to be arranged. There are many people who would like to be here, but then who is going to arrange for them? And if somebody else arranges for them, he will demand something in return.

The person says, "Even Christians don't ask for money; even they are not that bold." I know they are not that bold. They need not be; they have enough money. The Vatican has enough money; that is the richest party in the world. But then you have to pay – not in money, money is there – you have to pay with other things: you have to pay with your freedom.

Here I want you to be free. I don't want to hinder your freedom.

If you want to stay here without money, then I will have to ask some people who have money to give money to the ashram. But then they have their conditions. Then their conditions have to be fulfilled. Otherwise why should they give their money? They give money in return for something. Then you will not be free here. And I will not be free here. I will not be able to say what I want to say. Then they will dictate to me that this has to be said and this has not to be said.

Nobody is money obsessed. But the questioner is money obsessed: he has no money and he wants to be here. But what is money? Money is just that you have to pay for everything. You eat: you have to pay for it. You live: you have to pay for it. You need clothes: you have to pay for it.

And why should you not pay? Then somebody else will have to pay for you. Why exploit somebody else?

If you don't have money, then go and earn money and come back. *You* are money obsessed! But you think that Osho is demanding money. It is your problem.

Somebody has said, "I can't see the point why I have to pay when I come to the lecture. When I have to pay ten rupees for the lecture, then I cannot think of you as God." So the price of thinking of me as God is ten rupees! If he does not have to pay, he will think of me as God. What do you think? You are trying to bribe me? Pay twenty rupees and think of me as the devil, perfectly okay!

Why should you not pay? Why should you like to exploit?

And this is my understanding, that you hear only when you pay; otherwise you don't hear. When you have nothing to pay, there is no need to hear. The more you pay, the more alert you are – because those ten rupees are gone. If you don't listen it is your business; you remain a little alert. I know you are money-minded; those ten rupees will keep you awake.

And my godhood is not in danger, because I don't care what you think about me. That is not the point at all. It is not that you have made me a god. This is my declaration; it is not your recognition. If nobody believes in me, then too I am a god. If only I believe in me, that's enough. I don't need a single witness. This is *my* understanding.

Then again, the moment you think that this man is Osho, then he should behave in such a way and in such a way. Then he should be on a high pedestal. He should not behave like a human being.

Then you don't understand my concept of Osho. My concept of Osho is not that an Osho is a special being, that an Osho is a perfect being, that an Osho is not of this world. My concept of Osho is that God is a normal quality of existence. Just by being, you are God.

You are not a painter by just being. For painting, you will have to learn some skill, you will have to go to an art school. And then too your being a painter will depend on so many recognitions – people will recognize, may not recognize; the critics will appreciate, may not appreciate; a thousand and one things. If you want to be a musician, just by being, you are not a musician. You will have to learn; this is something which has to be learned.

When I say God, I mean you *are* God, just by being. It is not a specialization.

Then what is the difference between me and you? The only difference is that I recognize my godhood and you don't recognize yours. Otherwise there is no distinction. I am as imperfect as you are! Then what is the difference between me and you? The difference is that I enjoy my imperfection and you don't enjoy yours, that I am perfectly happy with all my imperfections and you are not happy with yours. You have a notion of perfection and I have none. I am perfect in my imperfections. I have accepted them totally, in toto. I am not trying to improve myself; I am simply the way I am. And I am happy the way I am.

The day you are also happy the way you are, the day you are also happy with all your imperfections, you are God. You are still God, whether you recognize it or you don't recognize it, but you have your ideas about God, and then you project those ideas. And if, sometimes, they are shattered – and they will be shattered again and again because I cannot keep to your expectations....

I am a free man. I live the way I live. And see the whole point: I am not expecting anything from you; still you go on expecting things from me. My whole effort here is to help you to be yourself, and your whole effort here is to make me something that you want me to be. Drop all this nonsense.

That's why I say even if you can forgive me, that will be enough. You need not even say a thank you.

It is very difficult to be safe amongst disciples; hence I need bodyguards. Because a disciple has "surrendered," now he will take revenge. And of course, if he surrenders to me, he will take revenge on me. Where else will he go to take the revenge?

Watch all these tendencies in you.

It was not Kovoor, it was not my criticism of Kovoor, that has hurt you. It is your idea of me, it is your expectation of me, that is feeling hurt. So drop the expectations; otherwise you will feel hurt again and again – I will find other Kovoors. Sometimes, even if they are not there, I can invent! But I am going to destroy all your expectations of me because if you cannot drop expectations about me, how can you drop expectations about yourself? It will be impossible.

And my whole work consists in a simple thing: to live a life without expectations, without hope, to live a life moment to moment, with no ideals.

Two men were chatting when the name of a mutual friend was mentioned. "Are you a friend of Harry's?" the first asked.

"Are we friends?" the man said. "Twenty years we are friends. There is nothing I would not do for Harry and there is nothing he would not do for me. In fact, for twenty years we have gone through life together, doing absolutely nothing for each other."

I am doing nothing to you. You, please, do nothing to me. Even if this can happen, there will arise a great friendship. You need not feel obliged; you don't owe anything to me.

*Meher Baba remained silent for the last forty-five years of his life. Please comment on its implications.*

There is nothing much in it. He just got fed up with the questions of his disciples.

And sometimes the idea arises in me too. So watch.

*Osho, there are a few words you always pronounce wrongly. Why?*

So that you can say to people that at least in one thing Osho is consistent.

My English is not that of the Englishman; my English is not that of the American; it is not even of the Indian. My English is just *mine*. So you have to tolerate it. And I am very reluctant to improve about anything.

And my English has been of a great help to me. I used to live in Jabalpur, for many years. The first day I was driving to the university, a woman, who lived next to me, an American woman, she wanted a lift. Now, this was going to be dangerous. This was the first day – and every day then I will have to carry her and tolerate her chattering for almost half an hour, going to the university and coming.

I had heard the American expression "Can I drop you off somewhere?" but I managed it into my English and I asked her, "Can I throw you down someplace?" And finished! She never asked again.

Once, another, an Englishwoman, got interested in me. I don't know what she saw in me, but she was almost in a fantasy. She was a lecturer in the same university, in the English department. She was after me. I was simply surprised as to what she saw in me because I don't see anything in myself; it is just emptiness there. But my English helped.

You know the expression...? I had read somewhere, in a novel, that a young man gazes into the eyes of his woman and says to her that "Your face, your beauty, your joy, your presence make time stand still." So I did the same to this woman.

I told her, "You have such a face that it would stop a clock." And finished! My English helped me.

Sometimes you will find it difficult too, because my structure of the sentences is mine, and sometimes the meaning I put into words is mine, the pronunciations are mine; sometimes you can't even get what I am saying. That helps you to keep awake. You have to listen attentively; you can miss. You cannot take me for granted.

One man was discussing with me about a politician, and I told the man, "That politician is a spherical S.O.B."

The man was puzzled; he said, "I have come across many S.O.B.'s in my life. But what do you mean by 'spherical'?"

"I mean," I said to him, "he is an S.O.B. any way you look at him."

"Spherical," that is my own word.

And my English has a certain reputation, and I am not going to destroy it.

A little lady from Fresno, visiting San Francisco, got quite a thrill out of attending a daring party in the Bohemia known as Telegraph Hill.

A friend who was showing her the sights pointed out a familiar-looking young couple and whispered, "Don't look now, but those two artists there are living in sin."

"Sin, my foot!" exclaimed the Fresno lady. "I know them. It is just Lois and Maurice, and they were married in the Fresno Baptist Church five years ago."

The young couple overheard and quickly drew the Fresno lady aside. "For God's sake don't tell anybody we are married," said the young man in a tense undertone. "It would ruin our artistic reputation."

I have a certain reputation of my English, hmm? And I am not going to change it in any way.

*What is pornography, and why does it have so much appeal?*

Pornography is a by-product of religious repression. The whole credit goes to the priests. Pornography has nothing to do with pornographers. The pornography is created, managed by the Church, by the religious people.

In a primitive, natural state, man is not pornographic. When human beings are naked and nude and man knows the woman's body and woman knows the man's body, you cannot sell *Playboy*. It is impossible. Who will purchase *Playboy*? And who will look into all that crap?

But religions have created a great profession of pornography. The whole credit goes to them. They have repressed so much that man's mind is boiling. The man wants to see the woman's body. Nothing wrong in it, a simple desire, a human desire. And the woman wants to know the man's body. A simple desire, nothing wrong about it.

Just think of a world where trees are covered with clothes. There are people.... I have heard about some English ladies who cover their dogs and cats with clothes. Just think, cows and horses and dogs dressed. Then you will find new pornography arising. Somebody will publish a *nude* picture of a tree – and you will hide it in a Bible and look at it!

This whole foolishness is out of religious repression.

Make man free, allow people to be nude. I am not saying they should continuously be nude, but nudity should be accepted. On the beach, at the swimming pool, in the home...nudity should be accepted. The children should take a bath with the mother, with the father, in the bathroom. There is no need for the father to lock the bathroom when he goes in.

The children can come and have a talk and chitchat and go out. Pornography will disappear.

Each child wants to know. "How does my daddy look?" Each child wants to know, "How does my mother look?" And this is simply intelligence, curiosity. And the child cannot know what the mother looks like, and the child cannot know what the father looks like; now you are creating illness in the child's mind. It is *you*, that *you* are ill, and the illness will be reflected in the child's mind.

I am not saying sit nude in the office or in the factory. If it is hot, it is okay, but there is no need to be naked, it should not be an obsession; but this continuous obsession of hiding your body is just ugly.

And one thing more. Because of the clothes, bodies *have* become ugly, because then you don't care. You care only about the face. If your belly goes on becoming bigger and bigger, who bothers? You can hide it. Your body has become ugly because it is not exposed; otherwise you will think a little: the belly is getting too big. Just let one hundred people stand nude, and they all will be ashamed, and they will squirm and they will start hiding themselves. Something is wrong. Why is it so? They know only about their face. The face they take care of; the whole body is neglected.

This is bad. This is not good. It is not in favor of the body, either.

Any country where people are allowed a little freedom to be nude becomes more beautiful; people have more beautiful bodies. If American women are getting more beautiful and have more beautiful bodies there is no wonder in it. Indian woman will have to wait long; they can hide their ugly bodies in the saris very carefully. The sari is a great help.

Nudity should be natural, should be as natural as animals, as trees, as everything else is nude. Then pornography will disappear.

Pornography is there as a sort of mental masturbation; it is mind masturbation. You are not allowed to love women, you are not allowed to love men, you are not allowed to make as many contacts as possible; the mind is boiling and starts a sort of inner masturbation. Pornography helps you; it gives you visions of beautiful women and beautiful men, to dream about, and it gives you a thrill.

Your alive wife does not give you any thrill. With your alive wife you suddenly go dead. There are people, even while making love to their wife, they are imagining some other woman; they are imagining some *Playboy* picture. They can make love to their woman only when in their imagination there is some other woman, some fantasy. Then they get thrilled. They are not making love to their woman, and the woman is not making love to them. She may be thinking of some actor or some hero or somebody. There are four people in each bed! Of course, it is too crowded, and you never contact the real person; those imaginary ones are standing in between.

You should know that masturbation – mental or physical is a perversion. It does not exist in nature. Homosexuality does not exist in nature, but in zoos it comes into existence. In zoos animals start masturbating. In zoos animals even start becoming homosexually interested. Wherever the situation is unnatural, unnatural perversions enter. In the military, in the army, people become homosexual, because it is an "all-boys" club, no woman available. Their pent-up energies start making them insane; they think they will go mad if they don't allow some outlet. In the boys' hostels, in the girls' hostels, where no boy can come, no girl can come, the other sex is not allowed, naturally pornography will be greatly enjoyed. It will help masturbation.

But these things have not been talked of directly. Now many will be offended – why am I talking about these things? I am here to make everything clear to you so that you can become more and more natural. The appeal for pornography simply says that your mind is in an abnormal state. It is perfectly good to be interested in a beautiful woman, nothing wrong, but to have a picture of a nude woman and to get excited about it is just stupid. That's what people are doing with pornography.

I have heard a beautiful joke. Listen attentively, don't miss it.

A husband was suspicious of his wife, so he hired a private detective to find out whether she had a lover or not. The detective, a Chinese immigrant, came back to report after only two days. His arm and nose were broken and his head was tied up in bandages.

"What happened?" the husband inquired eagerly. "Any proof yet?"

"Well," the detective answered, "I hid outside your house when you left in the morning. After half an hour a man came and let himself in with a key. I climbed a tree to see into the bedroom, and there was he holding she and she kissing he. So he play with she and she play with he; I play with me and I fall down from the tree."

That's what pornography is.

Beware of all sorts of perversions. To love is good; to dream about it is ugly. Why? When the real is available, why go for the unreal? Even the real never satisfies! So how can the unreal satisfy? Even the real, in the final analysis, proves to be illusory, so what to say about the illusory?

Let me repeat: Even the real, one day, proves to be just unreal, so what to say about the unreal?

Go into the real love, and you will become so aware one day that even the real love, the so-called real love, will disappear. And when a man is completely beyond sexuality.... Not that I am saying "*try* to go beyond," no, not at all, God forbid. What I mean when I say when a man "goes beyond" is that when a man has gone deeper into sex, into love, and has known and has found that there is nothing, that very finding takes him above. He starts floating above the earth, he grows wings. That transcendence is *brahmacharya*, that transcendence is celibacy. It has nothing to do with your effort; it has nothing to do with repression.

A repressed person can never attain *brahmacharya*; he will become pornographic. And there are a thousand and one ways of being pornographic. In the old Indian scriptures there are descriptions of great *rishis* sitting in meditation and beautiful women trying to seduce them, dancing around them, naked. And the stories say they are sent by the God of heaven to corrupt them because the God in heaven is afraid if they attain to their *samadhi* they will become competitors. The God of heaven is afraid of their competition, so when they are attaining closer and closer, coming closer to *samadhi*, he sends beautiful women to seduce them.

Now, there is no God, and no beautiful women come from heaven; this is mind pornography. These *rishis*, these so-called seers, have repressed sex so much that at the last moment, when they are really getting closer to their innermost center, that repressed sex bursts forth, explodes. And in that explosion their own images, mind images.... It is a mind panorama, it is very colorful, and it is so colorful and looks so real that even they are deceived; they think really women are there.

Just go in a cave for three months and be celibate and force celibacy. After three months you will be a great seer – and you will start seeing things. That is what a great seer is. You will start seeing damsels and beautiful *apsaras* from heaven coming and dancing around you seducing you. They are just your mind picture. When you are deprived of reality, your dreams start almost looking like reality. That's what we call hallucination.

In those old days *Playboy* magazine was not available, so the *rishimunis* had to depend on their own. Now you can have some support from the outside.

But beware: even the real is proved, finally, to be unreal. So don't move into the realms of the unreal. Go into the real, let it be a great experience. I am not against it, I am all for it, go into it, because only by going into it, one day, *brahmacharya*, one day, you simply get out of it.

Not that love will disappear. In fact, for the first time love will appear, but a totally different kind of love. Buddha calls it compassion – a cool love, with no sexual heat in it. Your being will become a benediction. Your very presence will make people feel your love. Your love will fall and shower on them. In your very presence, people will start moving into the unknown.

Yes, great compassion will arise in you. It is the same sexual energy, released from the sexual objects. Not repressed. Released. Not forcibly repressed, but understandably released. The same sexual energy becomes love, compassion.

And when love, compassion, arises you are fulfilled. Buddha

has said two things are the goals: awareness and compassion. And both come out of the sex energy; both are born out of it. Those two are the flowers, ultimate flowers, of sex energy.

That lotus is waiting in you to flower. Don't waste your energies. Use your energies to understand them, go into them deeply, meditatively, so that one day that lotus opens.

# Chapter 9

# You: the Greatest Lie There Is

*The official, Riko, once asked Nansen to explain to him the old problem of the goose in the bottle.*
*"If a man puts a gosling into a bottle," said Riko, "and feeds him until he is full grown, how can the man get the goose out without killing it or breaking the bottle?"*
*Nansen gave a great clap with his hands and shouted, "Riko!"*
*"Yes, master," said the official with a start.*
*"See," said Nansen, "the goose is out!"*

I do not seek, I find, says Pablo Picasso. And I say to you You need not seek, because if you seek, you will I ever find it. And you need not find it, also, because if *you* find it, it will not have been found at all.

Seeking means the truth is not and you have to seek it. Seeking means the truth is hidden and you have to seek it. Seeking means the truth is far away, distant, and you have to journey to it. And truth is herenow. No pilgrimage is needed; one has not to go anywhere. Truth is not *there* and truth is not *then*. Truth is here and now, so all seeking is going astray.

Seek, and you will not find, because in the very seeking you have missed the point, you have missed the first principle. In the very effort, you have gone away from the truth.

Seeking is a desire. With the desire comes in the mind — mind is nothing but desire. Seeking is in the future, and the future is not. Truth is always present, always present. Truth is always now; there is no other way for truth to be. You cannot say about truth, "Truth was," and you cannot say about truth, "Truth will be." That will be absolutely wrong. Truth *is* — and it is always so, and it will be always so, and it has always been so. Truth *is*.

How can you seek that which is? One seeks that which is not yet. Seeking is in the future. Seeking assumes it, that it is not here. You seek money, you seek power, you seek prestige, you seek heaven; but how can you seek truth? That's why, let me repeat. seeking, you go astray. Seeking, you become a victim of desire. Seeking, the mind becomes predominant. Seeking, the secondary becomes primary and the primary is lost track of.

And I say if *you* find it you have not found it at all. Because if *you* remain to find it, then it cannot be truth. Truth is found only when you are not. When truth is, you are not. You both cannot be present together. You are the greatest lie there is. If you are still there, then you will go on missing the truth. The very presence of you functions as a barrier. "I" cannot find; when the "I" is not there it is found.

That's why I say Picasso's statement is a half-truth. Half of it is true: "I do not seek." But that half is untrue when he says, "I find." It looks almost Zen-like, but it is not. A half-truth is more dangerous than a plain lie because you can see the lie as the lie sooner or later, but the half-truth can go on pretending to be the whole truth; at least it appears like the truth. Many have been deceived by Picasso's statement. It is almost Zen: "I do not seek, I find."

If he had said, "I do not seek, and it is found," it would have been Zen. If the "I" remains, then truth will remain clouded. The "I" functions as a cloud, and the sun goes behind. The "I" functions as a darkness, as a vale of darkness. The "I" is very noisy, and the voice of truth is very small, still. If the "I" is there beating its drums, then it is almost impossible to hear the whispering of truth.

Yes, truth is a whisper. You feel it only when you are absolutely not. In your absence it is present.

So this is the whole thing: if you are present, truth is absent; if you are absent, truth is present. To be absent is all that meditation is. To be absent is all that is involved in meditation.

How to become absent? How not to be? Yes, "To be or not to be" is the question. And ordinarily we decide to be. The moment we decide to be, the *samsara*. The moment we decide not to be, the nirvana. Yes, that is the basic question that encounters every human being: to be or not to be. A Buddha decides not to be.

And the paradox is that those who decide not to be, they become true, and those who decide to be, they become a lie. The lie can persist; you can go on feeding it.

Truth is, just is, only is. Seeking, you miss it. Seeking, you have started looking somewhere else. Seeking, you don't look *here*. Seeking, your eyes are turned upwards towards the sky. That's why whenever we think of God we look upwards towards the sky. It is very significant: God is far away, sitting in the seventh heaven, up. It is a long journey; only very rare people can do it – saints, mahatmas, ascetics. All nonsense.

God is where you are right now! Not in the seventh heaven, but within you.

But about those seven heavens, the metaphor of "seven" is beautiful. God is not in the seventh heaven somewhere, but is hidden behind seven layers of lies. There is a very strange incident in Bodhidharma's life, the founder of Zen. It is said that Bodhidharma collapsed seven times and arose eight times, when he realized enlightenment. Collapsed seven times and arose eight times. Very significant. Those are the seven layers of the ego, the seven layers of the "I". Each "I" will help you to collapse, and if you cannot rise eight times, that means if you cannot rise at least one time without the ego, you will not attain.

So the whole question is not that the truth is very far. It is very close, very, very close. It is in you, it is you, it is your intrinsic nature, it is your *dharma*. That is the first principle, but somehow, seeking, you have missed it.

Seeking, you have been for many lives. A seeker you have been. Non-seeking will reveal it.

That's why I say seeking, you go astray. Seeking, you go in dreams. How can you seek God? You have not known. How can you seek the unknown? You have never seen. How can you seek the unseen? Even if God comes across you, you will not be able to recognize him, because recognition is possible only if you have experienced him before. And you have not experienced him. He may have come across you many times in your life, and you will go on missing because how will you recognize him?

It is impossible to seek the unknown. Then what do you do? First you create a dream about the unknown and you start seeking the dream. The Hindu has one dream of God, the Mohammedan has another dream, the Christian has still another – but those are all dreams. The Christian will attain to his dream. That is the misery, because if you persist too much, your dream will start becoming almost a reality. If you pour your energy into your dream too much, then your dream will start becoming a reality; you will convert it into a reality. But it is not reality; it is still a dream.

The fight between Hindus, Mohammedans, and Christians is not the fight about reality. The fight is about their different dreams. Hindus have a certain idea of God, so have others, and they fight. They say, "Our dream is true." When a Christian meditates deeply, he comes to see Jesus. A Jaina never comes to see Jesus, never. A Buddhist never comes to see Jesus; Jesus never crosses his path. For a Buddhist, Buddha comes on the path. For a Jaina, Mahavira crosses his path. They are their dreams; they are dreams and projections and desires. And if you persist too much, the mind has the faculty to impart reality to the dream.

You do it every day, so it is not something very strange. Every day in the night when you fall asleep you dream, and in the dream you never recognize the fact that it is a dream. In the dream it looks true. In the dream it looks real – howsoever absurd. In the dream you see a dog is walking, and suddenly the dog becomes a cat, and you don't even doubt that it is possible. In the dream you accept even that. Your acceptance, your capacity to believe, is tremendous.

Even the people who think they are skeptical, people who think they are great doubters, logicians, rationalists, even in their dreams all their rationalism is gone and all their doubt disappears. In their dreams they believe absurd things. In the morning, when they are awake, they will be amazed, but then it is too late.

Just think of a person who is in a coma.... Once a woman was brought to me who had been in a coma for nine months.

Now think, if she is dreaming for nine months, she must be thinking they are realities. A man can be in a coma for nine years, or ninety years – or for nine lives. Then? The dream will look real. In fact, if this woman is awakened out of her coma for one minute and she looks around and falls into her dream again, which will be more real, her dream that has lasted for nine months, or the reality that she saw for one single minute? What will be her conclusion if she can conclude? She will conclude that she had fallen for one minute into sleep and she saw a dream and again the dream is gone, so she is awake and her reality continues.

The greatest possibility of the mind and the greatest capacity of the mind is imagination. It lives through imagination. The moment you start seeking truth you are moving in the direction of imagination. What are you seeking?

Zen says there is nothing to seek, because you don't know what is there. So if you seek, you will miss. Now, this is a very much higher standpoint. Jesus says, "Seek, and you will find." A very much lower statement, nothing to be compared with Zen. Meaningful, meaningful for those who are starting on the journey, but if you follow Jesus, one day or other, you will understand that by seeking, you cannot reach. Jesus was talking to people who were not highly evolved, people who had not even started seeking. He had to teach them: "Seek and you will find, knock and the door shall be opened unto you, ask and it shall be given to you." If you go to a Zen master he will smile; he will say, "Start," because his statement is a higher statement. When you have sought and you have not found, when you have struggled hard and nothing comes in your hands except dreams, then the Zen master's approach will become possible, you will be able to understand it. Then he will say, "Seek, and you will not find. Now, please, drop seeking. Drop seeking and find it herenow!"

But I am not saying that Jesus is wrong. I am saying it is a beginners' class. And unless you follow Jesus for a time you will not understand Zen. So Jesus will prepare you, Jesus will help you.

Jesus was talking to the Jews, who have been one of the most earthy races in the world. To talk Zen would have been impossible – they would have killed him even earlier. They didn't allow him much life, only three years of ministry. At the age of thirty he started his work; by thirty-three he was gone. They could not tolerate even a very primary statement about religion. It was not very rebellious, it was not very absurd. It was in tune with the Jewish thinking, but still they could not tolerate it. It was "otherworldly". He was talking about the world that he calls the Kingdom of God. Jews have been very worldly; that is their success. They are very down to earth, and this man was distracting them. They were seeking money and they were seeking power and prestige, and this man was talking about God. Jesus was trying to change their seeking towards religion. It is religion of the kindergarten class.

Zen people are talking about the highest statement. India's highest consciousness was transplanted into China, and China's highest consciousness, Taoism, met with Buddhism. These are two of the greatest flowerings of human consciousness. Never again has humanity reached such a peak as Buddhism, as it reached in Buddha; and never again has it reached anything like Lao Tzu. And just think: Zen is a crossbreeding of Taoism and Buddhism. It is a meeting of Buddha and Lao Tzu. It is a meeting of two of the highest peaks. Naturally Zen goes still higher. Zen goes higher than Buddhism and higher than Taoism because it contains all that was beautiful in these two cultures, the ancientmost cultures, the longest seekers in the world, who have staked all that they had for their seeking. Zen is the purest flower.

In fact, Zen is not a flower. It is essence, it is fragrance. Even a flower has something gross in it, something of the earth. So remember it, when Zen is saying something, it is to be understood at the highest level; otherwise there will be no understanding about it. You will misunderstand it.

Seeking, you go astray; seeking, you go in dreams; seeking, you go somewhere else; and truth is here. Seeking, you go then; and truth is *now*. Seeking, you are, and seeking, you are too much. The more you seek, the more you feel you are. The harder and more arduous the seeking becomes, the stronger the ego becomes.

Seeking, you are, and seeking, you are too much; and there

is no space for the truth to be. You fill the whole space of your being. Seeking, you are closed.

Have you not seen this happening in ordinary life too? A man is suddenly told that his house is on fire. He rushes towards his house from the office or from his shop: now he cannot see what is happening in the market, on the road. Somebody says, "Hello"; he cannot hear. Somebody comes and collides with him, but he cannot see who he is, and he will not remember that somebody collided. His whole mind is narrow now – his house is on fire. His mind is concentrated.

Seeking means concentration, and truth is never achieved by concentration. Truth is achieved by meditation. And the difference is vital, and the difference is great. And you have to understand the difference because ordinarily people who don't know anything about meditation, they go on writing books in which they write that meditation is concentration. Meditation is not concentration! Meditation is just the opposite state of concentration.

When you concentrate your mind is narrowed down; when you meditate, you mind is widened. When you concentrate, there is an object on which you concentrate; when you meditate, there is no object.

People come to me and they ask, "On what to meditate?" Then they are not asking about meditation. They are asking about concentration when they come and they say to me, "I cannot concentrate. Osho, can you help me?" Concentration means you want your mind to cling to something, you want your mind to remain with something. Concentration is a sort of attachment, so whenever your attachment is there you are concentrated.

Your wife is dying, and if you are attached to her, you will forget the whole world. Now nothing exists except your dying wife. You will be sitting by her side and you will be concentrated; your mind will not go here and there.

Or if you are driving a car and suddenly you see an imminent accident is going to happen – some madman is coming, driving his car madly, and on the turn you see now it is too late, it is going to happen – suddenly you will be concentrated, because you are too attached to life. There will be no thoughts any more. Just a moment before, you were thinking to see your girl friend, a moment before, you were thinking to go to the movie tonight, or do this or that; suddenly all has disappeared; there is no thought in the mind, no object. You are too attached to life. Because of this attachment, all other objects have disappeared. You are concentrated now only on your life; only one thing has remained: your life.

Dostoevsky has written a memoir. He was young and he was a revolutionary, and he was caught by the czar with twenty other people, and they all were sentenced to death. The day came, ditches were dug, and they were standing in front of the ditches and the man was getting ready with the machine gun. Everything was ready.

Just close by on a church tower there is a clock, and each moment is passing fast, and the life is disappearing. At exactly six o'clock, they will be shot dead. It is ten minutes to six.

You can imagine how concentrated they must have become. Dostoevsky writes, "Never again have I been so concentrated in my life. All else disappeared. I could hear my heart throbbing, I could see my breathing for the first time, I felt my body for the first time. I had never felt my body, never heard my heartbeat, never seen my breath. Everything became simply concentrated – and we could hear the clock moving.

Five minutes, four minutes, three minutes...and the concentration is becoming more and more and more. One minute...and everything else has disappeared.

When life is at stake, only life is in the mind.

And then comes a horseman, running, and the czar has pardoned them; their death sentence has been converted into a life sentence.

One man, at exactly six o'clock, fell in the ditch, Died! without being shot. Must have become so concentrated with the idea of death. Died! Nobody could believe it. The officers ran. He was taken out of the ditch, but he was dead. He believed it; he must have become hypnotized with the idea of death. Death is coming, death is coming, fifteen minutes, death is coming...It was coming for two, three months; now it was closer and closer and closer, and the mind became concentrated. The man fell and died.

Another man shouted, "I am dead!" He became mad. For his whole life he remained shouting, "I am dead. I have died, don't you know?" He will meet people and say, "Don't you know? I died on that day. Six o'clock they killed me. I am a ghost!"

Dostoevsky himself could not believe it, because it was unimaginable, that the czar was going to forgive them. But he writes in his memoirs that "Never again was I concentrated; that was the peak of concentration."

It is not meditation. If it was meditation, then Dostoevsky would have become enlightened. That peak of concentration?

It happens to you. When you are studying for an examination, as the examinations come closer, you become more and more concentrated. Just the night before, your mind functions so concentratedly. Once the examination is gone, the mind relaxes again.

Concentration is a mind thing; meditation is a no-mind thing. Concentration means pouring your whole energy onto one object. Meditation means not pouring your energy onto any object, but just overflowing in all directions.

For example, if you are listening to me you can listen in two ways. You can listen in the wrong way: the wrong way is the way of concentration; you can just remain tense, strained. Or you can listen in a relaxed, let-go way; you can remain relaxed. If you listen in a tense way – that is the meaning of the word "attention": "with tension, concentration" – then you will not listen to the birds singing in the trees. Then you will listen only to me, and everything else will be blocked out, bracketed out. That means only this small voice that is here is in your concentration and the whole existence has been blocked out.

Meditation is just the opposite: nothing is blocked out, you are open in all directions. You are listening to me; you are listening to the birds also. If the wind blows in the trees and the trees start a murmur, you will listen to that too. And there will be no distraction, remember. You are so open, you listen to me and the bird and the wind, and they all become one. And when you can listen in that way, you have listened to God.

When you listen meditatively, you listen to God – whatsoever you listen to, it is God, it is God's message. He has reached you through the tree, through the wind, through the bird, through me. He is coming from everywhere, because he is everywhere. He surrounds you. So when you are open to everything that is happening, to all that is happening, you are herenow, you are in meditation. And this state is a state of non-seeking.

Concentration is part of seeking; when you seek something you become concentrated. When you don't seek anything you become relaxed. When you seek something and you are concentrated, you are going away from yourself. Your object will be the goal, you forget yourself. Your arrow of consciousness goes only to the object. When you are not going anywhere, where will you be? When you are not going anywhere you will be where you are, you will be whoever you are. You will be simply relaxing and resting into yourself.

Ashtavakra says, "Rest in yourself, and you will attain all." Because resting in yourself you will know who you are.

So it is not a question of seeking. Seeking, you are too much. Seeking, you are so arrowed towards something that you don't see anything else, your eyes don't allow all to enter into your being, and then there is no space for the truth to be. Seeking, you become a cloud and the sun goes behind. Hence, seeking, there is night and darkness and death.

When you are not seeking there is life, eternal life, and light and God, or you can choose any name which you prefer. Buddha calls it nirvana, non-seeking: you have arrived. In fact, you had never gone anywhere else; you were only imagining.

"Tell us, master," a monk asked Daito....

Daito was a great Zen master.

"Tell us, master, when Shakyamuni Buddha saw the morning star, what did he see?"...

In Zen this is the legend, that Buddha was seeking and seeking for six years, then he got tired and fed up with seeking, and one day he dropped seeking too. As one day he had dropped his kingdom, his family, his *this* world, one day he dropped his *other* world too. As one day he had become disinterested in the material, a day came when he became disinterested in the spiritual too. And that was the night when he rested in himself – because there was nothing to seek. So he slept under a tree, the Bodhi tree; that became the most famous tree in the world. He rested under the Bodhi tree, slept well. There was no seeking, so there was no dreaming either. The whole night was just a peaceful rhythm, not even a thought, because the material world was gone, the spiritual world was gone. It was an absolute rest into oneself.

By the morning, the Zen legend says, his eyes opened. Not that he opened his eyes, because there was nothing to do now: he will not even open his eyes. The Zen legend says the eyes opened because the rest was complete. See the difference. You can open your eyes; then there is strain. You can close your eyes; then there is strain. When the eyes are closed by themselves there is rest; when the eyes open by themselves, then there is rest.

When a life is not a life of doing, but happening, then there is rest.

The eyes opened and he saw the last morning star setting, it was just disappearing, the last glimpse of it, in a moment it was gone, and he became enlightened. The last trace disappeared with the disappearing morning star, and he was utterly empty. He was utterly nobody. He became a nothingness, a pure nothingness, a content-less consciousness.

What is the significance of this last star disappearing? When the eyes opened and he saw the last star, there was a little concentration, a slight concentration, must be the old habit, thousands of lives of old habit. He must have become a little strained; a little concentration must have arisen. Looking at the last star, he must have become focused, his consciousness must have become narrow – just out of old habit. There was nothing to look at now. But then the star disappeared – it was the last star and the sun was going to rise soon, so the star disappeared – the star disappeared, and the last object of concentration disappeared.

Suddenly he was released from all concentration, suddenly there was freedom, there was no content. The last star disappearing took away the last trace of concentration. He was there – and he was not there. He was there for the first time authentically – and he was not there for the first time as an "I", as an ego.

Some seeker asked master Daito...

"Tell us, master, when Shakyamuni Buddha saw the morning star, what did he see?"...

Why did he become enlightened by seeing the last star?

Many people have copied it – people are foolish, people are monkeys. Many Buddhists sit, they even go to Bodhgaya – they come from China, from Korea, from Japan, from Ceylon – they go to Bodhgaya, they sit under the Bodhi tree, they try to rest the whole night, and they watch, many times it must be, in the night they must be looking: whether the last star is there or gone. And they must be closing their eyes again – it is still night and there are so many stars – and they must be afraid and tense: will they be able to see the last star, or will they miss? And they have to see the last star disappearing.

Once a Japanese man came and stayed with me. I said, "Why have you come from Japan?" He said, "To see the last star disappearing." I told him, "Can't you see a last star disappearing in Japan? Don't the stars behave the same way there? Don't they disappear in the morning? For what have you come here?" And he said, "I have come to sit under the Bodhi tree." But any tree will do. Buddha was not sitting under that tree specifically. It was just a coincidence, it was accidental. He had not searched for that tree. That tree was in no way special; it was as ordinary a tree as any tree.

You can sit under any tree and under any sky and in any country, but the question is not of country, not of the sky, not of the stars, not of the tree. The question is, "Has your attachment to things – and attachment to other-worldly things – disappeared, or is it still there?"

Now, in fact, you have come to sit under the Bodhi tree

because you want to become enlightened. The desire. The seeking. You have come as a seeker, and Buddha did attain because he was not a seeker that night.

This is how things go on and man goes on imitating and becoming foolish.

"Tell us, master, when Shakyamuni Buddha saw the morning star, what did he see?"

"Clean blank nothing," Daito replied at once. And then added, "But if a person has only so much as just one speck of dust in his eyes, he may look at a blank and see all sorts of imaginary things."

Just a speck of dust will do, just a small speck of desire will do, and then you will start seeing imaginary things. If you really want to see that which is, then the eyes have to be utterly clean, blank. With those blank eyes you are a Buddha – with those empty eyes.

Seeking, one never finds. Let it be a fundamental remembrance. So Pablo Picasso is true, but only half true.

And half-truths are really dangerous. They can pretend, they can masquerade as truths, as whole truths. That's what happens. Whenever a man like Buddha moves, walks on the earth, that's what happens – his truths become half-truths in our minds. A half-truth is a reflection of truth. A half-truth is a shadow of truth. In our monkey minds, in our imitative minds, we start imitating half-truths. And there is something which has to be understood. A half-truth deceives better.

But Pablo Picasso could not have done better, because art itself cannot go beyond the half-truth. That's the difference between art and religion. Art is the world of the shadows, the world of the reflections, the world of imagination, the world of dreams, the world of desires, the world of projections. Art cannot give you the whole truth, but the best art is always giving you half of it – that too the best art. I am not talking about the third-rate art. A third-rate art is simply a lie, a fantasy, a fiction. But Pablo Picasso is one of the greatest artists the world has ever produced. The best art always give you half; more is not possible through art.

The artist has glimpses of truth, reflected in the world of his dreams, in the world of his imagination. The artist is a pool of imagination, a lake of imagination. In that lake is reflected the full moon. And sometimes the moon in the lake looks far more beautiful than the real moon. On the glossy, silent surface of the lake, on the placid, silent surface of the lake, the moon looks even more innocent. But that is not a real moon – although the reflection belongs to the real.

That is the difference between the mystic and the artist. The best artist comes closer to the mystic than anybody else, but the artist is not a mystic. He is a shadow, a shadow mystic. William Blake or Pablo Picasso or Emerson or Rabindranath, they give beautiful reflections of the truth. And even the reflection is so enchanting, what to say about the original?

But if you jump into the lake to find the moon, even the reflection will disappear. You are not supposed to jump into the lake. And where the reflection is, you are not to go in that direction. You have to move exactly in the opposite direction, then you will find the real.

The artist has some quality of the mystic; he is on the way to becoming a mystic in some life. The mystic has all the qualities of the artist, plus.

Sometimes mystics have been artists, particularly Zen mystics. They have painted. They have written poems, haiku. They have carved wood, they have sculpted. They were great artists. In fact, all Zen masters have been creative people.

That should also be remembered. When you have attained to a state of consciousness, your consciousness has to create something, something visible. You have to materialize something of your consciousness into the world so that this world also becomes beautiful. And people who cannot understand religion at least can understand art. You may not be able to understand the meaning of the Upanishads, but the very poetry of it appeals, and if the poetry appeals, then the truth is making a way towards your heart. You may not be able to meditate, but if somebody is dancing with deep meditation, that dance may appeal, and through the dance, lingering by the side, something of the meditation will enter into your being.

Gurdjieff had prepared a group of dancers, and he took the

dancers to many great cities of the world. It was a rare opportunity made available. When in New York those meditators danced, people were suddenly amazed, they could not believe what was happening. The dancers created such meditative energy, such a great wave of energy, that those who had come just to see the dance suddenly forgot the dance completely. Something else was there by the side, a door opened through it.

And Gurdjieff used to do the "stop" exercise. The dancers are dancing, a group of twenty, thirty dancers, and they are going wild in their dance, and suddenly he will shout by the side, "Stop!" And they will all become just marble statues, as they were. If the hand was raised, it will remain raised. If one leg was up, it will remain up.

At one moment when he said, "Stop!" they were in such a position that they all fell – fell from the stage, in front of the audience in the hall. But not a single person moved; they fell as if dead. And one man who was watching, something inside him also fell. The very shocking incident, these people fallen as if dead, and something changed in his mind. He became one of the great followers of Gurdjieff and attained to greater heights of consciousness.

Looking at a Zen painting you will be surprised because the painting brings to you something of the man who has painted it. If you look at modern painting, that too brings something to you. If you look at a modern painting long enough, you will start feeling a little crazy. If you put too many modern paintings in your bedroom, beware, you will have nightmares. Those paintings will start entering into your dreams. You cannot look at a modern painting for long; you have to move. You start feeling weird, something is wrong, something is bizarre.

The modern painter is insane. He is painting out of his insanity. If you look at a Zen painting, a silence oozes out of it, suddenly something beautiful surrounds you. You are transported to another consciousness. The painting carries something of the touch of the master. The painting has been done in deep meditation; the painting has been done by one who has arrived.

Gurdjieff used to call such art "objective art". When somebody who has attained to consciousness does something, that something becomes objective art. Looking at that thing, you will have some glimpse of the master. The master may have been dead for three thousand years, that doesn't matter. The painting, the statue, the carving will represent him, and through it you can again become connected to him. If you know how to meditate with a painting, it will be easier.

Within these twenty years a rare thing has come to light because of too much use of drugs. The underground world of drugs has stumbled upon a very significant fact; they call it "contact high". It is exactly the meaning of *satsang*. Let me explain it to you.

A "contact high" is a state. Somebody has taken LSD and is turned on, and you love the man, you really love the man, or the woman, you really relate to him – the man or the woman is somebody who turns you on by her presence or his presence. The person has taken LSD. You simply sit by the side, and you love the person, and the person's presence turns you on, and by and by you will start feeling that the LSD is affecting you too, that somehow his consciousness is infiltrating your consciousness, that your space is being overpowered. And you will start feeling high. This is contact high.

This is the meaning of *satsang* too, on a different plane. If somebody has attained, just being with him in deep love, in deep gratitude, in deep relatedness, and you will start feeling that something, through him, reaches your heart, stirs your being, and you are put on a totally different plane, where you cannot go by yourself. You are transported, carried to it. Yes, it too is a contact high.

That's why in the East we have praised *satsang* so much, to be in the presence of a master, to attain contact high. And once you have started attaining through somebody, by and by you can find your own way.

This contact high is possible even after thousands of years, through objective art. Read some haiku of Basho, small haiku. Read one haiku, repeat it, sing it, chew it, swallow it deeply, and then sit silently, waiting for the meaning to be revealed. Don't think about it; thinking, you will go astray. Don't analyze it;

analyzing, you will go far away. Meditate, just be with it, let it be with you, and suddenly you will find something is changing in your consciousness. You are moving upwards, or you are moving deeper.

The very small haiku can turn you on. It can almost become an LSD trip because the haiku carries Basho's consciousness, condensed. It is no ordinary poetry. It is not written by a poet, not by an artist. It is done by a master.

And the master has put it almost like a mantra. If you simply allow it to spread its meaning on your being, its fragrance on your being, you will be in the state of contact high.

That's why I say Picasso's statement is a half-truth. "I do not seek" is the half-truth, and "I find" is the half-untruth, because it is never the "I" that finds it. "I" is the barrier, the cloud, the hindrance, the obstacle. Truth is found, but not by "I". Truth is found only when there is no "I", when there is nobody to find it. Truth is found only when there is nobody to seek it and nobody to find it.

Now, the "I" has seven layers, those seven times when Bodhidharma fell and again rose. You will also fall seven times before you can attain to enlightenment. The first layer consists of the past: "I" is memory. Go with me into it as deeply as possible because this will lead you to the first principle. The first principle cannot be said, but can be showed, how you can attain it.

The first layer of "I" consists of memory, the past. If you want to get rid of the "I" you will have to get rid of the past. Many people come to me and they say, "We would like to drop this ego." But they think that the ego is a non-complex thing, a simple thing. It is not. It is very complex, the most complex. In fact, the one who wants to drop it may be the ego itself. That is so subtle, it is so tricky. Layer upon layer. The first layer is the memory.

If you really want to drop the ego – and that is the only way to find the truth; all religion consists only of dropping these seven layers – don't live in the memory. By and by, the moment you catch hold of yourself, that you are moving in the memory, immediately slip out of it. Immediately. Don't waste a single moment. I am not saying repent about it, I am not saying feel guilty about it, no, because that too will be the past. I am simply saying the moment you find you were moving into a dream about the past, a nostalgia, the moment you find it so, just slip out of it. There is no need to fight with it. If you fight, you will be defeated. There is no need to feel angry about it. If you feel angry you will be defeated. You need not value it in any way, good or bad. You simply do one thing: the moment you find out, slip out of it.

And the one who finds it red-handed is your awareness. Eckhart says the one who finds is God, God within you.

Just try. Whenever you find your memory is hovering around you too much, the one who finds this sudden recognition that "Yes, I am again in the memory," that one, that awareness, is God within you. Slip out of the memory.

And I say slip out of it because there is no need to fight. Fighting, you will cling to it. Fighting, you will have to be there. If you have to fight with somebody you have to be there. Don't fight.

And you are capable of slipping out, just as a snake slips out of the old skin. Go on slipping out of the memory. Memory is an old skin. In fact, you have already slipped out of it; it is just in the mind, it is nowhere else.

The second layer consists of unawareness. We live almost in a drunken state. We live with the minimum of consciousness. You go on doing things, you go on moving, this and that, but you are not conscious. Have you ever had any moments of consciousness so that you can see, you can compare?

For example.... Just now! See what is there. Gather yourself together. Just be herenow and see what is there, and you will find your consciousness is more, you have come out of a fog. Soon you will again disappear into the fog. This fog surrounds you. Sometimes you come out of it. Sometimes something penetrates your fog, brings you out. But ordinarily, life is so monotonous, there is no surprise, nothing brings you out.

Whenever you are a little more aware, many things happen. If you watch you will understand. A beautiful woman passes by; suddenly you become more aware. A bird on the wing, you were watching an empty sky and a bird passes by....

Ramakrishna attained to his first *samadhi*, to his first satori, by seeing a row of cranes against the black clouds. He was very young, must have been thirteen. He was sitting by the lake of his town, it was cloudy, dark clouds were gathering, the beginning of the rain, and suddenly a row, many white cranes against the black clouds. Almost like lighting they were there and they were gone, and he attained to his first *samadhi*. For days he was drunk with the unknown, he danced, sang. His town's people, his family thought he had gone mad. But he was so happy.

That sudden experience. Something penetrated like a sword. Something was cut.

Sometimes it happens to you too. You don't take account of these moments, because you are afraid. You try to forget them. And they are so extraordinary and they are so exceptional and so rare that even to talk about them, nobody will believe it. So you don't take account of them; you think, "Must be a fantasy, an imagination." But one day in the morning suddenly the world is beautiful – for no reason at all. The reason IS there: the reason is you are more aware. Maybe you rested well in the night, it was a good sleep, the dreams were not too many, your stomach was not too full of food or hungry. Things somehow went well, and in the morning you felt on the top of the world. It is nothing but awareness.

With a friend you have not seen for many years, suddenly you become more aware. Anything that makes you more aware, watch it, take account of it, remember it, so that you can go more and more into it. Don't put it aside. Don't neglect it. It has to be fed and watered, taken care of.

The third layer of "I" is ambition, comparison with the others, where I am, higher or lower, inferior or superior, ahead or lagging behind – who I am. Watch it: never compare. You are you. And there is nobody like you, so comparison is not possible. And everybody is so unique and so different, how can you compare? Drop comparison. Whether you find yourself caught in comparison, immediately drop it, then and there. It is not good to carry these things in the mind longer; otherwise they leave traces, they make grooves in the mind. Never compare. Somebody is more intelligent, somebody is more beautiful, somebody is more healthy.... Don't compare. You are you.

And this is the way God wanted you to be. Feel fulfilled the way you are and accept yourself. Don't condemn yourself.

The fourth layer of "I" consists of future, always thinking ahead, what to do tomorrow or the day after tomorrow. Or people are so mad, they are thinking of what to do in the next life: where to go, to hell or heaven?

People come to me and they ask, "Osho, what do you say about life after death?" I say, "You are not alive even now, and you are talking about life after death? I don't even see life before death."

Man is not! Man only thinks that he is. Man has not happened yet. Rarely it happens. Once in a while, in a Buddha or a Bodhidharma a man is there; otherwise you are just a belief. And you are thinking about life after death? Think of life after birth! Think of life before death. Think of life now. Don't go into the future too much.

I am not saying that if you want to go to Bombay don't book a ticket – I am not saying that. Otherwise there are fools of that type too. One day I talked in the morning, "Don't think of the future," and by the evening I received a letter. One friend threw his passport into the river. "Why bother? 'Don't think of the future,' Osho has said." I am not saying that. There is a practical world, but that is not a problem at all. To carry a passport is not a problem.

To carry fantasies about the future is a problem. A passport is not such a burden. To think about tomorrow and to go and book a ticket is not a problem. These are factual things, ordinary, practical things. But to think that tomorrow you will be happy, not today, that tomorrow you will love, not today, that tomorrow you will sing, not today, is dangerous – because tomorrow never comes. Again when it comes, it will be today, and your old habit will say, "Tomorrow I will be happy." Tomorrow again and again, you will be happy, and you will never be happy.

What I am saying is psychological future has to be dropped. The ordinary future is okay, it is not a problem at all.

The fifth layer consists of conditionings. You have been conditioned – Hindu, Mohammedan, Jaina, Buddhist, English, German, Indian – these layers are there. Start dropping them.

Again, please, don't throw your passport!

These ideas from the mind – that I am a German or a Japanese or a Chinese – are just foolish. You were born just as pure consciousness and you will die as pure consciousness, and all these are just dresses, formalities, forms, what Hindus call *nam-rup*, name and form. But you are not confined to them, you are not contained in them; you are beyond them.

The sixth layer consists of arrogance, of non-humbleness. One has to learn humbleness because that is reality. We are interdependent, so how can we be arrogant? You cannot live without the air, you cannot live without fire, you cannot live without the sun, you cannot live without the trees, you cannot live without the woman, woman without the man – you cannot live at all independently. So all arrogance is just ignorance. We are interdependent, we interpenetrate each other, and everything is required.

If the sun sets tonight and never rises again we will die. Within ten minutes we will die. If all the forests disappear and the trees disappear we will die, we will not be able to live. We breathe through the trees, they are continuously working for us and we are working for them. Don't think that they are slaves and we are masters. Nobody is a slave here and nobody is a master; everybody is a master here and everybody is a slave here. This is humility. They go on releasing oxygen for you; they serve you. And you go on releasing carbon dioxide for them, they live on carbon dioxide; so you serve them. They serve you, you serve them.

We are servants of each other or masters of each other, but we are all in the same boat. The animals, the trees, the birds, the rocks, we are all in the same boat. We exist in a togetherness; that's the meaning of humbleness.

I am not saying become humble and start being arrogant about your humbleness and start saying that "I am the most humble man in the world." That will be arrogance again. Humbleness is an understanding, not a cultivation.

And the last layer of "I" consists of imitations. We learn to imitate – that's what I mean when I say we are monkeys. Somebody is doing something: we start doing that. Somebody is making something: we start making that. We learn through imitation. Good for the children because otherwise children will never learn, but when will you become mature, when will you start not imitating, and being true to yourself?

If these seven layers are dropped, you will simply become aware of who you are. You are God, as everybody else is God.

These seven layers are the "bottle".

Now let me tell you this beautiful anecdote. It is one of the most beautiful anecdotes in the Zen literature, and Zen has many beautiful anecdotes. This is one of the topmost. Listen to it.

*The official, Riko, once asked Nansen....*

Nansen was a great master. You must have heard another story, I must have told you sometime. A great professor comes to see Nansen. The professor was the head of the department of philosophy in a university. He comes, and immediately he asks, "Do you believe in God? Is there any life after death? Has man a soul?"

Nansen says, "Wait. Let me prepare tea for you. You are tired and you are perspiring. And there is no hurry; these problems can wait a little. Let me prepare tea for you." And he prepares the tea. This is the humbleness of a Zen master.

He brings tea. He goes on pouring the tea in the cup. The cup is full and the tea starts overflowing into the saucer, and then the saucer is full, and the professor shouts, "What are you doing? Are you mad? Now there is not any space, not even for a single drop, and you go on pouring and you go on pouring. It will start dropping on your floor!"

And Nansen laughs and he says, "So you understand. Now do you have any questions, still?"

The professor says, "Why, what do you mean? How does this explain my questions?"

And Nansen says, "Have you any space in your head? I can give you the answer, but there is no space. I don't see any space in your head. And you are alert, very alert; you can see that when the cup is full, no more tea should be poured in. Go, please, and clean your skull. Empty your skull and come back! Because these questions are such that they can only be answered to an empty skull."

Nansen is a rare man.

*The official, Riko, once asked Nansen to explain to him the old problem of the goose in the bottle.*

The problem is very ancient. It is a koan; it is given to a disciple, that he has to meditate on it. It is absurd; you cannot "solve" it. A koan is something which cannot be solved. Remember, it is not a puzzle. A puzzle has a clue; a koan has no clue. A koan is a puzzle without any clue. Not that more intelligence will solve it. No, no intelligence will ever solve it. Even if it is given to God, it will not be solved. It is made in such a way that it cannot be solved. This is a koan.

"If a man puts a gosling into a bottle," said Riko, "and feeds him until he is full grown, how can the man get the goose out without killing it or breaking the bottle?"

Don't break the bottle – and the goose has to be taken out – and don't kill the goose. Now, these are the two conditions to be fulfilled. The koan becomes impossible. The bottle has a small neck; the goose cannot come out from it. Either you have to break the bottle or you have to kill the goose. You can kill the goose, and piece by piece you can take the goose out, or you can break the bottle, and the goose can come out alive, whole. But the condition is the bottle has not to be broken and the goose has not to be killed. The goose has to come out whole and the bottle has to remain whole. Nothing has to be destroyed; no destruction allowed.

Now, how are you going to solve it? But meditating on it, meditating on it...one day it happens that you see the point. Not that you solve the problem, suddenly the problem is no more there.

> Nansen gave a great clap with his hands and shouted, "Riko!"
> "Yes, master," said the official with a start.
> "See," said Nansen, "the goose is out!"

Now, it is tremendously beautiful. What he is saying is that the goose has never been in, the goose has always been out. What is he saying, the moment he said, "Riko!"? What happened? Those seven layers of ego disappeared and Riko became aware. The shout was so sudden, the sound was so unexpected. He was expecting a philosophical answer.

That's why sometimes the Zen master will hit you on your head or throw you out of the window or jump upon you or threaten you that he will kill you: he will do something so that those seven layers of ego are immediately transcended and your awareness, which is the center of all, is alert. You are made alert.

Now, shouting "Riko!" so suddenly, for no reason at all – and he has brought a small puzzle to be solved and this master suddenly shouts "Riko!" – he cannot see the connection. And that is the whole clue to it. He cannot see the connection, the shout startles him, and he says, "Yes, master."

"See," said Nansen, "the goose is out!"

Those seven layers of the bottle are crossed.

"Yes, master" – in that moment Riko was pure consciousness, without any layer. In that moment, Riko was not the body. In that moment, Riko was not the mind. In that moment, Riko was just awareness. In that moment, Riko was not the memory of the past. In that moment, Riko was not the future, the desire. In that moment, he was not in any comparison with anybody. In that moment, he was not a Buddhist or a Mohammedan or a Hindu. In that moment, he was not a Japanese or an Indian.

In that moment, when the master shouted "Riko!" he was simply awareness, without any content, without any conditioning. In that moment, he was not young, old. In that moment, he was not beautiful, ugly. In that moment, he was not stupid, intelligent. All layers disappeared. In that moment, he was just a flame of awareness.

That is the meaning when the master says, "See, the goose is out – and I have not broken the bottle, I have not even touched the bottle." The bottle means the ego, those seven layers. "I have not broken the bottle, it is there, and I have not killed the goose. And the goose is out."

Now, there are three types of religions in the world. One which will destroy the bottle. Then you become very vulnerable, then you become very insecure, then great trembling arises in you, and then there is every possibility you may go mad. That sort of thing happens many times in India. There are methods which can destroy the bottle, easier methods. They destroy the bottle, and the goose is out; but then the goose has no house to abide in, no shelter; then there is every possibility the man may go mad. And many people in India, seeking, searching, working towards the unknown become mad. When the unknown comes into them, they have no protection.

Remember, you need protection even against God because God can be too much too suddenly. Those protections have not to be destroyed; practically, they have to remain there. Just think of a person who has no ego. Now, the house is on fire: he will not run out. For what? "I am not. The fire cannot burn me, because I am not." Just think of a man who has no ego, and he is standing in the middle of the road, and there comes a bus and the driver honks and honks, and he does not bother. He is the immortal soul, he is not the ego. This state can be dangerous. It happens if you destroy the bottle.

Zen says don't destroy the bottle. Use it when it is needed. Whenever you feel to have protection, the goose simply goes inside the bottle. Sometimes one needs rest, and sometimes the bottle is also useful. It can be put to a thousand and one uses. The ego can be used if you know that you are not the ego. Then the ego cannot use you, you can use it.

And there are methods which will save the bottle and kill the goose – self-destructive methods are there – so one becomes more and more unaware. That is what I mean when I say kill the goose: one becomes more and more unaware. Drugs can do that. Drugs have been used in India for thousands of years. They can kill the goose. The bottle remains protected, but the goose is killed. If you take some foreign chemicals inside your being and your nature is not ready to absorb them, by and by you will kill the goose, your consciousness will be gone, you may fall in a coma.

The first possibility, if the bottle is broken and thrown; you may go mad. The second possibility, if the goose is killed, or almost killed: you will become so unconscious that you will become a zombie. You can find zombies. In many monasteries there are zombies, whose goose is killed, or at least drugged. And there are mad people, maniacs.

Zen says avoid both. The bottle has to remain and the goose has to come out. This is a great synthesis.

> *"Yes, master," said the official with a start.*
> *"See," said Nansen, "the goose is out!"*

It must have been a moment of great discovery to Riko. He must have seen it, "Yes, it is out." He is fully aware. The trick worked, the device worked, the shouting and clapping worked. In fact, Riko must have been almost on the verge; otherwise shouting would not do. You can go on shouting. Clapping won't do. But the man must have been just on the verge of it. Just a small push, and he has jumped the barrier.

Meditate over it. This is the way to attain the first principle: to know that the goose can be out without destroying the bottle, that you can be God without destroying your humanity, that you can be God without destroying your ordinariness.

A disciple of His Divine Grace Prabhupad came to see me. Prabhupad is the founder of the Krishna Consciousness movement. Naturally, to be respectful to me, he also called me His Divine Grace. I said, "Don't call me that; just call me 'His Divine Ordinariness'."

The ordinary is the extraordinary. The ordinary has not to be destroyed. Once the ordinary is in the service of the extraordinary it is beautiful, it is tremendously beautiful.

Let me repeat: the trivial is the profound, *samsara* is nirvana. Whatsoever you are, there is nothing wrong with it. Just something is missing. Nothing wrong with it! Something is simply missing. Just that missing link has to be provided, that plus, and everything that you have becomes divine.

Love has not to be destroyed; only awareness has to be added to it. Relationship has not to be destroyed; only meditation has to be added to it. You need not go from the marketplace, you need not go to any cave and in the Himalayas; only God has to be called there in the marketplace.

The bottle is beautiful, nothing is wrong in it. You just have to learn that you can come out of it whenever you want and you can go into it whenever you want, that it is your pleasure. It is almost like the house. When you feel too cool or cold in the house, freezing cold, you get out under the sky, under the sun, to warm yourself. Then it becomes too warm and you start perspiring; you go into the house. You are free. The same door takes you out, the same door takes you in, and the house is not the enemy.

But if you cannot get out of the house, then something is wrong. There is no need to leave the house, there is no need to drop being a householder. There is only one thing needed: in the house become a sannyasin, in the world remain in such a way that the world is not in you.

See, the goose is out. In fact, the goose has always been out, just a recognition is needed.

## Chapter 10

# All Going Is Going Astray

*There are moments when I feel no hope, without feeling desperate, when there is recognition that the "I" has fought enough and cannot help anymore. Yet under these momentary covers lingers the one and only longing: to become my real nature, to experience truth and to live it in the world. My mind pleases itself to call this longing an authentic, genuine thirst. However, the suspicion is there that it is just a way to hide my plain greed.*

The question is from Gunakar. Yes, Gunakar, it is a way to hide the greed. And not only that, it is a way to avoid the real. It is not a thirst for the real; it is a way to escape from the real. All greed, all desire, is an escape from the real. The desire is for that which is not. That which is already there; you need not be greedy about it, you need not desire it. Whether you desire or not does not make any difference. It is there. By desiring, you will miss, because you will create a cloud around yourself.

This is how the mind goes on playing games. It can play the game in the name of reality too, in the name of God, in the name of enlightenment, nirvana.

One thing has to be remembered always, that you are not to become real, you are real. That which you are is the reality. Gunakar has said: Only one longing lingers, to become my real nature. But then who are you? You are your real nature. What else can you be? How else can you be? There is no way to go away from your reality. There is no way to go against it. There is no way to be anything else other than it.

But you can forget about it. You can start looking in some other direction. All that is possible is to be forgetful. You cannot lose contact with reality; you can only forget it. You can start looking in some other direction. You can put it at the back. You can avoid your eyes. You can pretend that you are not the real.

The first thing: you are the real. Whatsoever you are is your reality. It has not to be attained; it is already there. It has happened. Nirvana is not somewhere in the future. Either it is now or never. To seek it is to miss it. If you want to find it, don't seek it. Just be herenow. And when I say just be herenow, don't make a desire out of it. Don't start asking how to be here and now. Don't start planning that "I have to work hard to be here and now." You have moved away; that "how" takes you away.

You are your real nature. This is the great declaration of Zen. Other religions say you have to find God. Zen says you are. Other religions say long is the journey. Zen says there is no question of any journey whatsoever. You are already there! Maybe fast asleep, snoring, but you are there. The goal is where you are. You are the goal, you are the target.

You want "to experience truth and to live it in the world". That's what you are already doing. Drinking tea you are living the truth. Talking to a friend you are living the truth. Going for a morning walk you are living the truth. Even being angry you are living the truth. How can it be otherwise?

The ordinary is the extraordinary, and the trivial is the profound. The *samsara* is nirvana.

It is just a question of remembering.

"...to become my real nature, to experience truth and to live it in the world". That's what you are doing, Gunakar. Just the mind goes on playing a game. The mind says things can be better. The mind says life can be improved upon. The mind says there must be something more, you must be missing something – seek, search, do something. This is greed, and the greed is so subtle that it can hide in millions of ways. It can even start trying not to be greedy. Now, listening to me, your mind will say, "Right. Now I am not to be greedy at all because it is greed that is destroying my life. So I have to get rid of greed." Again the greed has come, from the back door.

"It was deep in the woods back yonder," began old Herman, the guide. "I was plodding along minding my own business when suddenly a huge bear sneaked up behind me. He pinned my arms to my sides and started to squeeze the breath out of me. My gun fell out of my hands. First thing you know, the bear had stooped down, picked up the gun, and was pressing it against my back."

"What did you do?" gasped the tenderfoot.

Old Herman sighed. "What could I do? I married his daughter."

But the bear or the daughter, it makes no difference. It is the same.

Just be aware of the ways of the greed. Don't try to get rid of it. Don't try to do anything. Just be aware of how greed takes a thousand and one forms. Watch it. There is no hurry.

And you are not losing anything. You are living the truth. You cannot lose, in the very nature of things. We are all winners. Here nobody can be a loser. God has managed the world in such a way. That's why mystics say this is the most perfect world. God has managed it in such a way that everybody is a winner, nobody is a loser. Everybody is a victor, nobody is ever defeated. Even in your defeat there is victory, and even when you think you are lost you are not lost. It is all dream. The day you become awake you will find you have never been outside your home, you have always been there.

The only thing is to become more and more alert. Just watch. You see greed arising in one way, watch it. Don't try to stop it; otherwise it will arise in another way. It may choose just the opposite so it can deceive you. Don't do anything to it; otherwise it will find another way. No need to fight with it. Just watch it, let it be there. Watch it. See it naked, through and through.

Awareness functions like an X-ray. It sees things through and through, and in that very seeing there is freedom. If you have seen the greed totally, in that very seeing greed disappears. Not that you make it disappear. It disappears. In that vision it is not found. In that light that darkness is no more there. Suddenly you are free of greed.

And when you are free of greed you know you have never left the home, you have always been there. You have never left

God. Adam has never been expelled from the garden of Eden. He still lives there; he just dreams that he has been expelled. This is the Zen interpretation of the biblical story.

I must have given you a thousand interpretations about the story. The story is so beautiful. Zen says Adam is still living in the garden of Eden. The snake has not tricked him into sin. The snake has only tricked him into a dream. And God has not expelled him. How can God expel you? And to where can he expel you? It is all his garden. Where will you be? Wherever you will be it will be his garden, so to where can he expel you? And how can God expel? Expelling Adam, God will be expelling himself, a part of himself. He will fall into parts. No, it is not possible.

Then what has happened? Adam has fallen asleep. Eating the fruit of the tree of knowledge, Adam has fallen asleep and is dreaming that God is very angry. It is his own dream. It is his own idea. It is his own guilt. It is his own mind, that "I have broken the rule," that "I had promised, and I have broken my promise." Now he is trembling and feeling guilty, and in the sleep the guilt is creating a dream that God is very angry. He is projecting his guilt on God. His guilt is becoming God's anger, in his mind. Naturally God must be very angry, and he is expelling him, and he has expelled him. The gates are closed, and Adam is thrown into the world.

But it is just a dream. The moment Adam becomes awake, he will laugh. He will have an uproarious laugh. He will roll down on the ground. His belly will start bursting with the laughter because he will see the whole absurdity of it: he had never been out.

Have you not dreamed dreams like this? In a dream you are being killed, and in that moment when you are being murdered, can you doubt it? It is so real. You shriek, you scream, and because of the shriek and the scream you become alert, you become aware. The dream is broken. Even after the dream your heart is beating louder, your breath is not in rhythm, your hands are shaking. You know now it was a dream, a nightmare, you are sitting in your bed and there is nobody, just your poor wife sleeping by your side – no murderer – the doors are closed, everything is silent, there has been nobody in the room, nobody was murdering you; but still you are trembling. The fear has been so deeply there, the idea of murder has penetrated so deeply in you, that even when you are awake, a little smoke of it continues to be there. But now you know you have never been out of the room and nobody is trying to murder you, there is nobody.

This is what I say to you. You are still in the garden of Eden. God has not expelled you. You have fallen asleep.

And the work of the master is to bring you back. Back, not from anywhere, but only from sleep. Back to awareness.

*Why do you talk only to your disciples? Why not to the masses?*

There is a beautiful Zen saying. Let that be the answer.

"I sing my songs to him who understands them. I drink my wine with the friend who knows me well."

*It all sounds so great, as perfect as can be articulated. But what the hell do you do in the meantime?*

You have missed. You have not understood what has been said to you. You have not heard. Again the greed has become a barrier. Listening to me you are listening through the greed.

When you listen to me, if I am talking about enlightenment and the joy of it, you become greedy. You start thinking, "When am I going to become enlightened?" So you say it is great – it all sounds great, "as perfect as can be articulated". Now, this greed creates a problem. You put whatsoever I am saying as a goal. Of course, the goal is far away. There is a distance between you and the goal, and the distance has to be traveled, so the second question arises: "What the hell do you do in the meantime?"

But there is no meantime. I am not talking about the goal; I am talking about the way. And I am not saying anything about the future or afterlife; I am saying something about *this* moment, this very moment! This is it! You think in terms of tomorrow. I am talking about today.

Jesus says to his disciples, "Look in the field. Look at the beautiful lilies. They don't think of the morrow, they toil not, they labor not. Look at these beautiful flowers. They are just herenow. Even Solomon attired in all his costly clothes was not so beautiful. Look at these lilies in the field."

I am talking about *this* moment. What do you mean by "meantime"? There is no meantime. This is it! These birds, this cuckoo, these trees, you and me: this moment. This is the moment of nirvana.

But you start thinking in terms of desire. You say, "It sounds great." In fact, a thing that could have released your celebration becomes a desire, and through desire you start feeling sad because the goal is far away.

The cuckoo is singing right now. And the trees have flowered right now. It is all beautiful this moment. It will never be more beautiful. It has never been less beautiful. Each moment is perfect. But you start thinking about the tomorrow. Then the whole glory is there, somewhere away from you, and here you are a miserable creature, crying and weeping for the goal.

You create the meantime. I am not talking about the meantime. I am not talking about time at all, so what to say about meantime? I am talking about the eternal moment, about eternity. You bring time in. The mind always brings time in. Time is a mind faculty.

The mind cannot be herenow. The mind says, "Right. Hoard this, whatsoever Osho is saying. Hoard it. Someday we are going to practice it, and one day we are going to attain to this buddhahood. It sounds great." Then the misery, then the sadness. Then you will remain miserable your whole life. This buddhahood will never happen, because you missed it in the first place.

You have become so miserable that you cannot trust me that the celebration is possible right now. You say, "First one has to prepare. First one has to become this and that. First one has to meditate. First one has to become a great saint. First one has to become virtuous." This is something which from the very childhood has been deeply conditioned on your mind.

The parents, the teachers, the schools, the universities, the priest, the politician, they all have been teaching you, "Get ready. Get ready; something is going to happen." And then you go on getting ready – and one day you simply die, just getting ready. It never happens. When you were a child they were saying, "Wait, grow up, first be educated. Go to the university, come back home." Thrilled, you go to the university and you suffer all sorts of tortures there, in the hope that it is not going to last forever, in the hope that now you are getting ready. You don't know what for, what you are getting ready for.

To listen to this cuckoo singing? To watch a bird on the wing? To see a full moon in the night? To hold a friend's hand? To love? For what? Because all this is available right now.

You go to the university, you go through a thousand and one imprisonments; by the time you come back home you are destroyed. It is very rare; very fortunate people come back from the university without being destroyed by the education system.

Then they come home. Then the father says, "Now find a job – and get ready. Get married, and get ready. Then everything is going to be beautiful." And you read the novels and you go to the movie and you see the film, and once the marriage happens, the story says, "Ever afterwards they lived in happiness." Have you ever seen anybody living after marriage and happy? But these stories circulate, they condition the mind: Get ready.

So one day you find a job. Another humiliation. One day you get married. Another distraction from the moment. And so on, so forth. Then you go on missing, it is not happening, so somebody says, "How can you have it unless you have a child?" Right. So get ready, have a child. And so on, so forth.

Finally you recognize the fact that the whole life has been a wastage.

I am not saying don't go to the university, and I am not saying don't get married, I am not saying don't get a job. Please, don't misunderstand me. What I am saying is: For happiness don't get ready, it is already here. Go to the university. Enjoy. Have a job, but enjoy it. It is not going to lead to happiness. Each moment is an end unto itself; it is not to be converted into a means towards something else. Love, and enjoy love. Don't think that you will be happy while you are married. Get married, and *be* happy. Don't think that when you will have a child and you will become a mother or a father then you will be happy. Have you not seen your mother and your father? So what are you hoping for? And don't wait and don't go on postponing.

The greatest calamity that has happened to humanity is postponement – always postponing. There are people who are always looking at the timetable and thinking about where to go on the holidays, what trains to catch and what planes to go by, this place or that, to the Himalayas or to the Alps, to Kashmir or to Switzerland. And they are always preparing and preparing, and they never go. What will you say about these people? You will think they are mad. They have all the guidebooks and all the maps of the world and all the literature that government information services go on publishing. They have a whole library, and they go on looking into it and they go on preparing, but they always prepare and they never go. What will you think about them? Will you not call them neurotic?

This is what the situation is with everybody. You always talk about God, you always talk about *moksha*, nirvana, heaven, paradise, you always talk about it, but it is always tomorrow. So you have to prepare. "Meantime" you prepare.

I am saying there is no meantime. God is available right now, just for the asking.

Start enjoying. Don't ask how to dance! Start dancing. Can't you move your body? It may not be very graceful. So who bothers? It may not be a trained, disciplined thing. So who bothers? Start dancing. Don't go on consulting manuals about love. Start loving. Don't go on and on in the mind. Start moving into existence, be existential. That is the message of Zen.

*Osho, are you really crazy?*

How can I be crazy? I have no mind out of which to go.

*As sin can be defined as "missing the mark," could one define Zen as "hitting the mark"?*

No. Sin means missing the mark. Zen means there is no mark to miss. There is nothing, no target. There is no destiny. It is all beautiful purposelessness. It is all beautiful meaninglessness. It is a song. It has no meaning. It has a rhythm, but no meaning. It has tremendous beauty in it, but no logic. And it is not a syllogism; there is no conclusion. It is an unconcluded existence, and it remains always unconcluded.

We are always in the middle. There has been no source, and there is no goal.

Sin exactly means missing the mark. That's why Zen people don't talk about sin. Christians talk about sin, because they think God has to be achieved, heaven has to be achieved, there is some goal. If you miss that goal, that is what is called sin; sin means missing the goal. Zen people don't talk about sin. The word "sin" exists not for them, because there is no goal to miss. You are already at it! The arrow has reached, the arrow has always been there, not for a single moment has it been otherwise. Zen is so profound. It gives you utter freedom to be. It does not yoke you to some ideology and doesn't yoke you into some guilt.

The moment you talk about sin, guilt arises. The moment you start thinking you are missing the mark, tension arises, anxiety arises, anguish arises: "So how not to miss?" Then there is great trembling, and then the fear you may go on missing. Who knows? – for so long you have been missing. So who knows, you may go on missing. You may go astray.

Christianity talks in terms of duality. You are separate from God, so you can miss him, you can move in a wrong direction, you can go astray. Zen is non-dual. It says you are in God, you cannot go astray. See the beauty of it. See the great declaration. See the declaration of freedom – utter freedom.

Freedom from the goal is utter freedom because the goal keeps you tied together in a direction. Zen has no direction. When you have a direction to move in, you will have to choose where to go. And the fear will always remain, whether you are going in the right direction or not. Who knows? – even your leader may be wrong. The one who is leading you may himself be misguided or may be a cheat. Who knows? And if you come close to your priest and your leader, you will become more suspicious.

Gurdjieff used to say that if you want to get rid of religion, live near the priests. Then you will get rid of religion because you will see they are trembling as much as you are trembling. Their public faces are different, their private faces are different. Live close to a priest, and you will be surprised. He is as much in the dark as anybody else. He just pretends. He is as blind as anybody else, but he goes to the masses and pretends to the blind people that "I have eyes."

And all religions depend on priests. Why don't the priests say the truth? They cannot, because their whole trade depends on one secret, that they have to go on pretending that they have eyes. That pretension is very basic to the trade of the priest.

And one priest may fight against another priest – the Hindu priest may say something against Christianity and the Christian priest may say something about Hinduism – but they never say anything against priesthood. Never.

I have heard a beautiful anecdote. Meditate over it.

The little island in the South Pacific was in an uproar when the American missionary visited the chief of the tribe. "What is the commotion?" demanded the missionary.

"There is a white baby born in the village," replied the savage, "and you know we don't like no man messing around with our women. Since you is the only white man on the island they is fixing to fry you alive."

The missionary was in a state of nervous collapse when he spied a flock of sheep on the hillside behind the village. Turning to the chief he cried, "Look there on the hillside, chief, you see that flock of white sheep?"

"I sure do," replied the chief.

"Well," said the missionary. "Do you see the black sheep in the middle of the flock?"

"I see it," responded the chief.

"There is no other black sheep and there never has been, has there?"

"Well?"

"Well."

The chief beckoned the missionary aside and whispered in his ear, "You not tell, me not tell."

This is how it goes on. They have to protect each other. They may fight about dogmas, they may fight about principles, philosophies, that is all okay. But they never say anything against the priesthood. The Shankaracharya of Puri will be as much in favor of the priesthood as the Vatican Pope. There will be no problem about that, no conflict about that. If priesthood is at stake, they will all fight for it.

When Buddha declared these ultimate truths in India, there were many religions in India. They all went against him. Not only Hindus, Jainas were against him. Not only Jainas, Ajivakas were against him. And so many others. Why? Whenever a real man is there, all priests will be against him because the real man will bring the message to you that you are being led by blind people: they don't know; you don't know. The blind are leading the blind.

Zen says there is no need to be led by anybody, because there is nowhere to go. This is cutting the very root of priesthood. Look at it. This is destroying priesthood totally. Zen does not say that one priest is right and another is wrong. If it is said that way, then priesthood is still protected. Zen says there is nowhere to go.

A man came to Nansen and asked, "What do you say? Is Zen the right way to achieve God?" Nansen said, "Zen is not a way at all, it is not a path, because a path leads somewhere. We don't lead. A path reaches somewhere. We don't lead you anywhere. We simply throw you to where you are. We simply throw you back to yourself."

If it is a path, then leaders will be there. If something has to be done, then you will find people mediating between you and God, between you and reality. Nothing has to be done, so nobody has to show and guide you. You alone are enough.

Zen is not "hitting the mark". Zen is knowing that there is no mark and nowhere to hit, that you are the target, and the arrow has always been in the target.

You must have heard the great Tibetan mantra *"aum mane*

*padme hum.*" It has many meanings. One meaning is "Look! The arrow is already in the target." *Aum* is just a shout, so that you can look; it is almost "See!" "Look!" – "Aum! mane padme hum." Literally it means "jewel in the lotus", "mane padme hum." Jewel in the lotus. Literally it means "Look! The jewel is already in the lotus." Metaphorically it means "Look! The arrow has already reached the target."

You are at home already, so it is not "hitting the mark," because "hitting the mark" will again be the same thing. Then you will ask, "How to hit it?" Then one has to learn archery, then one has to go through discipline, and then the whole priesthood comes in from the back door.

I have heard:

One summer's day when a man in a rowing boat caught a cramp and fell into the water – it was an ornamental lake – arms and legs wildly flailing, he screamed, "Help, Help! I can't swim!" Finally a bystander shouted back, "Stand up, you bloody fool!" The drowning man did so – and found that the water just came up to his waist.

But he was thinking he was drowning. The water just came up to his waist.

You are not drowning. Just stand up!

I have heard another story. A traveler lost his track one night in the hills. It was a dark night, and he was very much afraid. The hills were very tricky and dangerous and the track was very narrow, and he was afraid he could miss a step and could disappear forever in the valley. He could fall into any abyss; they were all around. So he was just creeping on his hands. Still he fell, he slipped. He caught hold in time of the roots of a tree. Now, he was very much afraid. He tried hard somehow to get out of that hole he was hanging in, but he could not. And it was getting colder and colder and his hands started becoming frozen, and now he was certain that it was a question of minutes. Once the hands are too cold, he would not be able to hold onto the roots, and he would die. That became certain. Now there was no way to escape.

He started crying and weeping, and he started praying, and

he had never been a theist, but in such moments nobody bothers about principles. He started saying to God, "Save me," this and that, and "I will not do this sin or that sin, and I will be straight now; I will not drink and I will not smoke," and all sorts of things he was promising. But no help came, and by and by his hands started slipping, and a moment came when he thought, "Now it is finished." And he fell.

And to his surprise, he was standing on his feet. There was no abyss there; it was just plain ground. For hours he was hanging between life and death.

Once you stop planning, you will suddenly be on plain ground. Once you stop thinking about the target and how to hit it, you will be at home. Zen says drop all ways, because all ways lead astray, because to God there is no need of any way. He is there in your heart. It is he who is listening to me, it is he who is talking to you. It is he who is breathing in you, it is he who is beating in your heart. God is not far away. God is not even outside. God is the innermost core of you.

So drop this sin-oriented idea of hitting or missing. Both are in the same category; both will create anxiety.

My whole effort here is to make you free of anxiety, free of guilt. Free of guilt, free of anxiety, you are a saint, because you are innocent then, you are a child again. You are born again.

*You confused me very much by saying that the samsara is the nirvana. Now, from where to begin?*

There is no need to begin. I am not sending you on a journey. Not even the first step is needed. Take the step, and you have moved in the wrong direction. It is not that any direction is wrong; all directions are wrong. Movement is wrong. It is not that a few people go astray and a few don't, no. All going is going astray.

Let this sink in your heart as deeply as possible.

When I say the world is *samsara*, I mean don't divide into the profane and the profound. Live the profound in a profound way, live the profane in a profound way. Don't divide into the material and the spiritual. Live the material in a spiritual way; bring the quality of the spirit to matter.

What do I mean when I say live in the ordinary world? I mean live the profane life in a new way, with a new being, with a new style, with a new flavor, the flavor of meditation.

I am not telling you to go away anywhere.

I am for God, but I am not against anything. And God, my God, is so vast, he includes all.

Yes, you can sip your tea in such a meditative way that it becomes prayer. Try it. You can love your woman in such a meditative way that love becomes ecstasy, that when you are lost with your woman or with your man, suddenly you are lost in God. Those moments become of tremendous value. Those moments become the first glimpses of divinity.

Start living your ordinary life in an extraordinary way. What is the extraordinary way? To bring awareness. Whatsoever you do, let it be soaked in awareness, let it be showered with awareness.

*What is maturity? How can I be mature?*

You will have to understand first what immaturity is. That will give you the idea of what maturity is. Immaturity has a few ingredients in it. One, immaturity is a sort of dependence. A child depends on the parents; he is immature. If you are still depending, you are immature. You may depend on God or you may depend on me, but it is immaturity. You are still seeking your parents. Maybe your parents are gone and lost; now you are projecting your parents.

There are many people who come to me and I can see immediately in their eyes they are searching for their father. It is not accidental that the pope is called the pope. "Pope" means "papa". People are looking for a divine daddy, continuously. This is immaturity.

When are you going to stand on your own feet? How long are you going to remain a dependent on the mother, on the father, on this and that?

These dependent people are very dangerous people because they can be exploited easily. Anybody who pretends to be their father, they will become victims to him. They will follow Adolf Hitler; the führer will become their father. The Germans used to call their country the "fatherland," others call their countries the "motherland," but it is all the same nonsense. We go on projecting. The country becomes the mother, the country becomes the father, or God the Father, or Kali the Mother. You go on projecting.

You want to remain a child; you don't want to grow. Growth is responsibility, and you don't want to take any responsibility.

People come to me and they say, "Osho, we surrender to you. Now you are responsible." How can I be responsible for you? Surrender can only mean that you have come to me to learn responsibility. Now you want to avoid responsibility. Surrendering to me can only be a way, a means, to learn to be responsible. But if you want surrender as a substitute for responsibility, your surrender is wrong, ill. It is not healthy, it is dangerous. And then you will start getting angry at me. If nothing is happening you will get angry. Because nothing is happening, you will think I am not doing anything.

Only you can do something. I can indicate, but the real thing is going to happen within you. Nobody else can do it. If I can do it, then I can undo it also. That will not be much of a gain. If Buddha can deliver you from your ignorance, then one day if he gets angry with you he will release all your ignorance again, back to you. That will not be of much use. Freedom is possible only when you learn responsibility, when you start standing on your own feet.

Of course, one feels very helpless. So what? It is how life is. That helplessness is not bad. It teaches you that ego is wrong, that you have to be humble, helpless. And yet there is no other way to stand: you can stand only on your own feet. Nobody can take you on his shoulders to God. You will have to enter into divinity on your own.

So maturity has to be understood through understanding immaturity. First thing: we are taught to be dependent on the parents, on the leaders, on the priests. Nobody wants you to be free, because people are afraid, the society is afraid, of free people. Free people will be rebellious. Free people will start doing *their* thing, and the society is very much afraid of such people. The society wants you to do things that the society wants. The society wants you to follow a certain pattern. The society has its own goals; they have to be fulfilled. The society does not want you to become a Buddha or a Christ, because they have always been dangerous people. The society wants just zombies. And an immature person can easily become a zombie because he is an imitator.

Have you watched small children imitating, and by imitation they think they are becoming grown-ups? Small children start smoking. Not that they feel very good about smoking, not that it is great or anything. When a child starts smoking he cannot even believe why people smoke, because his eyes start getting red, his throat feels irritated, and he starts coughing, tears come down his cheeks. It is really painful, but he will tolerate the pain because the cigarette gives a certain feeling that he is a grown-up. Only grown-ups are allowed to smoke, so the smoking becomes a symbol of grown-upness.

I have heard:

A man walking down the street noticed a small boy about ten years old sitting on the front doorstep of a house, smoking a cigarette. "Aren't you a little young to be smoking?" he asked.

"Of course I ain't," replied the lad. "I got a girlfriend and all."

"A girlfriend!" said the man.

"Yeah, Picked her up last night, I did. Smashing it was."

"Good Lord! How old was she?"

"I dunno. I was too drunk to ask her."

There are symbols of grown-upness. You need to have a girlfriend, you have to smoke, you have to drink, and even small children start learning these tricks. And then they never grow up, They only imitate, They imitate other, false grownups. And their children will imitate them, and so on it goes.

This world is a world of imitators, monkeys all. And it does not make much difference – you can be a chairman of the board of monkeys, that doesn't make much difference; or you can be a president of a monkey country, that doesn't make any difference – all the same you remain the monkey. Maybe you are more monkeyish than others.

A grown-up person is one who does not imitate, who starts

feeling his own way, who starts being in his own way, who starts looking into his nature: "Who am I? And what *really* do I feel?"

One woman came home, driving, she got out of her car, and fell down flat on the ground. The husband rushed, asked, "What is the matter? What happened? Why did you faint?"

She said, "It was too hot."

The husband looked at the car and he said, "But why didn't you open the windows?"

She said, "What! Open the windows, and let the neighbors know that our car is not air conditioned?"

One can die but cannot allow the neighbors to know that the car is not air conditioned. She had to keep the windows closed. She was fainting, but that is okay, but to keep the windows open hurts much more.

Listen to your being. It is continuously giving you hints; it is a still, small voice. It does not shout at you, that is true. And if you are a little silent you will start feeling your way. Be the person you are. Never try to be another, and you will become mature. Maturity is accepting the responsibility of being oneself, whatsoever the cost. Risking all to be oneself, that's what maturity is all about.

If you imitate you will again and again fall into a ditch because whatsoever you imitate never fits reality. Reality is continuously changing, it is a flux, nothing is ever the same. It is a river; it goes on flowing.

If you imitate your father.... Just see, your father lived many years before. Your father was a child maybe thirty years before or forty years before. He learned things in a different world. For example, your father, when he was a child, was not sitting five hours glued to the chair before the TV. Now, you don't know how much the TV has done to the small children. The father does not know. His childhood was not at all influenced by the TV. Five hours sitting before a TV is no ordinary phenomenon.

In fact, before TV happened, down the centuries, people had never looked into a source of light for five hours continuously. Now the scientists say that the whole nervous system changes because of those five hours of looking directly into the source of light. The TV goes on throwing strong rays on your eyes. It has never happened before. Five hours is too much. Scientists say if you sit near a color TV, four feet away, you will get cancer, you will suffer from many diseases which your parents had not known, ever. The eyes are eighty per cent of your life. Five hours of just strong light rays reaching into your head – your sleep will be disturbed. If America suffers from insomnia, it is natural. The TV is one of the basic causes.

Ordinarily man has lived with light, natural light. In a primitive society, the sun rises, people rise, and the sun sets and people set, people go to sleep. A natural rhythm with light. Now we are living too much with the light; the eyes are not made for that much light. The inner nervous system is disturbed; it becomes too loaded.

And a thousand and one things will happen. In America a new phenomenon is happening. Many places it has happened, and people have become really worried about it, what to do? In one place a woman was murdered, and twenty persons were standing there, almost paralyzed, not doing anything. A psychological investigation was done. What is the matter? Twenty young, healthy people standing there, and a woman was killed just in front of them and they didn't do anything – they didn't even shout, they didn't call the police. What happened? And you will be surprised. The finding is that it is because these twenty people have lived on TV for too long.

On the TV screen murder happens so many times. What do you do? You don't do anything; you remain glued to your chair. They have become accustomed to it. It was another TV scene. They have lost track of reality. The TV has become more real. For five hours you are not with anything else – and a continuous bombardment of light, and strong light, and things are moving in your head. You become a watcher. They were standing there just glued to their spots, paralyzed – just watching. They could not do anything, because they are no more doers.

Now, your father, who had a different kind of childhood, will not be able to understand it. You are living in a different world, in a world which is more of TV watchers than of participants.

Whatsoever he says will not be fit for your world; hence the generation gap. The father speaks a different language, you speak a different language. You live in a different world, he lived in a different world. Now, those two worlds never coincide.

If you are an imitator you will always be taking false moves. You have to learn to live in *your* world; you have to respond to the reality that surrounds you. Things have changed dramatically. They have always been changing, but the change has been too fast in this century. And it will be faster and faster.

You have to become aware of the situation and respond accordingly.

An experienced plumber was giving instructions to his apprentice.

"Working in other people's homes," he said, "can sometimes lead to embarrassing situations, but you can always get out of them by using tact. For example, the other day, I walked into a bathroom and found a lady taking a bath. I backed out saying, 'Excuse me, sir.' In that way, the lady thought I had not gotten a good look at her and it was all right."

The following afternoon, the apprentice staggered into the office in a beat-up condition.

"What happened to you?" asked the boss.

"You and your tact," cried the apprentice. "I went to the bridal suite of the Etter Plaza Hotel to fix a faucet. I was halfway through the bedroom before I realized there was a couple making love in the bed. The husband cussed at me, but I remember what you had said, so I tipped my hat and said, 'Excuse me, gentlemen'!"

If you simply follow and you don't understand, you are immature. Never follow. Try to understand. Let understanding be your basic law of life. Let things come out of your understanding, not out of your memory.

The immature person functions through memory. Whenever there is a situation he looks into his memory, into his past, and finds a clue. The mature person looks into the situation, puts his past aside, because the past is irrelevant. He brings his total attention to the present situation and functions out of that totality. His action is in the present. The immature person is always living through his past; the immature person is always turning his future into his past. He is repetitive, he is parrotlike, he is a shadow, a reflection. He is not real.

When a party of tourists climbed to the top of a famous echoing mountain, they saw an old man, sitting on a rock, an enormous telescope in his hands. Every few moments he let out a series of shouts.

The puzzled tourists watched him for some time. Then one of them went up to the old man and asked, "Why do you keep looking through that thing and then calling out as if you were in pain?"

The old man answered impatiently, "Don't talk to me. You will distract my attention and I will lose my job. I am the echo for this hill."

Many people have become just echoes. Watch yourself when something happens and you react. Are you reacting the same way as your father used to react in such a situation? Are you saying the same thing as your mother would have said if she were in this situation? Are your gestures the same as your teacher's in the school you loved so much? Just watch – your gestures, your words, your actions – and you will be surprised. Ninety-nine per cent they are just echoes, they are not true.

How can you be fulfilled with such echoes?

Your father is living through you, not you. Your parents are living through you, not you. Your parents' parents are living through you, not you. The whole of humanity and its past is living through you, but not you. This is immaturity.

Maturity means you discontinue with your past. With one stroke of the sword you become discontinuous with your past and your heritage and the tradition, and you start living independently. The gesture is yours; then it is meaningful, then it is full of significance, then it is not an empty gesture. The words are yours, not borrowed, not somebody else's; then your life becomes more and more authentic and real.

To live in immaturity is to live in a kind of dream. It is a shadow world. Your eyes are so full of fog, you don't have clarity.

A frustrated young man went to see his doctor.

"Doc," he explained, "every night I have the strangest dreams. Beautiful blondes, brunettes, and redheads appear, and one by one they try to kiss me and put their arms around me."

"So?" answered the doctor.

"So nothing, Doc. I keep pushing them away – every one of them."

"What would you like me to do?"

"Doc, please," pleaded the patient, "break my arms."

People are living in their dreams. They are ready to break their real arms for their unreal dreams.

Watch! You will find many times the same happening in your life. You are ready to kill your reality for some unreal ideal, some utopia, some ideology, some scripture. Somebody insults the Bible. Are you ready to fight? Then you are a fool. Somebody says something against Ram, and you are Hindu and you are ready to be killed or kill. Then you are a fool. Then you are living in shadows and you have become too attached to shadows.

In fact, a really alert man will not feel offended even if somebody insults him personally. Even if somebody says something against his name, he will not feel offended, because he will know, "I am not my name. The name is just an appendage, a label – useful, but not real, just a make-believe. Any other name would be the same." He will not feel offended.

A really alert man, even if you hit his body, will not feel offended, because he will know he is not the body. He will know he is not his mind. He will know that he is something transcendental, and he will remain in that transcendentalness. In that transcendence is his being.

Then life will have a totally new quality and it will become a new experience. That experience is divine. Maturity is the door to divinity. Immature, you remain asleep. Mature, you become awake.

The question is from Prem Anam. He has many things which are immature in him. His question is relevant, relevant to his being, and it is good that he has asked.

Now, Anam, watch, become more careful. Drop your childishness more and more.

I say again and again, I quote again and again, Jesus' saying that "Unless you are like a child, you will not enter into my kingdom of God." But remember, he does not mean childishness. Childishness is just the opposite of being *like* a child. A childish person is never like a child. He pretends to be a grown-up; he is a pretender. A childlike person is one who has become so mature, so alive, so aware, that he drops all pretensions. He is nude and naked, he is true, he is innocent.

Drop childishness, and become a child; and you will be mature. And you will be ready, ready to take the jump into yourself.

*I seem to be more interested in helping others reach enlightenment than reaching it myself; having grasped it intellectually. I lose no opportunity of talking about it. The ease, the joy, the peace, and the energy that I feel make me believe that I am on the right track. But am I? Or should I better be silent till...?*

The question is from Ajit Saraswati.

For Ajit Saraswati it is perfectly right. He can continue. But remember, I am saying so only to him, not to anybody else. It is a very personal question.

He has nothing of the ego. He can go on. In fact, this too is part of his humbleness, that he has asked.

It is good to help others, because there is nobody really who is other. Helping others, you are helping yourself because we are parts of each other, members of one another. We are joined together. If I help you to be happy, I become happy. If I help you to be miserable, I become miserable. Our life is together here; it is a togetherness; we are not separate. On the periphery we may be separate; at the center we are one.

Nothing to be worried about. If you have the feeling that you enjoy sharing whatsoever you have understood, howsoever little it is, if you have the feeling that you enjoy, you feel blissful, you feel joyful – and no ego arises out of it.... Let that be the criterion: if ego arises out of it, then you are not helping others, and you are destroying yourself meanwhile. If no ego arises – you simply feel peaceful and silent and happy that you shared something with somebody, a grace descends on you – then you are perfectly right. Then go on the housetops and shout. When you have, share it.

And there is no need to wait, that when you have the whole of it, then you will share it. Then you will not have the whole, ever. Share it, and you will get more. Give it, and you will get more.

But remember only one thing: the ego should not enter in. The moment you see ego arising, the moment you see you are feeling great, superior to others, holier than others, then something is going wrong. Then it is better to wait. You are not to wait for the whole of God to happen to you, but you are to wait for the whole of the ego to go.

With Ajit Saraswati, it is already the case. The ego is not there. Slowly, slowly that rock has disappeared. I have been falling on him like a waterfall. Yes, the ego was there one day. And the water is very soft, so the rock never feels worried, but the water goes on falling, goes on falling, goes on falling, and by and by, unaware what is happening, the rock slowly, slowly disappears, becomes sand, and is taken far away.

The rock was there, but is not there. So enjoy it, delight in it, rejoice, share.

*Osho, can you give me two very fundamental rules for the seekers?*

Here are two ancient rules, very ancient:
First, that you must be like a man who has been bitten by a snake and knows he has not a moment to lose.
And second, that you must be like a man who has awakened

to find that his horse has been stolen and it is too late to lock the door and there is no hurry.

*Osho, what is the first principle?*

If I were to tell you, it would become the second principle.

# ABOUT OSHO

Osho defies categorization, reflecting everything from the individual quest for meaning to the most urgent social and political issues facing society today. His books are not written but are transcribed from recordings of extemporaneous talks given over a period of thirty-five years. Osho has been described by the *Sunday Times* in London as one of the "1000 Makers of the 20th Century" and by *Sunday Mid-Day* in India as one of the ten people – along with Gandhi, Nehru and Buddha – who have changed the destiny of India.

Osho has a stated aim of helping to create the conditions for the birth of a new kind of human being, characterized as "Zorba the Buddha" – one whose feet are firmly on the ground, yet whose hands can touch the stars. Running like a thread through all aspects of Osho is a vision that encompasses both the timeless wisdom of the East and the highest potential of Western science and technology.

He is synonymous with a revolutionary contribution to the science of inner transformation and an approach to meditation which specifically addresses the accelerated pace of contemporary life. The unique Osho Active Meditations™ are designed to allow the release of accumulated stress in the body and mind so that it is easier to be still and experience the thought-free state of meditation.

## Osho International Meditation Resort

Osho International Meditation Resort has been created so that people can have a direct experience of a new way of living – with more alertness, relaxation, and humor. It is located about 100 miles southeast of Mumbai in Pune, India, on 40 acres in the tree-lined residential area of Koregaon Park. The resort offers a variety of programs to the thousands of people who visit each year from more than 100 countries. Accommodation for visitors is available on-campus in the new Osho Guesthouse.

The Multiversity programs at the meditation resort take place in a pyramid complex next to the famous Zen garden park, Osho Teerth. The programs are designed to provide the transformation tools that give people access to a new lifestyle – one of relaxed awareness – which is an approach they can take with them into their everyday lives. Self-discovery classes, sessions, courses and meditative processes are offered throughout the year. For exercising the body and keeping fit, there is a beautiful outdoor facility where one can experiment with a Zen approach to sports and recreation.

In the main meditation auditorium the daily schedule from 6:00 A.M. up to 11:00 P.M. includes both active and passive meditation methods. Following the daily evening meeting meditation, the nightlife in this multicultural resort is alive with outdoor eating areas that fill with friends and often with dancing.

The resort has its own supply of safe, filtered drinking water and the food served is made with organically grown produce from the resort's own farm.

An online tour of the meditation resort, as well as travel and program information, can be found at: www.osho.com

This is a comprehensive website in different languages with an online magazine, audio and video webcasting, an Audiobook Club, the complete English and Hindi archive of Osho talks and a complete catalog of all Osho publications including books, audio and video. Includes information about the active meditation techniques developed by Osho, most with streaming video demonstrations.

The daily meditation schedule includes:

Osho Dynamic Meditation™: A technique designed to release tensions and repressed emotions, opening the way to a new vitality and an experience of profound silence.

Osho Kundalini Meditation™: A technique of shaking free one's dormant energies, and through spontaneous dance and silent sitting, allowing these energies to be redirected inward.

Osho Nadabrahma Meditation™: A method of harmonizing one's energy flow, based on an ancient Tibetan humming technique.

Osho Nataraj Meditation™: A method involving the inner alchemy of dancing so totally that the dancer disappears and only the dance remains.

Vipassana Meditation: A technique originating with Gautam Buddha and now updated for the 21$^{st}$ Century, for dissolving mental chatter through the awareness of breath.

No Dimensions Meditation™: A powerful method for centering one's energy, based on a Sufi technique.

Osho Gourishankar Meditation™: A one-hour nighttime meditation, which includes a breathing technique, gazing softly at a light and gentle body movements.

# Books by Osho in English Language

**Early Discourses and Writings**
A Cup of Tea
Dimensions Beyond The Known
From Sex to Super-consciousness
The Great Challenge
Hidden Mysteries
I Am The Gate
The Inner Journey
Psychology of the Esoteric
Seeds of Wisdom

**Meditation**
The Voice of Silence
And Now and Here (Vol 1 & 2)
In Search of the Miraculous (Vol 1 &.2)
Meditation: The Art of Ecstasy
Meditation: The First and Last Freedom
The Path of Meditation
The Perfect Way
Yaa-Hoo! The Mystic Rose

**Buddha and Buddhist Masters**
The Book of Wisdom
The Dhammapada: The Way of the Buddha (Vol 1-12)
The Diamond Sutra
The Discipline of Transcendence (Vol 1-4)
The Heart Sutra

**Indian Mystics**
Enlightenment: The Only Revolution (Ashtavakra)
Showering Without Clouds (Sahajo)
The Last Morning Star (Daya)
The Song of Ecstasy (Adi Shankara)

## Baul Mystics
The Beloved (Vol 1 & 2)
Kabir
The Divine Melody
Ecstasy: The Forgotten Language
The Fish in the Sea is Not Thirsty
The Great Secret
The Guest
The Path of Love
The Revolution

## Jesus and Christian Mystics
Come Follow to You (Vol 1-4)
I Say Unto You (Vol 1 & 2)
The Mustard Seed
Theologia Mystica

## Jewish Mystics
The Art of Dying
The True Sage

## Western Mystics
Guida Spirituale (Desiderata)
The Hidden Harmony (Heraclitus)
The Messiah (Vol 1 & 2) (Commentaries on Khalil Gibran's The Prophet)
The New Alchemy: To Turn You On (Commentaries on Mabel Collins' Light on the Path)
Philosophia Perennis (Vol 1 & 2) (The Golden Verses of Pythagoras)
Zarathustra: A God That Can Dance
Zarathustra: The Laughing Prophet (Commentaries on Nietzsche's Thus Spake Zarathustra)

## Sufism
Just Like That
Journey to the Heart
The Perfect Master (Vol 1 & 2)

The Secret
Sufis: The People of the Path (Vol 1 & 2)
Unio Mystica (Vol 1 & 2)
The Wisdom of the Sands (Vol 1 & 2)

Tantra
Tantra: The Supreme Understanding
The Tantra Experience
 The Royal Song of Saraha
 (same as Tantra Vision, Vol 1)
The Tantric Transformation
 The Royal Song of Saraha
 (same as Tantra Vision, Vol 2)
The Book of Secrets: Vigyan Bhairav Tantra

**The Upanishads**
Behind a Thousand Names
(Nirvana Upanishad)
Heartbeat of the Absolute
(Ishavasya Upanishad)
I Am That (Isa Upanishad)
The Message Beyond Words
(Kathopanishad)
Philosophia Ultima (Mandukya Upanishad)
The Supreme Doctrine (Kenopanishad)
Finger Pointing to the Moon
(Adhyatma Upanishad)
That Art Thou (Sarvasar Upanishad, Kaivalya Upanishad, Adhyatma Upanishad)
The Ultimate Alchemy, Vol 1&2
 (Atma Pooja Upanishad Vol 1 & 2)
Vedanta: Seven Steps to Samadhi (Akshaya Upanishad)
Flight of the Alone to the Alone
(Kaivalya Upanishad)

**Tao**
The Empty Boat
The Secret of Secrets
Tao:The Golden Gate (Vol 1&2)

Tao:The Pathless Path (Vol 1&2)
Tao: The Three Treasures (Vol 1-4)
When the Shoe Fits

**Yoga**
The Path of Yoga (previously Yoga: The Alpha and the Omega Vol 1)
Yoga: The Alpha and the Omega (Vol 2-10)

**Zen and Zen Masters**
Ah, This!
Ancient Music in the Pines
And the Flowers Showered
A Bird on the Wing
Bodhidharma: The Greatest Zen Master
Communism and Zen Fire, Zen Wind
Dang Dang Doko Dang
The First Principle
God is Dead: Now Zen is the Only Living Truth
The Grass Grows By Itself
The Great Zen Master Ta Hui
Hsin Hsin Ming: The Book of Nothing
I Celebrate Myself: God is No Where, Life is Now Here
Kyozan: A True Man of Zen
Nirvana: The Last Nightmare
No Mind: The Flowers of Eternity
No Water, No Moon
One Seed Makes the Whole Earth Green
Returning to the Source
The Search: Talks on the 10 Bulls of Zen
A Sudden Clash of Thunder
The Sun Rises in the Evening
Take it Easy (Vol 1 & 2 )
This Very Body the Buddha
Walking in Zen, Sitting in Zen
The White Lotus
Yakusan: Straight to the Point of Enlightenment
Zen Manifesto : Freedom From Oneself
Zen: The Mystery and the Poetry of the Beyond

Zen: The Path of Paradox (Vol 1, 2 & 3)
Zen: The Special Transmission
Zen Boxed Sets
The World of Zen (5 vol.)
Live Zen
This. This. A Thousand Times This
Zen: The Diamond Thunderbolt
Zen: The Quantum Leap from Mind to No-Mind

**Zen: The Solitary Bird, Cuckoo**
of the Forest
Zen: All The Colors Of The Rainbow (5 vol.)
The Buddha: The Emptiness of the Heart
The Language of Existence
The Miracle
The Original Man
Turning In

**Osho: On the Ancient Masters of Zen** (7 volumes)*
Dogen: The Zen Master
Hyakujo: The Everest of Zen–
With Basho's haikus
Isan: No Footprints in the Blue Sky
Joshu: The Lion's Roar
Ma Tzu: The Empty Mirror
Nansen: The Point Of Departure
Rinzai: Master of the Irrational
*Each volume is also available individually.

**Responses to Questions**
Be Still and Know
Come, Come, Yet Again Come
The Goose is Out
The Great Pilgrimage: From Here to Here
The Invitation
My Way: The Way of the White Clouds
Nowhere to Go But In
The Razor's Edge
Walk Without Feet, Fly Without Wings and Think Without Mind

The Wild Geese and the Water
Zen: Zest, Zip, Zap and Zing

**Talks in America**
From Bondage To Freedom
From Darkness to Light
From Death To Deathlessness
From the False to the Truth
From Unconsciousness to Consciousness
The Rajneesh Bible (Vol 2-4)

**The World Tour**
Beyond Enlightenment (Talks in Bombay)
Beyond Psychology (Talks in Uruguay)
Light on the Path (Talks in the Himalayas)
The Path of the Mystic (Talks in Uruguay)
Sermons in Stones (Talks in Bombay)
Socrates Poisoned Again After 25 Centuries (Talks in Greece)
The Sword and the Lotus
(Talks in the Himalayas)
The Transmission of the Lamp
(Talks in Uruguay)

**Osho's Vision for the World**
The Golden Future
The Hidden Splendor
The New Dawn
The Rebel
The Rebellious Spirit

**The Mantra Series**
Hari Om Tat Sat
Om Mani Padme Hum
Om Shantih Shantih Shantih
Sat-Chit-Anand
Satyam-Shivam-Sundram

**Personal Glimpses**
Books I Have Loved

Glimpses of a Golden Childhood
Notes of a Madman

**Interviews with the World Press**
The Last Testament (Vol 1)

**Intimate Talks between**
Master and Disciple – Darshan Diaries
A Rose is a Rose is a Rose
Be Realistic: Plan for a Miracle
Believing the Impossible Before Breakfast
Beloved of My Heart
Blessed are the Ignorant
Dance Your Way to God
Don't Just Do Something, Sit There
Far Beyond the Stars
For Madmen Only
The Further Shore
Get Out of Your Own Way
God's Got A Thing about You
God is Not for Sale
The Great Nothing
Hallelujah!
Let Go!
The 99 Names of Nothingness
No Book, No Buddha, No Teaching, No Disciple
Nothing to Lose but Your Head
Only Losers Can Win in This Game
Open Door
Open Secret
The Shadow of the Whip
The Sound of One Hand Clapping
The Sun Behind the Sun Behind the Sun
The Tongue-Tip Taste of Tao
This Is It
Turn On, Tune In and Drop the Lot
What Is, Is, What Ain't, Ain't
Won't You Join The Dance?

## Compilations
After Middle Age: A Limitless Sky
At the Feet of the Master
Bhagwan Shree Rajneesh: On Basic Human Rights
Jesus Crucified Again, This Time in Ronald Reagan's America
Priests and Politicians: The Mafia of the Soul
Take it Really Seriously

## Gift Books of Osho Quotations
A Must for Contemplation Before Sleep
A Must for Morning

## Contemplation
India My Love

## Photobooks
Shree Rajneesh: A Man of Many Climates, Seasons and Rainbows
through the eye of the camera
Impressions... Osho Commune International Photobook

## Books about Osho
Bhagwan: The Buddha for the Future by Juliet Forman
Bhagwan Shree Rajneesh: The Most Dangerous Man Since Jesus Christ by Sue Appleton

Bhagwan: The Most Godless Yet the Most Godly Man by Dr. George Meredith
Bhagwan: One Man Against the Whole Ugly Past of Humanity by Juliet Forman
Bhagwan: Twelve Days That Shook the World by Juliet Forman
Was Bhagwan Shree Rajneesh Poisoned by Ronald Reagan's America? by Sue Appleton.
Diamond Days With Osho
by Ma Prem Shunyo

Books by Osho in English Language

*For any information about Osho Books & Audio/Video Tapes please contact:*

**OSHO Multimedia &Resorts Pvt. Ltd.**

17 Koregaon Park, Pune – 411001, MS, India
Phone: 020 4019999 Fax: 020 4019990
E-mail: distrib@osho.net Website: www.osho.com